Walking
Since Daybreak

Books by Modris Eksteins

Theodor Heuss und die Weimarer Republik

The Limits of Reason: The German Democratic Press
and the Collapse of Weimar Democracy

Nineteenth-Century Germany: A Symposium
(edited with Hildegard Hammerschmidt)

Rites of Spring: The Great War and the
Birth of the Modern Age

Walking Since Daybreak: A Story of Eastern Europe,
World War II, and the Heart of Our Century

Walking
Since Daybreak

◆

A STORY OF EASTERN EUROPE,

WORLD WAR II, AND

THE HEART OF OUR CENTURY

Modris Eksteins

A PETER DAVISON BOOK
HOUGHTON MIFFLIN COMPANY
Boston • New York
1999

For information about permission to reproduce selections from
this book, write to Permissions, Houghton Mifflin Company,
215 Park Avenue South, New York, New York 10003.

Library of Congress Cataloging-in-Publication Data

Eksteins, Modris.
Walking since daybreak : a story of Eastern Europe, World
War II, and the heart of our century / Modris Eksteins
p.   cm.
"A Peter Davison book."
Includes index.
ISBN 0-395-93747-7
1. Baltic States—History—1940–1991.
2. Eksteins, Modris.   I. Title.
DK502.74.E39   1999
947.9—dc21   99-17856 CIP

Printed in the United States of America

Book design by Robert Overholtzer

QUM 10 9 8 7 6 5 4 3 2 1

For Theo, Roland, Oliver, and Andra

Contents

Latvia

150 km
100 miles

★Tallinn
(Reval)

Hiiumaa
(Dagö)

Haapsalu
(Hapsal)

Saaremaa
(Ösel)

E S T O N I A

°Kuresaare
(Arensburg)

Gulf of
Riga

Valka
(Walk)

Valmiera
(Wolmar)

Ventspils
(Windau)

Gauja

Cēsis
(Wenden)

Venta

Tukums
(Tuckum)

★Riga

LATVIA

R
U
S
S
I
A

Jelgava
(Mitau)

Iecava
(Eckau)

Iecava R.
(Eckau)

Liepāja
(Libau)

Dobele
(Doblen)

Tetele
(Tetelmünde)

Code
(Zohden)

Krustpils
(Kreuzburg)

Rēzekne
(Rositten)

Daugava
(Düna, Dvina)

Stalģene
(Stalgen)

Mežotne
(Mesothen)

Bauska
(Bauske)

Daugavpils
(Dünaburg)

Lielupe (Aa)

Klaipeda
(Memel)

Šiauliai
(Schaulen)

L I T H U A N I A

Daugavgrīva
(Dünamünde)

B E L A R U S

Prologue

History is the most dangerous product evolved from the chemistry of the intellect. Its properties are well known. It causes dreams, it intoxicates whole peoples, gives them false memories, quickens their reflexes, keeps their old wounds open, torments them in their repose, leads them into delusions either of grandeur or persecution, and makes nations bitter, arrogant, insufferable, and vain. History will justify anything.

PAUL VALÉRY

History is not truth. Truth is in the telling.

ROBERT PENN WARREN

There is no such thing as *was* — only is.

WILLIAM FAULKNER

SHATTERED CITIES. Smoldering ovens. Stacked corpses. Steeples like cigar stubs. Such are the images of Europe in 1945, images of a civilization in ruins.

At the end of the fury that was the Second World War there was stillness. Alan Bullock, the British historian and biographer of Hitler, recalls traveling to the center of hell at the end of the war: "I remember going to the Ruhr — this was the heart of Europe as far as industry was concerned — and there was silence everywhere. There wasn't a single smokestack. There were no cars, no trains."[1] Ruth Evans, née Mönckeberg, returned to Hamburg, city of her youth, after the war: "Had it not been for the two rivers, the Elbe

and the Alster, I would not have known where I was . . . Most of
the familiar landmarks had vanished: factories, houses, churches,
schools, hospitals — which ghastly ruin belonged to which? Not a
living soul in the streets, no trees, no birds, not even a stray dog or
cat. Nothing."[2]

Silence. Nothing. Emptiness at the heart of civilization. "All the
poems that sustained me before are as rigid and dead as I am myself," wrote a German mother to her children.[3] All the rhymes, all
the metaphors, all the harmonies, they meant nothing, or they were
lies. Reflection, analysis, and even language itself seemed inadequate, indeed improper, when one was confronted by the magnitude
of the horror. The muses had been silenced. Only the second-rate
had the courage to speak. Only the mindless claimed to understand.
"Everything was false," wrote Charlotte Delbo, "faces and books,
everything showed me its falseness and I was in despair at having
lost the faculty of dreaming, or harboring illusions; I was no longer
open to imagination, or explanation."[4]

However, beyond the corpses, beneath the rubble, there *was* life,
more intense than ever, a human anthill, mad with commotion. A
veritable bazaar. People going, coming, pushing, selling, sighing —
above all scurrying. Scurrying to survive. Never had so many people
been on the move at once. Millions upon millions. Prisoners of war,
slave laborers, concentration camp inmates, ex-soldiers, Germans
expelled from Eastern Europe, and refugees who had fled the Russian advance — a congeries of moving humanity. A frenzy. Apt subjects for Hieronymus Bosch. But he was nowhere to be found.

And so, silence and frenzy.

Sights and sounds for a century.

The year 1945 stands at the center of our century and our meaning.

How did we get there, to this silence in the eye of the storm, to
this moment of incomprehension when life was reduced to fundamental form, scurrying for survival?

We arrived twice: in reality, and subsequently in collective remembrance. The reality is now beyond our reach, the remembrance
constitutes history. Our historical sense is derived in turn from two

directions: from the buildup that were the events of the pre-1945 past, with its inherent notions of agency and cause, and from the confusions of our own end-of-century, end-of-millennium present, with its immediacy and contradiction. We arrive, on the one hand, from a prior imperial age whose gist was coherence, and on the other hand, from a postcolonial present whose logic is fragment. The past and present converge in 1945 with poignancy and symbol *sans pareil*.

Most of us arrive at 1945 not as agents, leaders, soldiers. We arrive as hangers-on or as victims, in crowds, pushed and pulled by events over which we feel we have no control. But as Franz Kafka suggested earlier in this century, the very notion of the victim is redolent of compromise and guilt. Violence was perhaps prefigured in the cultures of the victims, in the provocation they represented. At the same time the violence of 1945 remains our violence, our burden, our shame.

But how does one tell a tale that ends before it begins, that swirls in centrifugal eddies of malice, where the margin is by definition the middle, the victim the agent, where the loser stands front and center? Perhaps Theodor Adorno was right. He foresaw the very "extinction of art" because of the "increasing impossibility of representing historical events."[5]

If the tale is to be told, it must be told from the border, which is the new center. It must be told from the perspective of those who survived, resurrecting those who died. It must evoke the journey of us all into exile, to reach eventually those borders that have become our common home, the postmodern, multicultural, posthistorical mainstream. "God, it must be cool to be related to Aztecs," said the Berkeley undergraduate to the Mexican-American writer Richard Rodriguez.[6]

The tale must reflect the loss of authority, of history as ideal and of the author-historian as agent of that ideal. What we are left with is the intimacy not of truth but of experience.

The story, as a result, becomes a pastiche of styles, an assemblage of fragments, appropriate to an age. It becomes a mélange of memory, reflection, and narrative. The tale begins at two extremes and journeys to its center. It begins in the 1850s in the border provinces of western Russia and simultaneously in the intellectual border-lands of contemporary North American academe. It moves both forward and backward, through parallel migrations, disjunctures, and upheavals, to its conclusion in the maelstrom that was Germany in May 1945.

Germany at the end of World War II is the ultimate "placeless" place — defeated, prostrate, epicenter of both evil and grief, of agency and submission. It is here, in a swampland of meaningless meaning, that our century has its fulcrum. It is to Germany in May 1945, to its milling millions, its smashed armies, its corpses and debris, that we must journey.

The principal *dramatis personae* in this tale of disintegration, and yet liberation, are of necessity the author's family — my family. (In the collapse of category that marks our age, can I present any other list of characters?) We begin in the middle of the last century with Grieta, my maternal great-grandmother, Latvian chambermaid to a Baltic-German baron. She was seduced, made pregnant, and then rejected by her master. Her subsequent life, of spiteful and vengeful disquiet, merged with a burgeoning Latvian self-affirmation that was more often directed at the perceived foe, represented directly by the dominant Baltic-German nobility and in the background by Russian imperial authority, than at self-cultivation.

My grandfather, Jānis, born 1874, married the youngest of Grieta's daughters. He used her tiny dowry to set up a small fiacre business in Mitau, the capital of Kurland. This urban-entrepre-neurial spirit was again representative of a stage of social, eco-nomic, and ethnic development in the Eastern European border-lands that now coincided with the onset of a merciless whirlwind of violence, engendered by imperial rivalries and yet fueled by indige-nous interests, too — the Great War and the brutal civil war that followed. Jānis could have been born of Bertolt Brecht's imagination: with his cart and horse he became a latter-day Mother Courage, an itinerant, salvaging life and future for himself and his family amidst the chaos of murderous conflict. In the postwar world, when Latvia achieved independence, owing less to her own effort, significant as that was, than to the collapse of empire (Hohenzollern, Hapsburg, Romanov, Ottoman), Jānis finally got his own plot of land, a few kilometers from Jelgava, the former Mitau.

My father, Rūdolfs, born 1899, represented the hopes and aspirations of the "successor states" of Eastern Europe. He fought in the civil war of 1918–20 against Bolshevik incursion. He went on to study in England and America. He regarded himself as a cosmopolitan spirit in a new cosmopolitan age of youth and vitality.

Artūrs, my uncle, born 1910, son of Jānis, exuded the new energy in a more down-to-earth manner, but also the fears and resentments of the newly independent Latvia. He joined a nationalist organization, avid of uniform and prone to intolerance.

When the Russians returned, in 1940–41, my uncle was killed, while my father survived. The reasons for the survival were — as Rudyard Kipling said of his own conundrum — "known unto God." Latvians, like other Eastern Europeans, were either incinerated in the inferno that was the climax of imperial conflict — that between fascism and communism, Germany and Russia — or they fled.

We fled.

My mother, Biruta, born 1917, led the way. She dirtied her hands. She bartered and begged. She, the eternal woman, clawed her way to survival, for her family first and foremost and then for herself, like so many other women in wartime. My father, meanwhile, wondered about the spiritual and intellectual dimensions of it all.

The author was born, entr'acte, in late 1943. He was trapped with his mother and sister between German and Russian front lines in the summer of 1944, grazed along the temple by an exploding shell, and subsequently so eager to understand his and his family's fortunes that he became, alas and alack, a historian.

Such are the characters in this drama that is a mix of Agatha Christie and Luigi Pirandello, characters in search of a culprit, indeed in search of a clue.

The book began its life as an academic analysis of *Stunde Null*, hour zero, as the Germans called 1945, an attempt to portray the cultural landscape of Europe after the firestorm. As I dug into my own family's experience of that year, I was sidetracked by the story of Grieta. Her fate was at once trivial and yet resplendent with suggestion. I became mesmerized by her and the figure of her lover, the German baron. I went in search.

Appropriately, I found traces of Grieta, but I never found the baron. I did, however, become intrigued by the possible connections between Grieta, the baron, and the holocaust that followed. This book is the unconventional result of that intrigue. Its subject is disintegration and loss. But in the very quest for meaning, its essence is of course hope.

1

The Girl with the Flaxen Hair

There is something mean and common in the fall of man
and the loss of paradise.

FRIEDRICH VON SCHILLER

I plunge my gaze into the eyes of passing women, fleeting and
penetrating as a pistol shot, and rejoice when they are forced
to smile.

ERNST JÜNGER

Not everyone can live in palaces and skip about at dances — some
must live in tiny huts without a chimney and look after our
mother-earth! And which is the happier, heaven only knows.

M. E. SALTYKOV

The Maiden and Her Prince

BEAUTIFUL SHE WAS, everyone said. Temperamental and strong-willed, too. And in the next breath they mentioned her hair, long and blond. Everyone noticed her hair.

She, the peasant girl, caught the eye of the baron. It may have been at harvest time, as his barouche flew past the field where she and her family were working. It may have been winter, cold, damp, and endless, as his equipage and sled bounced by on the frozen road. But most likely it was during summer, when every year he spent several months on his estate. Perhaps it was midsummer's night, long and bright, as he greeted the families of local tenant farmers.

He was enchanted by the young girl with the azure eyes, the flower chaplet, and the splendrous hair.

One day he asked if she would like to come and work for him at his manor house. She was willing. Her duties as the baron's chambermaid were straightforward and not unpleasant. The baron treated her well. Her duties took her into his bedchamber. One day, she did not refuse his advances. After that, intimate favors became a normal part of the employ of *la fille aux cheveux de lin*.

The girl with the flaxen hair, Grieta Pluta, was my maternal great-grandmother. Born in 1834, she was the daughter of tenant farmers near Bauske (Bauska),* in the Baltic province of Kurland. She came from a long line of peasants, generation after generation of humble folk, beginning where, no one knew for certain, and heading where, few were inclined to ask. They were like the seasons, these generations of simple people — inevitable, necessary, occasionally admired and more often cursed. They had no recorded history. Their permanence was their history. And that which is permanent bears little interest.

As a result, of Grieta Pluta we know little. She left few traces. She left no heirlooms, no photographs. Hard evidence of her presence on this earth is difficult to come by. She seems to exist only in stories and impressions — about her hair, character, and fate — passed on orally across the generations and presumably colored by each raconteur to fit the occasion. When as a youth I first heard the story of Grieta and the "German baron," it was told in hushed tones, punctuated by titters, as if it were a deep, ignoble secret. I laughed and assumed that it was a bit of exaggerated family lore, designed to make us, the family, a little less insignificant historically. Grieta, I thought skeptically, had been turned into a family wish.

Much has changed since. Grieta remains a figment of the family imagination, as does the "German baron." But in her symbolism she

---

*For place names I have used the name and spelling most widely employed in the international community at the given time, with the best known alternative(s) in parentheses. Thus in dealing with matters prior to Latvian independence in 1918 I shall refer to Bauske instead of Bauska, Mitau instead of Jelgava, the Dvina instead of the Daugava or Düna. For the period after 1918, in keeping with the shift in political and social power, I shall use the Latvian, instead of German or Russian, names. A Concordance of Place Names can be found on p. 224.

has grown in stature over the years and transcended the immediate family, while he has palpably diminished in importance; she has achieved the status of historical icon while he has lost face. From our vantage point at the end of the twentieth century, Grieta is in fact more suggestive of her age, its dynamics and thrust, than the baron who "made love" to her. It was she who won that social and emotional encounter. It was what she exuded and represented — despair, resentment, alongside a vindictive and self-promoting energy — that pulled the baronial empire down, with its grand palaces and time-honored customs.

Grieta was like Artemis of Greek myth. After Actæon, the hunter, had seen her bathing, naked, Artemis turned him into a stag and had his own hounds tear him apart. Grieta seemed to do the same to her Actæon. She demanded bloody sacrifice. The dimensions of this sacrifice, however, were to exceed her wildest imaginings.

Ghosts

I, GRIETA'S GREAT-GRANDSON, sit and write, a century after her death, in another part of the world. I have escaped the borderlands of her strife, yet I inhabit new borderlands. The ghosts of her empire dance about me and refuse to release me. I know it's old-fashioned of me, but I'd like to know who that German baron was. I'd like a name. The master narratives, we are told, are gone; the great ideas dead. And yet I hear their spirits prance. In exile. On the border.

Who was that baron?

The view from my third-floor study in north Toronto looks out on a symbol of empire, an elementary school, an imposing stolid edifice completed in 1921 and named in honor of an exemplary citizen of the city, John Ross Robertson. Robertson's civic accomplishments were formidable. He started a newspaper; he founded a hospital; he was a member of parliament; he was an author. His world was connected, his sense of duty clear. He stood for Anglo-Saxon achievement and virtue. He stood for what used to be called "bottom": responsibility and reliability, a persona nourished by civic pride.

The ghost of John Ross Robertson, inhabiting the school across the street, would be companionship enough. But the house I occupy, the street on which I live, the university at which I teach, and the subject of history which I profess are full of similar ghosts. They natter in the pages of bibliographies, smirk on the walls of college halls, chatter in property registers, and warm themselves behind our fireplace mantels.

They are everywhere, these ghosts of empires past. I live in a haunted world. The question is: Have I joined the ghosts or have the ghosts joined me?

Who was that baron?

Grieta's Curse

ONE DAY while working for the baron, Grieta learned she was pregnant. She told him. His response was decisive. Within weeks he had her married off to a young boy of Estonian background, Gederts Kuiva. Gederts, too, worked for the baron. His main responsibility was the drying kiln — to dry clothes and grain — which he kept supplied with firewood and heat. He was a sturdy, quiet lad with a round face and brown eyes. The baron installed the young couple on their own farm. The terms were generous. Neither family saw reason to protest.

At the outset, the young husband found his new responsibilities overwhelming. To be married suddenly to a woman already with child was difficult enough; to manage independently a sizable farm was terrifying. Gederts could not cope. He ran away.

When the baron heard that Grieta had been abandoned, he sent out a search party. A frightened Gederts was found, delivered to the baron, and promptly thrashed. The physical beating was not the end of the baron's intervention, however. Whether out of affection for Grieta or spite toward the youth who had let him down, he moved the couple yet again, this time to a larger house with more land, on the estate of Zohden (Code). This may have been a neighboring estate rather than the baron's own.

For whatever reason, the young Ģederts now rose to the challenge. He became a respected landlord, farmer, and family man. He sired four children of his own. He hired laborers to assist in the fields and domestic help for the house, but he never denied his own humble background, never adopted airs. He made a point of working alongside his staff, particularly when strenuous labor was involved. His gentle equipoise became renowned in the district.

His wife, the beautiful Grieta, was a different matter. She seemed unable to disengage from her fling with fable and fortune. She exuded pretense and prejudice toward the household help and even her own family. As her beauty faded, she became miserly and bitter. She stinted on food for the staff and had little positive to say about anyone or anything.

The firstborn of the couple was a girl. They called her Lavīze. She was the baron's daughter. She grew plump and round, a large child. She eventually married a gamekeeper called Zvirgzds and they had two sons.

To Grieta there followed two daughters, then a son, and, in the summer of 1877, a last daughter. Three months after the birth of this child, Ģederts died unexpectedly on returning from a day of work in the fields. He was forty-nine. By this stage, in the wake of agrarian reforms in the 1860s, peasant farmers were permitted to own land; Ģederts died the owner of the farm known as Pūrīcas.

After her husband's death Grieta continued to manage the farm, though with growing difficulty and decreasing interest. Toward her own children she seemed incapable of showing any deep affection. Her obsession with social airs left them cold. When one of her daughters declared her love for a local servant boy, Grieta was appalled and forbade further meetings between the two. The daughter ignored her mother, married the lad, and severed ties with her own family.

Some years later, with two young children of her own, this daughter was helping her husband at harvest. They were storing hay in a makeshift rick-shelter in the field. She was atop the high stack, he below pitching the hay up to her. When day's work was done, the mound was high, and he, bidding his wife to stay put, went off in search of a ladder so that she could climb down without harm and without disturbing their carefully arranged stack of hay. When he did not come back as soon as she wished, she decided she would slide down from the haystack after all. The husband returned to find his wife writhing on the ground, skewered on the pitchfork he had left propped up against the mound. "What will become of my children?" she is said to have moaned. In a panic he yanked the pitchfork from her. She died shortly afterward. In the family it was said that she had died because of her mother's curse.

Grieta's offspring could be as headstrong as she. When her son, Jēkabs, was nineteen, he married an older woman. Grieta, tired of managing the farm, signed it over to him and his new wife. He, however, turned out to be an incompetent, spending most of his time at the one pub on the Zohden estate, drinking and gambling away the family savings. In no time at all his debts were such that Pūrīcas had to be put on the auction block to pay off the publican.

The older daughters had by then gone their own way, but Grieta and her youngest girl, Paulīne, were forced to move out. Before leaving her old home, Grieta cut down her favorite tree in the apple orchard. Ģederts had planted it. Like the cherry orchard in Chekhov's play, Grieta's apple tree was not to survive her passing. Love and hate were emotions closely linked in this woman's life. That this was Grieta's nature goes without saying. But a world and a social system had nurtured her as well. The German baron always loomed large in the saga. The emotions he evoked were always intense.

Grieta moved in with relatives, while Paulīne, now fifteen years old, found employment, much to her mother's chagrin and shame, as a servant, first to a local farmer and then to the von der Pahlens at their huge estate of Gross-Eckau (Lieliecava), twenty-one kilometers northeast of Bauske on the Eckau (Iecava) River. Grieta never revisited her home at Pūrīcas. Nor did her son.

Not long after, Grieta fell ill with yellow fever. As she lay dying she ordered Paulīne to take scissors to her hair, to cut those tresses the baron and everyone else had admired. She wanted her youngest daughter to sell the hair so that it could be made into watch bands, a practice common at the time.

The daughter refused to comply. Grieta, her soul fractured but her hair uncut, died in 1894, the year the last tsar of Russia ascended the throne.

Plus Ça Change . . .

BOMBS EXPLODE. Invective spurts. The mayor of Moscow accuses Latvia of genocide. This is not 1945. This is 1998. The politics of the last atrocity continue.

Yuri Luzhkov, mayor of a city whose population is four times that of Latvia, claims that this small state is trying to wipe out its resident Russian population. Most of these Russians arrived in Latvia after the Second World War, as managers of Russian enterprises or as military personnel. They gravitated to the cities, especially Riga. After Latvian independence in 1991 they were denied Latvian citizenship unless they could pass a strict language test. Most of the older generation cannot. As their Soviet passports expire, these Russians become stateless.

A demonstration in Riga by Russian pensioners protesting the cost of heating is dispersed roughly by baton-wielding police. A small bomb explodes near the Russian embassy. A monument to the Soviet victory in the Second World War is damaged. About five hundred elderly veterans of the Latvian Legion, who fought against the Russians under the aegis of the German SS, parade in Riga, with the blessing of a few dignitaries.

Yuri Luzhkov compares the present government of Latvia to the murderous regime of Pol Pot in Cambodia.

Sword of Gideon

GRIETA PLUTA lived her entire life in Kurland, near Bauske. She was a Latvian surrounded by German and Russian power. Kurland was a border province over which Germans, Russians, Swedes, and Poles had fought since the late twelfth century.

In antiquity a handful of travelers from the Greco-Roman world had come north and recorded a few impressions of the area. The Vikings in turn left traces of their presence here and to the east. But the first chronicles date from the twelfth and thirteenth centuries. From the perspective of Western civilization, with its crucible in that much larger, warm-water sea to the south, the Mediterranean, the Baltic was an inhospitable pool in the frozen north. When descendants of the "Germanic" invaders, who had flooded westward in the great tribal migrations of the fourth and fifth centuries, eventually adopted the political structures of the Romans and created a Holy Roman Empire, led by German emperors, they also inherited other assumptions, among them the idea that anyone from the East was a "barbarian."

The Baltic land was not rich. Glacial activity had flattened and scarred much of it, leaving countless shallow lakes and long moraines. Except for a fertile basin in the middle, watered by two rivers, the Dvina (Düna, Daugava) and the Aa (Lielupe), both of which emptied into the sea, the soil was poor. North of the Dvina valley, boggy highlands replaced meadows, and oak, ash, birch, and elm gave way to a thick pine. Elsewhere, a low rolling plain stretched from the western coastline into the interior until it encountered swamps and marshes. The sea to the west and the marshland to the east had served as a natural frontier, isolating and protecting the tribes that had settled here at the eastern end of the Baltic Sea.

The Ests, Livs, and Ingrians may have come from the Ural region as early as 5000 B.C. and settled, respectively, to the south of the Gulf of Finland, around the Gulf of Riga, and next to Lake Peipus. Part of the Finno-Ugric language group, these peoples were related to the Finns to the north and Magyars far to the south. The "Baltic" group of tribes, consisting of Letts, Lithuanians, and Prussians, appear to have arrived from White Russia, from the area between Minsk and Smolensk, about 2000 B.C. The Letts, in turn, were a loose grouping of various tribes, Sels, Semgallians, Kurs, and Latgallians. Linguistic evidence — the archaic structure of the languages and the ties of

Latvian and Lithuanian to Sanskrit — suggests that these tribes had originally come from much farther south and that their language once had been the same. These tribes were distinct from the Slavic and Germanic peoples to the south and east and from their more immediate Finno-Ugric neighbors.[1]

If the land was not rich, the territory still held promise. Amber was the initial attraction. The product of pine resin, this precious stone had been coveted for centuries for its beauty and its association with healing. The ancient Greeks made necklaces of the "stone of the sun." Roman ladies, noted Martial, carried it in order to cool their hands. Pliny the Elder wrote: "An amber figurine, however small it may be, as long as it suggests the likeness of man, commands a higher price than a live and vigorous man."[2] Culpeper's *Dispensatory* of 1654 would note that amber was of help in treating coughs, nosebleeds, gonorrhea, and even hysteria.

Amber may have headed the list of desirable items, but the German merchants appreciated the honey, wax, and leather of the area as well. Furthermore, the rivers of the Baltic, especially the Dvina, were a gateway to the Russian interior, to its furs and pelts. After negotiating the Dvina, you could sally north to Novgorod with its renowned fur market or venture south to the Dnieper River, which would lead you to the Caucasus, the Black Sea, and eventually the warmth of the Mediterranean.

And so traders came first, in the twelfth century, from Visby, that vibrant trading post on the island of Gotland in the middle of the Baltic, from Bremen on the river Weser, and particularly from Lübeck at the western end of the Baltic. At the base of the Schleswig-Holstein peninsula and at the mouth of the Trave River, Lübeck became the capital of German commerce in the Baltic and the point of departure for hardy emigrants heading east. Its gabled merchant houses, towering church spires, and bustling mercantile spirit were to be duplicated in Riga, Reval (Tallinn), Danzig (Gdansk), Memel (Klaipeda), Stettin (Szczecin), Rostock, and other cities which later formed that great Baltic trading union, the Hanseatic League.

To acquire local goods from the eastern Baltic and beyond, the traders brought with them cloth, glass trinkets, and weapons of iron. The first natives the Germans encountered were the Finno-Ugric Livs who had settled around the Gulf of Riga, and so the entire coastal territory, including the islands in the gulf, the visitors designated as Livland (Livonia), regardless of who else resided there. The southern part, where the Kurs dwelt, would in time be called Kurland, and the northern section, inhabited by Ests, Estland.

It soon became apparent that the promise of the area was not only commercial but spiritual too. The Baltic offered opportunities equal to the Holy Land for saving souls. On the heels of the traders, churchmen arrived. The elderly but determined missionary Meinhard came around 1180. At Üxküll (Ikšķile), a village some distance up the Dvina, he built first a small wooden church and then, in symbolic sequence, a large stone castle.

Finally, in that remarkable progression that has been so characteristic of Western civilization, the churchmen, when they encountered difficulty or saw exceptional opportunity, summoned warriors, knights of the sword. Meinhard's successor, the Cistercian abbot Berthold, brought some crusaders in 1198, but when he was killed in a clash with natives, the Church stepped up its efforts. Albert von Buxhoeveden, a canon of Bremen Cathedral, aimed from the start at not only Christianization but colonization of the area. With support from Innocent III, the most aggressive of the medieval popes, he proceeded to preach a crusade across the German territories of Westphalia and Saxony. The northeastern edge of Christian Europe might be less glamorous as an object of crusading than the Holy Land, but the goal, of bringing God to these heathenish peoples who worshiped trees, ancestors, and woodland spirits and who had turned down repeated offers of salvation, was just as laudable. Paganism, or, from the vantage point of the Roman Church, the equally odious alternative of conversion to a Byzantine Orthodoxy coming from the Russian interior, could not be tolerated. Forced Christianization was necessary. In 1199 twenty-three vessels, each with about a hundred fighting men, set sail for Livland. The Baltic Crusade had begun.[3] By 1204 Bishop Albert had achieved for his crusade a status equal to that of the concurrent expedition to Jerusalem.

The knights, drawn mainly from the lesser nobility of northern

Germany, often landless nobles from the *ministeriale* or service class, regarded the indigenous peoples of the Baltic coastland with a disdain that not even the Turkish infidel merited — the Saracen at least had only one god, the Baltic peoples countless ridiculous ones — and they unleashed in the name of Christianity and civilization a *furor Teutonicus* that would resound through the centuries. As first the Order of Swordbrothers, whose white mantles were embroidered with a red sword below a red cross, and later the Order of Teutonic Knights reduced the local populations to a feudal dependence, these warrior monks built forbidding monastic castles to dot the countryside and signal their power and purpose. This petty German nobility found mission and reward — the latter in land and authority — in the Baltic; their war cries and ruthless exploits became the stuff of legend, the essence of the German *Drang nach Osten*, the push to the East.[4] "In the unfortunate collisions of mutually hostile races the murderous ferocity of a brief war of extermination is more humane, less shocking," insisted Heinrich von Treitschke later, "than mistaken leniency which does nothing to raise the conquered above the status of brutes."[5]

Bishop Albert founded Riga in 1201 and moved his headquarters there. The newly conquered territory he received from the German emperor as a fief, and he himself was proclaimed a *Reichsfürst*, a prince of the Holy Roman Empire. In his office the sacred and the profane merged.

As in all instances of forced conversion, incomprehension and then anger were the response of the objects of the effort. "It is no wonder that the simple idolaters had as little relish for the unexplained God of their invaders as for the heavy tribute by which they announced his presence," wrote the attentive and ebullient Elizabeth Rigby on hearing, during a visit to Estland about the time of Grieta Pluta's birth, the story of the crusaders' exploits and the fate of their victims. "Contented with their unexpensive deities of forest and dell," she wrote of the latter, "they resisted to the utmost; only declaring themselves converts after their huts were razed, their land plundered, and their best hunters slain; relapsing the moment their new brethrens' backs were turned."[6]

The cruelty was hardly one-sided. The local tribes had intense rivalries; warfare and butchery were endemic in the area. Weaker tribes frequently turned to the crusaders for assistance against stronger neighbors. With their technological superiority, their armor, crossbows, catapults, and stone towers, the knights, even if few in number, were almost always the decisive force in battle. In conflict with the godless, the question of mercy did not arise. Outraged by native resistance, the chronicler Heinrich von Lettland bellowed: "They deserve to be killed, rather than to be baptized."[7] Johann Gottfried Herder, the Enlightenment man of letters who taught in Riga for a number of years late in the eighteenth century, would compare the German impact on the Baltic with the Spanish conquest of Peru, where most of the natives were wiped out.[8]

From her home near Zohden, Grieta Pluta could walk to sites of German conquest but a few kilometers away, at Mesothen (Mežotne) and Bauske. The conquest of Grieta Pluta by the German baron was to be a consequence of the earlier exploits of the Germanic knights.

War and Peace

WHEN THE BERLIN WALL was pierced in 1989, and when communism subsequently collapsed in Eastern Europe and the Soviet Union, many of us were caught up in an extraordinary wave of optimism. The era of violence launched by the outbreak of war in 1914 was over. The age of the tyrants had ended. A new springtime of peoples was beginning.

But before we could catch our breath, the front pages of our newspapers filled up with items stemming from the age of horrors: stories about war criminals, looted art, Swiss banks and Nazi gold, the Catholic Church and the Holocaust. It was as if we had returned suddenly, through time warp, to the moral and historical dilemmas of 1945, dilemmas that the Cold War had frozen in place. The age of violence, particularly the Second World War, refuses to leave us in peace.

Before we can move forward, we must come to some kind of

terms with 1945, with what it represents. A start would be the recognition that 1945, with its devastation, displacement, and horror, was the result not just of a few madmen and their befuddled followers, not just of "others," but of humanity as a whole and of our culture as a whole. Nineteen forty-five is not our victory, as we often like to think; 1945 is our problem.

"Boris Petrovich Has Acted Splendidly"

WHILE IN POLAND, Bohemia, and Hungary the German military advance in the Middle Ages was followed by an influx of German artisans, traders, and even peasants, seeking opportunities, a similarly variegated social infrastructure did not move up into the Baltic. Some German architects, masons, and craftsmen did come to build cities like Riga and Reval; a German middle class of merchants, doctors, apothecaries, and teachers did eventually emerge in the towns. But the German peasant never came. In the Baltic, far more so than in other areas of German migration into Eastern Europe and Russia, the Germans remained an isolated elite, officers without men.

The first phase of German influence in the eastern Baltic ended in the middle of the sixteenth century, when the religious and political strife of the Reformation engulfed Central Europe. As the Holy Roman Empire fragmented over the next century, the Baltic lands were pulled repeatedly into the vortex of neighboring rivalries and battered mercilessly by Swedish, Polish, and Russian armies. War seemed constant. Yet through all the strife, the Baltic nobility, the German barons, managed to retain their rights and privileges.

The Livonian War, which dragged on from 1557 to 1582, was followed by a century of Swedish influence in the north and Polish in the south. Kurland became a duchy under the suzerainty of Poland. Russian power, under Peter the Great, came next. The Great Northern War, fought between 1700 and 1721, devastated much of the eastern coastal area. Initial Swedish military success was followed by repeated Russian counterblows. As he pursued the Swedes through the Baltic, the Russian commander, Sheremetyev, had no concern for the local inhabitants. In one of his reports to the tsar, he noted: "Everything is destroyed. Aside from Pernau and Reval, and the odd manor house by the sea, nothing remains. From Reval to Riga everything has been eradicated root and branch." Tsar Peter was pleased. "Boris Petrovich," he said of his commander in the Baltic, "has acted splendidly."[9] Those the soldiers spared, plague, pestilence, and famine did not. By some estimates two thirds of the Baltic peasantry was wiped out during the Great Northern War. The effect on landowners and townspeople was only slightly less devastating. By the Treaty of Nystadt, in 1721, Estland and Livland, including the islands of Ösel (Saaremaa) and Dagö (Hiiumaa), became Peter the Great's "window on the West."

Russian attention shifted westward. Not only did Peter move his capital from Moscow to St. Petersburg, he brought droves of experts and advisers to Russia. Impressed by the efficient administration of the Baltic provinces and eager to have the Baltic Germans on his side, Peter struck a deal with them, leaving them to run their own affairs unhampered in return for loyalty and service to the crown.

The first two partitions of Poland, in 1772 and 1792, by the major powers that surrounded her — Prussia, Austria, and Russia — did not affect the eastern Baltic, but the third, in 1795, did. In that partition Kurland finally became a part of Russia. But while all the Baltic provinces were now incorporated into Russia, they continued to enjoy administrative autonomy. The Germans owned the land; the vast majority of the native population was landless, much of it in feudal bondage to the Baltic barons.

Death of History

THE UNDERSTANDING of human behavior in the past has always been the raison d'être of history. Because of this, history has prided itself on being a progressive discipline. Historians like to think that they have been to the modern world what theologians were to the age before enlightenment. They have provided meaning.

In so doing, they have made the world a better place. History has been not only a subject of study; it has been a moral force. History, one could argue, has been the essence of the Enlightenment project.

Historians have been conceptualizers and explicators, and since their mission has been to bring the unknown and the marginal into the fold of knowledge and understanding, they have been empire builders too. Thomas Carlyle called history "the only study," and likened it to the "universal Divine Scripture."[10] History would be the basis of universal understanding and of a universal morality. History would achieve transcendence.

Our century, however, has not been kind to conceptualizers and empire builders. Our century, likewise, has not been kind to history and historians, though it did take some time for the sense of crisis to seep into the guild itself. Michel Serres once called history the last ideology, the last and most stubborn of them all.[11]

But all that has changed. History has died a thousand deaths of late, at least history as progressive vision and imperial dream. History has become at most histories, accounts that point less to the order of things than to their disorder; accounts that place their emphasis on questions rather than answers, on the quest rather than the discovery.[12] History has become, in the words of Pierre Nora, "the deciphering of what we are in the light of what we are no longer."[13]

After all the horrors spawned by ideological rigidity in our century, the notion of a variety of histories, as opposed to a single history, is to be celebrated. Friedrich Nietzsche had such a vision, as did Ernst Troeltsch and Martin Heidegger. Troeltsch, the prominent German historian and theologian, admitted in an essay written in 1916 in the midst of war that he could no longer adhere to any concept of the unity of history. Not only that: the various histories that would be written in the future would not understand one another.[14] Heidegger went further. The dismantling of pretense he saw as the fundamental development of the West, and that would also invariably include the dismantling of history. "Nihilism," he wrote, "is the world-historical movement of the peoples of the earth who have been drawn into the power realm of the modern age."[15] If for an earlier generation the loss of a sense of unity was an admission of intellectual crisis, for our own era, more than a half century later, such visions of diversity can be interpreted as appeals for humility and respect.

We must accept a variety of histories, but we must also accept variety within our history. It is not possible to write history without preconception. It is possible, however, to write history with layers of suggestion, so that history evokes, history conjoins, it involves. History should provoke, not dictate meaning. It should be a vehicle rather than a terminus. Beware, in Jacob Burckhardt's famous admonition, the terrible simplifiers. "I believe it to be a barbarism," he added elsewhere, "to keep birds in a cage."[16]

The Baltic Baron

THE BALTIC OVERLORDS were descendants of a warrior elite. They were proud of their heritage, its implications and responsibilities. They were energetic and ruthless administrators. Their superior education and managerial talents took them to the highest offices of tsarist Russia, where their influence in the civil and military services far exceeded their numbers. If Peter the Great had enormous respect for them, so did his successors. Empress-to-be Anna Ivanovna married Friedrich, duke of Kurland, and when he died, her lover and favorite was the Baltic-German Duke Ernst Johann Biron. During her ten-year reign, 1730–1740, the government seemed to fall largely into the hands of Germans.

On her accession in 1762, Catherine II, herself born in Stettin in Pomerania as a princess of Anhalt-Zerbst, reinforced the trend by bringing the Baltic barons not only into the upper echelons of government but into the service of the greater empire. When she introduced a new statute for provincial administration in 1775, a sudden need for educated and able administrators arose in all areas of public life, and numerous Baltic Germans were invited to serve. They were, noted Elizabeth Rigby, "the best and most favoured officers" in all the Russian services.[17]

The German-speaking population in the Baltic provinces would never exceed 8 percent of the total, yet they controlled economic, political, and cultural life. Their religion, after the Reformation, was Lutheranism — in a sea of Catholicism and Orthodoxy. All clergy-men were German-speaking. German was the language of higher education and of high culture. The Latvian and Estonian languages, with their various dialects, were regarded by the Germans as peasant vernacular, not vehicles of literature and genuine culture. Latvians and Estonians were looked on as a lower social order rather than separate nationalities. "There are no educated Latvians," declared a German newspaper editor. "Those who are educated and call them-selves Latvian only deceive themselves . . . To be both Latvian and educated is an impossibility."[18] With their land, their influence, and their prestige, the Baltic aristocracy were in an enviable situation. Their lot, said Elizabeth Rigby, "is one of the happiest that man can desire."[19]

A good number of the Baltic barons were descendants of the Teutonic Knights. Among the best-known names were Keyserling, Manteuffel, Ungern-Sternberg, Lieven, and von der Pahlen. They were among the largest landowners in not only the Baltic but all of Russia.[20] The last two families, the Lievens and the von der Pahlens, enveloped Grieta Pluta. Their estates surrounded and enthralled her.

Dystopian Visions

DISMEMBERMENT. Displacement. Discord. As the Soviet Un-ion, Yugoslavia, and Czechoslovakia came apart in the 1990s, Canada threatened to do the same. In Quebec the separatist leadership took encouragement from developments in Eastern Europe and Russia. The events in the Baltics, culminating in 1991 in independence for Estonia, Latvia, and Lithuania, fascinated them.

A referendum in Quebec in October 1995 brought Canada to the brink of disintegration. Regionalist and partisan interests through-out the country took heart. On Canada's 130th birthday, in 1997, Toronto's *Globe and Mail* editorialized: "If the land is strong today, the spirit is weak. Canada is suffering from a fading sense of com-munity, an erosion of self-awareness and a retreat into sectionalism and ethnicity . . . Ambiguity is not new to Canada, nor is it all bad. The trouble is that it mixes today with a noxious envy, anger, ignorance and indifference. Against this corrosion, our leaders are helpless."[21]

The question of identity has always troubled Canada. "The Canadian," J. B. Priestley once asserted, "is a baffled man" when asked to "make plain" his distinction.[22] Canadians are inclined to describe themselves in negative terms: We are not Americans, we are not British, we are not French. More recently Canada has been described as the premier postmodern nation because of its inability to define itself in economic, political, geographical, and, least of all, racial terms.[23] Canada has been called "a nation-less state" and "the world's largest country that doesn't exist."[24] Lucien Bouchard, the leader of the separatist Parti Québécois, has echoed those views: Canada, he says, is not "a real country."

And yet the United Nations has repeatedly graded Canada as the most agreeable country in which to live. The country that is not a country is the best. Therein resides the postmodern dilemma. Ah, how the ghosts chortle.

The developments in Canada underline a broader tendency. If the twentieth century has had one principal theme, it is the collapse of authority, or at least the "de-centering" of authority. We have fled to the borders, of our cities, of our values, of our minds. All previous forms of representation, be they in art or politics or law, have become suspect.

Can we ever achieve focus again? Or is dystopia our fate? Are we bound to forge a world peopled only by exiles and tourists, bonded by disparity, diversity, and disagreement, a lonely world?

"Where is Hollywood?" asks a German sociologist. He answers: "Everywhere."[25]

Baron and Friends

THE ESTATE OF ZOHDEN, on which Grieta was settled by the German baron, was actually owned at the time by a Russian family. This modest property, of some 1,300 hectares (about 525 acres), had been in Baltic-German hands for centuries but in 1821 had been sold to "Lord Grand Master of the Horse" Count Ivan Kutaisov. A few years later he passed the property on to his daughter. She had married a Golitsyn, and so this distinguished Russian family, which for centuries had provided governors, ministers, and administrators for the tsar, took proprietorship of Zohden. Still, though owning Zohden, the Golitsyns do not appear to have spent much time there; they had grander estates elsewhere. Zohden was administered by a series of German and Latvian estate managers. In 1911 the Golitsyns would sell Zohden to the Lievens.

The properties adjacent to Zohden were owned by the Lievens and the von der Pahlens. They, in contrast with the Golitsyns, did use their Kurland estates. Both families belonged to the so-called Russian party within the Baltic-German nobility. In recent memory they had always sided actively with Russian interests in the Baltic. Both families had excellent relations with the Golitsyns, whom they saw frequently during the winter season in St. Petersburg. Did a Lieven or von der Pahlen persuade the Golitsyns to house Grieta and her husband on their estate?

The Lieven family seat was at Mesothen, at the site of a famous crusaders' battle in 1220 against the Semgallians. Tsar Paul I had awarded the estate, consisting of some 7,000 hectares and including the ruins of the old crusader castle, to his children's governess, Charlotte von Lieven, in 1796. The family owned countless other estates in the Baltic and in Russia.

The most renowned of all the Lievens was Dorothea, née Benckendorff. She had married Christoph von Lieven, a son of Charlotte, in 1800. In 1812 Christoph was sent as Russian ambassador to London. The Lievens would remain in England for twenty-two years. Dorothea would hobnob with the high and mighty: King George IV, the Duke of Wellington, Earl Grey, Lords Castlereagh and Aberdeen, and the royal Dukes of Clarence, Cumberland, and York. Her paramours were legion — counts, grand dukes, foreign ministers, and prime ministers. In 1818 she took Metternich, "the coachman of Europe," as her lover, at the apex of his political power. The Austrian foreign minister was at the time the most celebrated man in Europe, architect of the post-Napoleonic peace. François Guizot, who in 1847 became French prime minister, was a later conquest. "I quite like prime ministers," Dorothea had written to Metternich in 1820.[26]

This woman, though hardly a beauty — "nose too strong, ears enormous, neck too long, mouth disgraceful"[27] — nevertheless exuded an indefinable attraction. Her physical demeanor was said to be exquisite. Attired always at the height of fashion, she was a talented pianist, superb dancer, and scintillating conversationalist. She introduced the waltz to Britain. She had, remarked Charles Greville, "the faculty of turning everyone to account, and eliciting something either of entertainment or information from the least important of her acquaintance."[28] Men stumbled over each other to pay their compliments. Her intrigues and meddling in British politics would reach a point in 1834 where Lord Palmerston felt obliged to insist to St. Petersburg that she and her husband be recalled. The Russian foreign office complied. Prince Lieven returned to Russia and accepted the post of governor to the tsarevich. Four years later he was dead.

After the high diplomacy, politics, and social whirl of London, Dorothea could not bear the return to Russia. Within months she had departed, *sans mari*, for Paris, where she remained until her death in 1857, at age seventy-three. At the end she had taken Talleyrand's former apartment, in the rue Saint-Florentin, and died in the very same room as he. Her remains were transported from Paris to the family estate at Mesothen and buried there beside her two youngest sons.

Her private life was, not surprisingly, quite the reverse of her glamorous public performance. "I am so wedded to sorrow," she confessed to Lady Palmerston in 1839.[29] By then her husband and four of her six children had died. By the end of his life Christoph had sundered all ties with her. Together they had had a daughter followed by five sons. Dorothea clearly found the children a nuisance. To her lover Metternich she wrote in March 1825: "I have a fifth son; it is very stupid."[30]

The daughter died before the age of three. Two of the boys, Georg

and Arthur, would die in March 1835, within days of each other,
of scarlet fever. A third son, Constantine, died in the same year
as her husband, 1838, while in America, to which he had fled because
of an ongoing quarrel with his father over gambling debts and
family honor.[31] Only two of the sons, Alexander and Paul, survived
Dorothea. Both of them found their relationship with their mother
difficult. Alexander, who lived until 1886, was without a legitimate
heir. He fathered at least one child though, a daughter, by the Countess Manteuffel.

Dorothea's life was not typical of the Baltic nobility, far from
it; but it did express grandly the place of performance in social life
and did comment on the relationship between power and morality
within those aristocratic circles that touched Grieta.

When Dorothea died, the master of Mesothen was her nephew
Paul, son of Christoph's eldest brother, Johann Georg. The nephew
followed the family tradition of service, becoming an elected marshal of the Livonian nobility and, briefly, master of ceremonies at
the imperial court in St. Petersburg. He remained a bachelor until
middle age. He was shy. He was a bit of a flake. He had a stutter. And
he was extremely handsome. His biographer felt it necessary to
remark on "a certain unsteadiness in his existence" and to point out
how much Prince Paul enjoyed the summers at Mesothen. "Only
toward the end of his life would he be granted a desired stability
thanks to the blessings of a happy family life."[32]

This family life commenced in 1871, on October 20, when the
landlord of Mesothen married. Prince Paul wed Natalie Countess
von der Pahlen. He was fifty, she twenty-nine. She came from another illustrious Kurland family. The marriage of a Lieven to a von
der Pahlen was a typically Baltic-German union. The two families
were neighbors. The von der Pahlens owned Kautzemünde (Kauc-
minde), but a few kilometers from Mesothen. Not only were the
families neighbors; their paths had crossed on a number of dra-
matic occasions.

Two generations earlier, Peter Count von der Pahlen had been
military governor of St. Petersburg under Tsar Paul I and perhaps
the most powerful political figure of his day in Russia. In 1796, the

same year the Lievens received Mesothen, Count Peter was accorded the adjoining estate of Kautzemünde. This became the von der Pahlen family seat. He also received Gross-Eckau, a huge property of 17,713 hectares, twenty-one kilometers northeast of Bauske, and Hofzumberge (Tērvete), to the west, on the site of another monastic castle of the Teutonic Knights. It was at Gross-Eckau that Grieta's daughter Paulīne would find work in the early 1890s.

Despite these imperial favors, Count Peter was an ingrate. He became a principal conspirator in the plot that led to the murder of Emperor Paul in March 1801. The ruler was so unpredictable in his attitudes and policies that many thought him mad and hence a danger to the state. According to Elizabeth Rigby and other early commentators, von der Pahlen himself strangled the tsar with his handkerchief, and hence came to be known in Baltic-German circles as "Schnupftuch Pahlen" (Handkerchief Pahlen). There seems little evidence now that Count Peter had a direct hand in the killing — he was fifteen minutes late for the conspiratorial assignation and may thereby have sought to distance himself from the plot should it fail — but nonetheless he was one of the two masterminds behind the plan to overthrow, if not necessarily murder, the tsar. At von der Pahlen's insistence, the messenger of woe who awakened Empress Maria Feodorovna with news of her husband's cruel death was the children's governess, Charlotte von Lieven.

As the wife of a minister of the tsar, Dorothea von Lieven, though only fifteen at the time, knew all the conspirators. Von der Pahlen impressed her greatly. "I always saw him with infinite pleasure," she noted shortly after the death of Paul. "He never failed to make me laugh and took delight in doing so."[33] In the wake of the murder, the empress was unforgiving, even if her hands were tied by her son Alexander's involvement in the conspiracy. She drove the conspirators from the Russian capital. Von der Pahlen was banished to his estates in Kurland and denied the right to visit St. Petersburg or Moscow ever again. According to Dorothea, he got blind drunk on every anniversary of the murder.[34]

Schnupftuch Pahlen had two sons, Peter Johann Christoph and Friedrich Alexander. Both had sterling careers in Russian diplomatic service — unaffected, it appears, by their father's fate. Peter was appointed ambassador to Paris in 1835, the same year Dorothea arrived in the French capital. He became a regular at her salon.[35] To Lady Cowper, the future Lady Palmerston, Dorothea described Peter as "a great man, and our leading general. Very upright, very honest, very simple in his manner, most distinguished-looking."[36] Peter was to remain single his entire life.

His younger brother, Friedrich, served as Russian plenipotentiary in Washington, Rio de Janeiro, and Munich. Administrative and political duties followed. In 1832 he became a member of the Imperial Council. At age fifty he finally married. Natalie von der Pahlen, bride-to-be of Paul von Lieven, was his daughter. She grew up on the estate of Hofzumberge. Like her mother, she would marry a fifty-year-old man.

Since her uncle Peter had no recognized offspring, on his death in 1864 the family seat at Kautzemünde and the estate at Gross-Eckau passed to his nephew Konstantin, a future minister of justice in the Russian empire.[37]

Grieta Pluta knew all these people. Natalie Princess von Lieven, mistress of Mesothen, used to invite her and Pauline for visits during the summer season when the family was on the estate. In the decade between her marriage in 1871 and her husband Paul's death in 1881, Natalie had five children, two sons and three daughters, several of whom were close to Pauline in age. Grieta and her child seem always to have been welcome. Why should Grieta have visited Mesothen so often? Why should Natalie have invited her?

Born into the Russian Orthodox community, Princess Natalie turned a few years after her marriage to a fervent evangelical Christianity. In 1874 she was converted to a nondenominational evangelicalism by the British peer Lord Radstock, who made several successful missionary tours of Russia. Radstock was often a guest of the princess at the Lieven mansion, on the rue Morskaja in St. Petersburg, with its magnificent pillars and cornices made of malachite stone from the Urals. In the spacious white drawing room the British guests were invited to address the Russian aristocracy, usually in French.[38] Preaching a gospel stripped of all dogma, Radstock had such success in these circles in the 1870s that a Russian Orthodox priest commented bitterly: "Not to be a Radstockist meant to lower oneself in the eyes of society and risk the danger of becoming labelled a backward person. To take exception with the teaching of the English Lord in a private home was considered equal to insulting the host."[39] Among Radstock's adherents were prominent families such as the Shuvalovs and Chicherins, but also the Golitsyns who owned Zohden. Natalie's sister, Princess Gagarin, and her uncle Konstantin von der Pahlen became converts. Central Kurland became in fact a pocket of enthusiastic Radstockism. Church authorities and those close to the tsar were not amused.

When Grieta and young Paulīne used to visit Mesothen, Princess Lieven taught the child hymns. Some of these the girl would remember and later teach to her own children. Princess Lieven became so hostile to the official world from which she had plucked her husband that she refused to present her three daughters at court because she believed that court society was, in the words of her great-grandson, both "a den of iniquity and a prime location for contracting venereal disease."[40]

In 1892, at age fifteen, Paulīne went to work as a handmaiden on the von der Pahlen estate at Gross-Eckau, where this evangelical Christianity also held sway. Princess Lieven, born a von der Pahlen, no doubt helped Paulīne find that position.

Fictions of Fact

OUR FAMILY has always thought that the name of Grieta's first daughter was Lavīze. However, an 1859 census document in the Latvian State Historical Archive in Riga records that daughter's name as "Lihbe,"[41] a transliteration of the German "Liebe." *Liebe* means love. Love? Did Grieta love the baron? Was her daughter a love child? Did she first call her daughter Lihbe and only later change the name to Lavīze?

But there is a smudge in the *b*, as if the census transcriber had started to write an *s* and then changed it to a *b*. Did he get confused?

Did he begin to write Lihse and then change to Lihbe? Lihse —
transliterated later in Latvian as Līze — was a common name, a
short version of Lavīze.

Did you love him, Grieta? Is that why the frustration turned to
fury?

"Cheaper than Niggers"

WHO WAS GRIETA? Though we know little about her, we know a
good deal about her social and cultural world. After the conquest
by German knights, the local populations of the Baltic had gradually been reduced to the status of serfs. This thralldom was to last
in law until the early nineteenth century. In 1777 a German clergyman noted of the local Latvian serfs: "These men go cheaper than
niggers in the American Colonies. A man servant can be bought
for 30 to 50 roubles, an artisan, cook, or weaver for anything up
to one hundred roubles. The same price is asked for a whole family; a maidservant rarely costs more than 10 roubles, and children
can be bought for 4 roubles each. Agricultural workers and their
children are sold or bartered for horses, dogs — and even tobacco
pipes."[42]

The peasants could be used for any practical purpose. One way to
break the chill of a ballroom on a country estate was to drive a horde
of peasants into it. Their body warmth would raise the temperature.
"The result," commented the Englishwoman Peggie Benton when
she heard of the practice, "probably smelt no worse than the stair-
cases of Versailles."[43] Similarly, what better way to warm a bed than
to have a pretty chambermaid occupy it first?

When Karl Marx wrote of "the idiocy of rural life," he had in
mind the kind of peasant existence that had been lived in Europe
since the onset of feudalism and which then still occupied the mass
of humanity in Central and Eastern Europe and in Russia. By "idiocy" he meant the subservience to nature and to routine and the
inability to transcend, in imagination let alone reality, the limita-
tions of one's immediate situation.

In this life rooted in the soil, people and nature were intimately intertwined. Before Christianization, the natives had as many gods as there were objects in nature and pursuits in life. This attachment to nature and to the act of creation survived over the centuries through folk customs, oral traditions, and family names. When the serfs were liberated and needed surnames, these were invariably taken from nature. In the 1930s the list of faculty at the agricultural college at Jelgava included the names Eglītis (little fir tree), Āboliņš (little apple), Krūmiņš (little bush), Tauriņš (little butterfly), Briedis (stag), Gailis (rooster), Lapiņš (little leaf), Lācis (bear), Ozoliņš (little oak tree), Rožkalns (rose hill).

Birth, marriage, the rising sun, and spring evoked religiosity and celebration. The white of the birch, of the Baltic sand, and of fresh snow, like Grieta's flaxen strands, were symbols of innocence, fertility, and goodness. Elizabeth Rigby noted that flaxen hair was "a feature that the hearts of the peasants are never known to resist." Girls so endowed, she was informed by her hosts, were "the surest of husbands."[44] The surest of princely interest too, the hosts might have added, with a wink and a grin.

But genuinely blond locks, like brightness and rejoicing, were in fact rare. For the most part, life was not fair; it was dark and, like the heavy rye bread of the region, sour as well. Life consisted of incomprehension, travail, and evil spirits. Well into the nineteenth century pagan rituals were regularly enacted by the peasants to placate or ward off these spirits, or "lords of the house," as they were called. One buried eggs, rooster feathers, bones, and coins in honor of these spirits. In general, pleasures were few, hardships many. The climate was not kind: rain, mist, and darkness dominated. Why even the Baltic Sea was known to freeze solid on occasion between the mainland and the large islands off the coast. "They," remarked the traveler Le Clerc of the Baltic peasants in 1785, "are afraid of everything except death."[45]

This was indeed a people without a formal history and with largely an oral culture. That culture, however, was extraordinarily rich: several hundred thousand folksongs, thirty thousand melodies, thirty-five thousand fairy tales. This oral tradition was a substitute for "history." The folktales and songs are plaintive, whimsical, and sad — "There once was a king so cruel . . ." Revenge and passion are rarely the motif; it is more often a stoical endurance of fate.

The tale of Rose of Treiden (Turaida) bears this out. Rose lived during the period when the Swedes ruled the land. A Swedish lord took a fancy to her and demanded affection, but she swore allegiance to her true love from whom she had received a kerchief. Her kerchief, she said, had magical powers born of love; it would protect her from all evil. She placed the kerchief on her breast. The implacable Swede aimed his pistol at the kerchief and fired. She died.

The folk culture expressed itself most powerfully in music and dance. Song was everywhere, in religion, in politics, in education, in the home. "They sing of their faith in a militant song," wrote one observer of the Riga working class.[46] Almost all ritual involved becostumed dance as well.

Although the Bible had been translated into Latvian in 1687, the language was still not written according to any agreed-upon rules when Grieta was born and would not be until the last quarter of the nineteenth century. Only in 1908 was the present orthography adopted.

The rather small corpus of Latvian literature exudes longing and melancholy. Joy is never shrill, always quiet, because it cannot last. Beauty, too, is fleeting. Oppression, exile, pain, and dreams that dissolve into illusions are standard themes. In Aspazija's poem "The Princess," the child declares: "They have told me so many fairy tales / I do not believe them anymore."[47]

That a Latvian culture and language survived, instead of dying out as did the Liv and Old Prussian cultures, might be explained by the aloofness of the German colonizers and the general subservience of the Latvians. Because they considered the Latvians inferior, their language a patois of kitchen and stable, and their folk culture shallow, the Germans made no systematic attempt to assimilate them.

The odd rural disturbance notwithstanding, the future was not an issue for most Latvian peasants. Poor harvests, famine, pestilence, and even cruel landlords were attributed to fate. Little could be done to alter fortune.

The Return

FRANKFURT AIRPORT, Sunday, July 11, 1993. The boarding call for the flight to Riga has not yet been made, but a flashing light at the gate indicates that the bus that will take us to the airplane is waiting. I descend to the bus along with a middle-aged German-speaking couple, she fat and puffing, he small and sallow. We board the bus but remain alone for some minutes. The woman begins to fuss and mutter, wondering whether we are on the right bus. Finally more people appear. "We're right after all," she exclaims with relief. "There are people coming. They all look like Baltic Germans!"

She knew what she was looking for; she trusted her senses. I, by comparison, was less certain, of anything. I returned to Latvia in 1993, forty-nine years after I had left. The Lufthansa flight from Frankfurt am Main to Riga covered in ninety minutes a distance it had taken my parents six months to cross during the fury of 1944–45. My fortnight's sojourn was a difficult one, fraught with emotion. I saw the church where my father had preached as a minister in Riga; the apartment that had been my first home; the street in Liepāja where my father had grown up; the farm outside Jelgava where my mother was raised; the cold-cellar where we had hidden when we were suddenly trapped between the Russian and German front lines in late July 1944. I walked through Old Riga, which was rapidly being restored to its former Hanseatic color and vitality. I visited Mežotne, seat of the Lievens, and Iecava, estate of the von der Pahlens. I strolled through the grand palace at Jelgava. I found Code (Zohden) and even Pūrīcas, the farm where Grieta had lived.

But did I make contact with history, as my Baltic-German companion on the airport bus set out confidently to do? No. I could not distinguish between the Baltic Germans and the Latvians on the bus. I was surrounded by apparitions. Perhaps the baron's descendants were among us.

Liaisons

IN THE EIGHTEENTH and early nineteenth century a girl from the aristocracy who had reached the age of fourteen was thought suitable for marriage. Catherine the Great received her first proposal, from an uncle ten years her senior, at fourteen and married the Russian heir Peter Ulrich at sixteen. Dorothea Princess Lieven was married at fifteen. Georg Reinbeck, a German inhabitant of St. Petersburg, insisted, for that matter, that "a girl of eighteen in Russia is almost past the desirable age."[48] Grieta, when she went to work for the baron, was just past that desirable age. She was nineteen.

To say that she was abused by the baron is a rough shorthand that leaves no room for either her personality or the historical background of the baron's behavior. She, it is clear from family lore, was an ambitious and even willful woman who readily fantasized about social advancement. Notable precedents for such advancement were not lacking and were well known in peasant culture. Empress Catherine I, for instance, was the daughter of a Lithuanian peasant. The lover and closest adviser of Empress Elizabeth was Count Razumovsky, a simple peasant from the Ukraine renowned for his good looks: "He was one of the handsomest men that I have ever seen in my life" was the assessment of Catherine II, no slouch herself when it came to appreciating virility.[49]

As for social achievement in general, the example of Napoleon Bonaparte loomed over the entire nineteenth century. From his humble roots among the impoverished nobility of Corsica, Napoleon had, through sheer will and effort, risen to a position of power never before attained by any ruler in Europe. Napoleon's Grand Army, in its march toward Moscow in 1812, had advanced over the very ground Grieta inhabited. Bauske was the site of a major battle, which spilled over to Mesothen in late September. For this campaign Maréchal Jacques Macdonald, who commanded Napoleon's Tenth Army, set up his headquarters at the Stalgen manor house on the river Aa, halfway between Bauske and Mitau, only a few kilometers from Mesothen. Napoleon, whose name became a synonym for ambition, was a legendary figure in the Bauske neighborhood.

As for the baron, even if serfdom had been abolished in Kurland in 1817, and even if the feudal *ius primae noctis* — the right of the lord to deflower the bride of a vassal — no longer functioned in literal terms, a related *ius dominorum* — the master's right — still obtained in judicial and police matters in the Baltic provinces. The master was exactly that, the master. The servant was to provide service. As for convention, to sleep with a servant girl was a practice as old as social distinction itself; it involved no shame for the noble-man; it merely confirmed a natural, hierarchical social order.[50] Sons of the nobility and even of the upper bourgeoisie were encouraged to have their first sexual experiences with servant girls.

That said, and questions of culpability aside, such social behavior did not encourage harmonious relations between classes and nation-alities in an age of transition and burgeoning ambition. Grieta's fate was the fate of a peasant class increasingly influenced by visions of change and self-assertion. Grieta's fate was also the fate of a small national group, the Latvians, whose growing self-awareness over-lapped with a sense of abuse and exploitation.

Bullet Holes

IN MARCH 1990 a poster for the Latvian People's Front read: "Eternal Glory to the Communist Party of the Soviet Union, Fallen in the Fight for Communism."[51] Less than a year later, during the night of January 20–21, 1991, the Black Berets, a special unit under the command of the Soviet minister of the interior, stormed the Latvian Ministry of the Interior in Riga. Five people were killed, ten wounded. Among the dead was Andris Slapiņš, Latvia's foremost film cameraman. He filmed his own death. Those clips were broad-cast around the world.

In a referendum in March 1991, residents of Latvia voted on a simple question: Did they want Latvia to be independent? Eighty-eight percent of eligible voters turned out. Seventy-three percent voted yes. Some of those who voted yes were Russians.

When the coup attempt in Moscow against Mikhail Gorbachev and his policies of *glasnost* and *perestroika* failed that August, the Soviet Union disintegrated. Latvia achieved independence from Russia. For a second time.

The last Russian troops withdrew from Latvia at the end of August 1994. In October of that year the Friedrich Ebert Foundation of Germany commissioned a poll of Russian military officers. Among the questions was one that asked the respondents to rank foreign states according to the threat they posed to Russia. That a German foundation should put this question to Russian soldiers a half century after the horrendously brutal war between Germany and Russia was understandable. The results of the poll were, however, most surprising. Germany was not to be found among the top five enemy states. In fifth position was the United States, in fourth Estonia, third Lithuania, and second Afghanistan. The grand prize went to Latvia. Forty-nine percent of the officers polled considered Latvia to be their chief enemy.[52] A country with a population of fewer than 3 million was deemed the principal foe of a state with some 150 million people.

The bullet holes in the Latvian Ministry of the Interior ooze.

Autumn

THE BALTIC ARISTOCRACY CAME, by the end of the nineteenth century, to be enveloped in an autumnal melancholy. Eduard von Keyserling's novels expressed this mood brilliantly. His characters, with cosmopolitan first names like Boris, Billy, and Betty, live lives full of an inexpressible longing bordering on despair. "Oh God, if only we knew what we are waiting for," sighs Countess Betty in the 1909 novel *Bunte Herzen*.[53]

In 1874 Prince Paul von Lieven had added another property to the family realm. He had acquired the old crusader castle, now little more than a ruin, at Bauske. He had then set about developing gardens around the castle and restoring its walls and towers. Constantin Mettig, a Baltic travel writer, visited the castle toward the end of the century. From the towers, he wrote, one had "a worth-

while view of the pleasant and peaceful countryside, which so
often in the past had been the scene of conflict of different warring
peoples."[54] Mettig described the turbulent history of Bauske in a
manner, quiet and composed, that suggested better times ahead.
Never could he or his fellow Baltic Germans have predicted the
fate that would befall them and this corner of Europe in the next
fifty years.

Grieta would have her revenge.

2

A Man, a Cart, a Country

Every beginning works hardship, but worst is the start
of a household.

JOHANN WOLFGANG VON GOETHE

To prolong the death agony of German life in this country to the
last possible moment is all we Balts of German descent can do.

COUNT ALEXANDER VON KEYSERLING

Entrepreneur

A TALLY OF the day's earnings and expenses, that was the business of
every evening. Each night after supper the young entrepreneur,
Jānis Vajeiks, methodically assembled the necessary tools: pocket-
knife, pencil, account book, and family. First he sharpened the pencil,
with a concentration befitting the preparation of a weapon for a life-
and-death struggle. The pages of the account book he then turned to
the appropriate place with gestures purposely exaggerated so as to
make certain everyone noticed how important the task at hand was.
And finally came the moment all awaited: onto the table he emptied
his purse.

A peasant might bite his coin to test its metal. But for this budding bourgeois it was paper that elicited a smile at once earnest and
jubilant. Paper currency, not coin, was the future. "This came from
an aristocrat's pocket," he would announce. "It has the scent of a
baron." He then passed the note to wife and children; each in turn
sniffed it with an air of reverence.

The counting began, aloud. A sum for income was determined; a verbal statement on expenses followed. Then came the final tally for the day. These closing calculations and entries were done with special pride, to impress the family yet again that its head was no paltry peasant but a budding businessman and that he, through this ritual, was pointing the way to a bright future for all family members. Writing and arithmetic, the ritual was meant to say, were no mean accomplishments. They represented a step into the modern world of enterprise and progress. The excitement of this new world would not be lost on the children. They would later speak with pride of their father, the independent entrepreneur.

Born in 1874, Jānis Vajeiks, my maternal grandfather, was the son of a peasant farmer. His mother had died when he was three, but his father had remarried. While the son's education was basic — he had spent only the three requisite winters at the village school — he had nevertheless learned to read, write, add, subtract, and multiply. Not, however, to divide. That would have come during the next winter's lessons, which he did not attend since in the 1880s only three sessions of schooling were mandatory.

Still, literacy had been achieved. In this Jānis Vajeiks was not alone. All the Baltic provinces had a far higher rate of literacy than Russia as a whole. In the tsar's empire at the end of the nineteenth century more than two thirds of the population were still illiterate. In Livland and Estland, by contrast, more than 90 percent of the inhabitants could read and write at the time of the census in 1897, and literacy levels exceeded those of some parts of Western Europe. In Kurland the rate was around 80 percent. Literacy became a source of pride to Latvians and Estonians.

The Swedes, during their occupation of Livland in the sixteenth and seventeenth centuries, had taken the initial steps to encourage the education of the native population. The vibrant Swedish king, Gustavus Adolphus, had established gymnasia in Reval, Dorpat, and Riga, and a university at Dorpat, with explicit orders that gifted peasant children benefit from these institutions. However, the primary responsibility for the high rate of Baltic literacy belonged to the Baltic Germans, and more specifically to Lutheranism.[1] "See to it that ye set up schools, for then Satan will be sure that he is in a bad way," Luther had ordained.[2]

Jānis Vajeiks met Paulīne Kuiva, Grieta's daughter, while both were on the staff of the von der Pahlen baronial estate at Gross-Eckau. On this mammoth property, assembled by the Treyden family in the sixteenth century and given to the von der Pahlens by Catherine II for their assistance in incorporating Kurland into Russia in 1795,[3] both Jānis and Paulīne worked as domestic servants. The estate was renowned for its manor house, built in classical style, for its distillery which produced a fine liqueur, and for being another site of battle in 1812 during which Napoleon's troops destroyed the elegant pastor's manse dating from 1567. By mid-nineteenth century the modern age had come to Gross-Eckau. A little more than three kilometers from the manor house stood the railway station, a stop on the Mitau–Kreuzburg (Jelgava–Krustpils) line.

The regime at the estate was severe. Amorous relationships between servants were discouraged. Paulīne was forbidden to see Jānis. Their trysts had to be secret affairs. When she baked bread for the household in the morning, she always put some aside in a hiding place for Jānis.

If the morning air was still, the train could be heard from the manor house, and to Paulīne, whose mother had left her with many visions, the lure of town life and the prospect of greater freedom, so short a distance away, were irresistible. She had a relative in Mitau who worked as a domestic for the family of a banker. "Bank Lizzie" her friends called her. She found Paulīne a position in town as a servant to a Russian family, and so the young girl left the von der Pahlen estate and moved to Mitau, the capital city of Kurland. A Russian master replaced a German one.

After her move a despondent Jānis made weekly trips from Gross-Eckau to Mitau, a distance of some thirty kilometers. Before long he proposed, Paulīne accepted, and in 1900 — in time for the new century and all its spectacular promise — they married.

Where would they live? What would they do? Since Paulīne quite liked her new position, they decided to stay in Mitau. Thus the two workers from the feudal regime of the countryside became a modern urban couple.

Jānis found the transition more difficult than Paulīne. He worked for a time in a confectionery factory, then in a brewery. Finally, craving independence and sensing opportunity in city life, he decided to strike out on his own. He himself had no money, but Paulīne had brought a small dowry into the marriage, 300 rubles. This was her share of the old family farm at Pūrīcas. Jānis decided to risk it in a business venture. He invested the savings in a cart and horse and started up a droshky service. The cart was old, but the horse was young.

His decision, as it turned out, was a clever one. By the end of the century Mitau was growing. Previously the towns and cities of the Baltic had been predominantly German. That was now changing. Jānis and Paulīne were an example of a broader trend, the influx of the native population into the cities, as the Baltic provinces of Russia began to experience industrialization and social movement. As a result, Jānis's little enterprise bore a modest profit. One day when his eldest daughter offered to teach him how to divide, a skill he had not learned in school, he replied that division was not necessary. In this atmosphere of burgeoning capitalism, multiplication sufficed.

Annus Mirabilis

THE YEAR 1989 was so remarkable that we in the West resurrected a Latin term for it that had not been used with such gusto for a century and a half, since 1848: *annus mirabilis*. Of all the striking images of that year — the huge throngs of young people in Tiananmen Square in Beijing in June; the one million Estonians, Latvians, and Lithuanians who literally joined hands from Tallinn through Riga to Vilnius on August 23, the fiftieth anniversary of the Hitler-Stalin Pact; the three hundred thousand people who paraded after Monday evensong in Leipzig in October; the crowds of young people dancing on the wall of walls, that supreme symbol of our arrogant and mutilated century, the Berlin Wall, on November 9 — of all the striking images, perhaps the most evocative are those pictures of Lenin statues being removed by cranes from the city centers of Eastern Europe. In Bucharest, around the statue's neck, like a noose, were several strands of metal cable.

That figure strung up from the crane in the Rumanian capital — reluctant as we were to admit it at the time — was not just Lenin. It was all politicians, statesmen, diplomats, academics, and, indeed, historians — all of us systematizers, synthesizers, prognosticators, and scientists, particularly of the social sort. None of us had predicted any of this. None of our bright and garrulous analysts had called this one. We were all outspoken proponents of balance and gradualism. A measure of liberalization, yes, we supported that, but we never envisaged the wholesale collapse of the Soviet Union, along with the unification of Germany and the reemergence of independent states in the Baltic.

In January 1993 in The Hague, an East Timor delegate to the General Assembly of the Unrepresented Nations and Peoples Organization stated: "The Soviet empire has crumbled. We too can be free."[4]

Mitau

BY THE LATE NINETEENTH CENTURY, Mitau had some light industry, but its main role was as the chief market town for the farm produce of the province. Mitau was by nature an intermediary. This part of Kurland was the agricultural heartland of the Baltic. In its rich soil, watered by the Aa, wheat, rye, oats, barley, and potatoes grew well. Fine pastureland provided fodder for dairy cattle and horses. The brown-earth plain on which Mitau stood stretched far into Lithuania. It was a natural route for travelers, and invaders.

Founded in 1265 by the German colonizers, Mitau had been the seat of power of the dukes of Kurland for more than two centuries. Holding their land in feudal tenure from the Polish rulers to the south, the dukes nonetheless exercised relative autonomy. If the

German manner on the land was dour, German town life could show flourish.

In the seventeenth century, one duke, Jakob, brought special renown to the duchy. He showed enterprise worthy of a latter-day robber baron. Since Kurland was a maritime province, he decided to build and maintain at the port of Windau (Ventspils) a small war fleet. In view of the size of the duchy, a few ships might have made the appropriate point. Jakob, however, had grander dreams. He built forty-four ships, a veritable fleet. This extravagance elicited respect and even declarations of neutrality from the sea powers of the day, Holland and England.

But Jakob was not finished. His fleet was neither gesture nor toy. He proceeded to seek out colonies suitable for a small European state with an imperial outlook, and for a while, thanks to the neutrality accords with the principal imperial powers, he exercised suzerainty, from 1651 to 1664, over a coastal part of Gambia in Africa and, from 1640 to 1690, over the Caribbean island of Tobago. From Gambia Jakob imported coffee, indigo, ebony, spices, ivory, and gold, and from Tobago, whose current capital, Scarborough, was first called New Mitau, tobacco, sugar, ginger, and rum. He even entertained the idea of colonizing Australia.

In Jakob's grand scheme Mitau was to become a center of East and West Indian trade.[5] If the duke's achievements never rivaled Queen Victoria's, the entire operation had a manic brilliance. This was not lost on the Swedish King Charles X Gustavus, who noted wittily that Jakob had become too rich to remain a simple duke but was still too poor to be a king. Jakob had to be taught a lesson in humility. The opportunity arose in the course of the First Northern War, 1655–1660, between Sweden and Poland. The Swedes conquered Mitau in 1658; Jakob, the Polish vassal, was captured and imprisoned for two years, until the end of the war. When he returned to his duchy, his world had been shattered. The ships were gone, the colonies in tatters, his own land destitute. A standard of rule had, however, been set.

His successor, Friedrich Casimir, felt obliged to make his own mark. He brightened up life in Mitau in a different but more obvious way: he established an Italian opera house, a court orchestra, and a falconry society. The taste, while garish, was attuned to Western styles.

Jakob's grandson, Friedrich Wilhelm, was perhaps the most astute, if short-lived, of Kurland's dukes. He saw that marriage was synonymous with opportunity. He wed the niece of Peter the Great, but on the return journey from St. Petersburg to Mitau, presumably overcome by his own accomplishment, he fell dead. The object of his affections, Anna, became first the duchess of Kurland, setting up a Russian court in Mitau, and then in 1730, in an extraordinary leap on the branches of the family tree, tsarina of Russia. On her departure for the Russian capital, she left Kurland in the charge of her lover, Count Ernest Biron.

The count was no idler when it came to great ambition. Aware that his chance to make a mark on history was fortuitous, he hired the architect Bartolomeo Francesco Rastrelli, whose accomplishments included the Winter Palace in St. Petersburg, to build him a grand rococo château at Mitau. The palace, begun in 1738, was completed only in 1772, after Rastrelli's death.

In the wake of the annexation of Kurland by Russia in 1795, Mitau lost its former glamour, albeit not immediately. The palace, already in need of repair owing to a recent fire, was still sufficiently grand to house the court of the exiled Bourbon heir, the Comte de Lille (later Louis XVIII). He had fled the revolution that had devoured his French homeland. Tsar Paul I invited him to stay, and the French pretender occupied the palace from 1798 to 1801 and again from 1804 to 1807. The French police sarcastically referred to the Comte de Lille as *"le roi de Mitau."*[6]

During Napoleon's advance on Moscow in 1812, Mitau was occupied by his Tenth Army, consisting largely of Polish, Prussian, and other German units. First contact with the Russians took place at Eckau on July 19. Other battles in the vicinity followed. The palace at Mitau served as an army hospital, a practice that would be repeated in the next century. When news reached General Jacques Macdonald that the Grand Army, on its retreat from Moscow, had been destroyed, he is said to have sunk back into a chair in the

Ritterhaus in Mitau and whispered, *"O quelle honte!"* (Oh, what shame!)[7]

If Mitau's brilliance faded in the nineteenth century, its symbolic stature did not. It now became emblematic of the modernizing process, the center of a growing network of communication in the Baltic. Mitau was on the new highway from the West to Riga and St. Petersburg. By 1868 a railway link connected it with Riga. The town also figured prominently in the growth of a Latvian cultural awareness. In 1815 the Kurland Society for Literature and Art was set up in Mitau to foster the study of local Latvian culture, language, and oral traditions.[8] A few years later, in 1822, a clergyman named Karl Friedrich Watson — he was born in Kurland of Irish background — began to publish a weekly newspaper, *Latviešu avīzes* (Latvian Papers), in Mitau, meant for Latvian readers, the first venture of its kind.

In the census of 1897 the population of Mitau numbered 35,131. By 1914 that had grown to 45,700. As late as the middle of the nineteenth century, Germans still far outnumbered Latvians in urban centers; by the end of the century, however, as Latvians like Jānis and Paulīne Vajeiks moved off the land and into cities in growing numbers, the ratios had changed drastically. Of the roughly thirty-five thousand inhabitants in Mitau in 1897, almost half were Latvians. The rest consisted of Germans, Russians, Jews, Poles, and Lithuanians, in descending numbers. Riga had similar proportions among its population of a quarter million.

In this lively atmosphere, a coachman could make a living. Paris and London might by then have been a mix of motorized and horse-drawn traffic, but in Mitau even bicycles were still a novelty and a sign of status. In 1923 there would be only 422 automobiles in all of Latvia.[9]

The coachman would of course have to speak the languages of most of his clients, German and Russian. Latvian-speaking riders would be few. Despite changes transpiring in the social and economic order, Latvian speakers remained at the bottom of the social ladder in the land in which they were in the majority. Latvians with social pretensions spoke German. Those who moved upward in status often assimilated to the German-speaking culture. As a Latvian cultural identity evolved, the rate of assimilation, rather than decreasing, actually rose.[10]

Jānis Vajeiks lived in Mitau through these years of growth. He and Paulīne assisted the population increase. They were to raise four children, three of whom were born in Mitau: Rūdolfs in 1901, Leontīne in 1905, and Artūrs in 1910.

The Summer of 1989

THE YEAR 1988–89 my family spent in Europe. We were in France, Britain, and Germany. In the summer of 1989 we rented a house in the Baltic resort town of Travemünde so that I could work in the archives and libraries of neighboring Lübeck. We were within binocular sight of the barbed wire and guard towers of the East German border.

After Travemünde and Lübeck I left the family with my wife's relatives in Holland and then spent time in archives in Koblenz, Freiburg, and finally Berlin. To reach Berlin I drove through "the zone," as Russian-occupied East Germany was often called, passing through checkpoints at Helmstedt and Dreilinden. I noticed little that was different from previous trips. The East German border police were as unfriendly as ever. No one ever smiled, no one ever indulged in polite pleasantry. Automatons these officials were, as close to machines as human beings could get. On a trip some years earlier, my car was disassembled after a zealous border guard, in flipping through a manuscript in the back seat, had found a footnote reference to Hitler's *Mein Kampf.* She was convinced that I had either copies of the forbidden text or uniformed fascists stashed under floorboards and fenders.

In that summer of 1989, I, a child of Eastern Europe and a historian of Germany, noticed nothing to suggest the events to come. Konrad Adenauer, a founding father of the Federal Republic of Germany and its first chancellor, had had little respect for historians who could make no sense of the future: "Naturally I don't demand prophecy from a historian, but I do think that his work, especially that of a historian of contemporary history, is only really done if he points to future developments that might follow from current events."[11] Had he lived to experience the events of 1989, Adenauer would have been overjoyed by the world-historical drama unfolding but at the same time dreadfully disappointed by the historical profession.

A Time of Troubles

IN 1905 RUSSIA BURST INTO FLAME. A mismanaged and unpopular war against Japan brought social and political discontent into the open. Strikes erupted in the Baltic provinces, too. Latvian workers had become steadily politicized since the 1880s. In 1904 the Latvian Social Democratic Party had been founded. On January 13, 1905, four days after the Bloody Sunday massacre of protesters in St. Petersburg by the tsar's troops, a large crowd of strikers and demonstrators in Riga was brutally dispersed. Some seventy protesters were killed and more than two hundred wounded. In the young poet Jānis Akurāters outrage turned to resolve. He penned words that became the Latvian revolutionary hymn in 1905 and again in 1917: "With battle cry on our lips . . ." A fortnight later, on January 27, one of the most famous of all Latvian plays, Aspazija's *The Silver Veil*, opened in Riga. In it, a usurper king shouts: "I want more blood!" The audience erupted in cheers.[12]

But whose blood? Russian? Royal? Anger turned on the Baltic Germans and their symbols of culture and authority. That spring, churches burned and churchmen were attacked. A hot summer followed. German baronial manors in Kurland and Livland were plundered and razed, including the von der Pahlen palace at Kautzemünde: altogether some 140 manor houses were destroyed either partially or completely by marauding peasants. A British journalist, Henry W. Nevinson, described the fate of an old parson in Mitau: "His chief delight had been the collection of Lettish songs, riddles, proverbs, and legends. Over this labour he had gone blind . . . Suddenly the peasants attacked his parsonage, shot his sexton, threatened his daughter, burnt his library, smashed his china, trampled on his harpsichord, and made a bonfire of his furniture in the garden, kindling it with his manuscripts."[13] More than six hundred Russians and Germans were killed in these various outrages and close to a thousand others injured. One of the dead was the grandson of Grieta's German baron, son of Lavīze and the gamekeeper Zvirgzds. He had grown up to become a district official, despised by the local populace for his ill temper and impatience. In our family it was said that he had the baron's blood in him. But maybe it was that of Grieta. One day during the "troubles" he was found murdered.

The thread connecting the strikes, attacks on clergy, and assaults on manor houses was hatred of the Germans. The Baltic Germans were, from the workers' point of view, the capitalists; they were, from the landless peasants' viewpoint, the baronial exploiters; they were, from the vantage point of the small coterie of Latvian literati, the cultural imperialists. They were the enemy.

The tsar's manifesto in October 1905, promising reforms and a parliament, quieted matters. Then came the reprisals. In the Baltic a vengeful local aristocracy armed with long lists of culprits organized "punitive expeditions." People were seized and executed without trial: 2,041 Latvians were shot or hanged; more than one thousand received corporal punishment; three hundred peasant farms were burned, more than double the number of manor houses destroyed by the insurgents.[14] Henry Nevinson, visiting Riga, was horrified: "Every day little groups of Letts — men, women, and boys — were hurried by escorts of Russian soldiers away to the sandhills to be shot, usually with a crowd following, much as a crowd follows sheep or bullocks to the slaughterhouse. I saw boys bayoneted before my hotel window, and shot against the wall of the old castle tower."[15] When Walter Duranty of the *New York Times* visited Latvia after the 1914–18 war and saw villages in Livland that had been burned to the ground, he assumed at first that the destruction was from the war, until he was informed that it dated from the punitive expeditions of 1906.[16]

The upshot of those two years, 1905 and 1906, was a constant tension between peasant and estate owner.[17] "The hatred which the Lettish peasantry in the Baltic provinces feels against the German landowners," wrote the British historian of Polish extraction, Lewis Namier, in 1915, "is unequalled anywhere in Europe."[18]

Cold War

FOR DECADES the Cold War held us in its viselike grip. It squeezed political life of complexity and variety; it tried to negate accident and surprise, and in doing so conjured up visions of ultimate surprise. It turned to solid ice the difficulties and conundrums, moral, political, and economic, that had led to, and resulted from, the horrific massacres of the first half of the century.

Despite its world-historical implications, the Cold War produced a form of isolationism. In a grand process of reduction, everything was made simple. Basic polarities were set up — subject/object, slavery/freedom — dressed by both sides in the rationalist finery of the Enlightenment.

The most famous station of the Cold War was Berlin's Checkpoint Charlie — off the Kochstrasse, at the Wall — with its ominous multilingual signs: "SIE VERLASSEN . . . VOUS SORTEZ . . . YOU ARE LEAVING . . ." The Cold War divided the world into Them and Us. It also, however, merely delayed the process of coming to terms with the realities of 1945 — the reality of, above all, displacement, not only of a few million refugees or strangers but of an entire civilization and its intellectual foundations.

Great War

THE 1914–18 WAR changed everything. German energy and ambition provoked the war. United as recently as 1871, Germany was the first new power of the modern age. Wary of German designs on the East, Russia joined the British and the French in opposing German expansion.

The Baltic Germans, as citizens of Russia, were confronted with decisions of horrifying magnitude. Should they fight for the tsar against the state representing their cultural heritage in the hope of retaining their privileged position in the Baltic, or should they furtively support Germany, and her ally Austria-Hungary, in the hope of German advancement in the East? At the Battle of the Masurian Lakes in early September 1914, the generals on both sides had German names: Hindenburg, Ludendorff, Rennenkampf.

The indigenous peoples of the borderlands were faced in turn with an old but no more soluble problem: what to do when their imperial neighbors went to war. In 1914 sympathies lay with Russia. The events of 1905–6 had turned a deep-seated resentment toward the German baronial overlords into an urgent hate. Latvians decided in 1914 to join with the Russians to destroy their common enemy, the German.

But the war did not develop as planned, on any of its fronts. What everyone had foreseen as a quick victory turned to nightmare. By 1915 the western front had stalled. In the East the Germans had more success. By early May they had pushed into the Baltic area and were just kilometers from Mitau. Here the Russian Fifth Army had its headquarters, and here the German advance was finally halted, with the help of Latvian rifle regiments, recruited in desperation by the Russian authorities and thrown into the breach at the last minute.[19]

Propaganda and paranoia mushroomed in tandem. Russian propaganda portrayed the Germans as barbarians who raped and plundered. At the same time, because of past history, the Russians looked on the peoples of the Baltic not as friends but as potential enemies, likely at the moment of decision to side with the Germans. Thus, as the German army approached, the Russians took to driving local inhabitants from their homes, destroying crops, and burning farmsteads and villages. Men of military age they deported to Russia.[20]

As the fighting approached Mitau, Jānis Vajeiks was compelled by the military authorities to provide his cart and horse for official duties. He complied, working long days, ferrying goods and men to and from the central train station. But as parts of the town began to burn, the chances of being caught in a crossfire became real. Terrified by rumors of what the Germans might do to him, the collaborator, and to his wife and children, but afraid also of being seized and deported by the Russians, Jānis Vajeiks quietly loaded up his prized cart one night and took his family the forty-one kilometers to Riga.

He was not the only one to flee. Much of Mitau's population left, either voluntarily or by force. Of the forty-five thousand prewar inhabitants only a little more than eight thousand, mostly old people, stayed through the German occupation, which began on August 1, 1915, and lasted until the German defeat in the West in November 1918. The front line hovered around Mitau for two years, running between Mitau and Riga and then along the Dvina, until the Russian collapse in 1917.[21]

Most of the Kurland refugees, driven by the retreating armies like leaves in a wind, headed north and east, into Livland, Lettgallen (Latgale), and finally Russia. By mid-1915 Russia was confronted with close to three million refugees from Poland, Lithuania, and Kurland. They were discouraged from settling in major cities and told to move ever eastward, into Siberia and Central Asia. Many of these migrants never returned.

When Jānis Vajeiks arrived in Riga, he found a city inundated by refugees. Food was short. The Russian military administration had no sympathy for the newcomers. On June 18, a decree ordered all those who had not been residents of the city before the war to leave. The only route to safety was north.

The cart trundled northward and halted in the middle of Livland, in the town of Wenden (Cēsis), with its imposing medieval fortress built by German knights. In recent years Wenden had developed into a spa and sports center, and owing to its picturesque setting in hilly terrain, came to be called the Davos of the Baltic. It had hospitals, sanatoria, and garrison quarters. During the war it had become a staging and supply center for the Russian army.

"I have learned," says Mother Courage in Bertolt Brecht's play, "that nothing has to come as expected, not even the seasons." Jānis

Vajeiks might have said the same of his fate. Like Mother Courage with her cart, Jānis found opportunity in the crisis of war. In a town bloated with refugees and military personnel, his little cartage business prospered. But the risks were considerable, especially the threat of typhus, the standard illness of war. About eight million people died of typhus in Central and Eastern Europe during and immediately after the Great War. Spread by lice and filth, the disease took a high toll among soldiers, and even if death was not the immediate result, serious complications for heart and lungs were common. The illness caught up with both Jānis and his elder son. Rūdolfs would die prematurely in 1920, at age nineteen.

As the front line moved, so did the supply and support positions in the rear. After a year in Wenden the work dried up. Late in 1916 Jānis Vajeiks decided to risk a return to Riga. As the city came under threat of German attack, its numbers shrank. When the German army entered it in the first week of September 1917, virtually all industry had been dismantled and shipped off to Russia, along with most of the labor force. Of 87,000 factory workers, only 3,400 remained. In 1914 Riga had had a population of half a million; six years later the number had dropped to well under 200,000. The city was a skeleton of its former self. Its many steeples reaching for the heavens were now suggestive of supplication instead of celebration.

Nevertheless, all the movement and upheaval translated into business for a resourceful carter. Jānis Vajeiks purchased a second wagon and horse that Rūdolfs now drove. The youngster's schooling was abandoned; father and son competed for profit. Not surprisingly, much of the time the sixteen-year-old youth bettered his parent.

As the Russians withdrew from Riga, they pillaged and burned much of it. German artillery and native looters added to the damage. One witness noted that a snarling dog, baring its teeth to approaching looters, was the only creature behaving with integrity.[22] This time the Vajeiks family could not flee. Paulīne was in late pregnancy. Shortly after the German arrival, a fourth child was born, a daughter, Biruta. She, my mother, came into the world on a makeshift bed of hay in the back room of a church, to which Paulīne had been brought by a midwife.

Culture and History

I BEGAN TO TEACH at the University of Toronto in 1970. The history I taught for several decades was steeped in liberal values, particularly of an Anglo-Saxon stripe, which I had absorbed as a student in Canada and England. This history was the essence of an Enlightenment tradition that has always assumed that to be cultured is to be historically minded, and to be historically minded is to be free.

These notions of the inseparability of culture, history, and freedom were rooted in eighteenth- and nineteenth-century visions of progress. Culture was associated with cultivation, growth, and refinement. Culture was all that was good, indeed all that was best in society. In Matthew Arnold's famous dictum, culture was "sweetness and light." The antithesis of culture, said Arnold in his classic mid-Victorian statement, was "anarchy."

Despite the efforts, from the late nineteenth century on, by anthropologists and sociologists — those modern levelers — to suggest that culture was some sort of glue that keeps groups together and hence is to be associated with the ordinary rather than the extraordinary, the earlier idealistic notion of culture, as all that is good and heroic, could not be dismantled easily. Culture had nothing to do with the mediocre, vulgar, or banal, let alone with the negative qualities of incompetence, misfortune, or defeat. Certainly in the Anglo-American tradition, culture and catastrophe did not mix.

Although doubts about the life-giving and emancipatory properties of culture and history had become widespread in continental Europe between the world wars, even the Second World War could not dispel the triumphalist aura that surrounded British and American thinking on the subject. The ideal of a British civilizing mission to the world lingered even as decolonization picked up speed in the post-1945 era. And while American interpretations of "manifest destiny" had lost territorial precision, the idea of an American world mission — a crusade for freedom — was fortified by the outcome of World War II.

Scylla

WHILE IN THE WEST the military front remained stalled through 1917, in the East all kinds of possibilities seemed to arise. With the capture of Riga in early September, German spirits rose. In November Lenin and the Bolsheviks seized power in Russia. On their instructions the Russian army surrendered. In March the Treaty of Brest-Litovsk truncated the Russian empire. German spirits rose further.

Whereas neither the German government nor the German military had had any clearly defined territorial designs when the war began, as the fighting progressed, annexationist fantasies flowered. Most Germans did come to expect some form of expansion eastward. The Mitteleuropa concept, with Germany dominating a huge Central European federation stretching from the French to the Russian border, was widely discussed. In annexationist circles the Baltic was regarded as an inevitable prize of victory, indeed part of at least a minimal program. Theodor Schliemann, the archeologist who had rediscovered ancient Troy, Paul Rohrbach, the journalist, and Johannes Haller, the historian, were among the Baltic Germans living in Germany whose strong voices supported German expansion eastward. Russia must cede her western borderlands to Germany, retreat to her pre-Petrine frontiers, and cease to be a European power.

In August 1915 General Ludendorff decided to set up an administrative unit consisting of occupied Lithuania and Kurland that would be called Land Ober-Ost, with the Prussian bureaucrat Alfred von Gossler in charge. After an initial tour of his realm of responsibility, Gossler was impressed: "A glorious land . . . which must under all circumstances be reunified with the old motherland." Several months later Prince Joachim von Preussen told the German commanders in the East that Kurland was "a pearl that we will add to the crown of the German emperor."[23] The view put forward by the Baltic-German lobby in Berlin was that if Germany did not annex the Baltic peoples, Russia would slaughter them.[24] In early 1916 Ludendorff issued orders that steps be taken to settle German peasants in the Baltic; in April 1917 Kurland was designated as an area of future colonization by demobilized German soldiers.

Kaiser Wilhelm himself was intent on reestablishing German dominance in the Baltic provinces. In 1915 a group of nobles, presenting themselves as a self-styled Baltic Committee of Confidence, called on the kaiser to adopt the title Duke of Kurland. Wilhelm visited Mitau twice, in May 1916 — "the German sword will never again surrender Kurland," he promised — and again in July 1917 when he met a delegation of local nobility and assured them that Kurland would be German. On September 6, 1917, three days after its "liberation," he visited Riga; and then on March 15, 1918, twelve days after the Treaty of Brest-Litovsk, he acceded to the earlier request and announced the re-creation of the Duchy of Kurland.[25]

According to the Treaty of Brest-Litovsk, between Germany and the new Bolshevik regime in Russia, Kurland, Lithuania, and Poland ceased to be part of the Russian imperium, and Russia was forced to acknowledge a separate peace agreement between the Central Powers and Ukraine. In August 1918 additional agreements were signed that removed Estland and Livland from Russia. The goal of forcing Russia back to its pre-eighteenth-century borders was temporarily accomplished.

After the Bolshevik coup d'état in Russia, the mood among the German community in the Baltic was unequivocally pro-German. Johannes Bredt, a legal expert on the staff of the German Headquarters Ober-Ost, visited Kurland late in 1917 to plan the constitutional arrangements for the "attachment" of the territory to a greater Germany. When he arrived in Mitau he was advised that, in order to get a proper sense of the situation, he should visit the countryside. Soon an invitation arrived from Prince Lieven to spend some time on the Lieven estate of Senten (Zentene). "We experienced several wonderful days on this spectacular noble estate," wrote Bredt. "You could still imagine what it meant formerly to be an aristocratic German family with property in Kurland. It was probably the most pleasant form of lordly existence anywhere in the world. We drove through the beautiful forest, danced in the evenings, and spoke about the war." In Mitau, where everyone seemed sure of German

victory, and where the tsar's portrait had been replaced by the kaiser's, Bredt was treated to a vibrant social scene. Many of the noble
families had houses on the Palaisstrasse, where they entertained on
jours fixes. Here, too, the Lievens were prominent. Bredt had fond
memories of Princess Lieven's salon.[26]

When in the summer of 1918 Bredt proposed a constitutional
arrangement for Kurland whereby a Baltic-German upper house
would have veto power over any legislation emanating from a lower
house elected by universal suffrage, the chief representative of the
Kurland nobility protested that this proposal was far too liberal: the
Latvians, he said, should have no say whatsoever in their government.[27]

Oxford

CECIL RHODES, one of the world's great imperialists, established scholarships for Oxford University whose purpose was to
train leaders for the English-speaking world. I, great-grandson of
Grieta Pluta, grandson of Jānis Vajeiks, was a recipient of one of
these munificent awards. I arrived in Oxford in the late summer of
1965. When the city's spires came into view from the train just after
Didcot, they proclaimed grandeur and virtue, history and culture. I
attended a college, St. Antony's, founded by a French entrepreneur,
Antonin Besse, who had amassed a huge fortune in Aden.[28] If the
careers and bequests of Rhodes and Besse harbored moral ambiguity, that did not concern me.

I spent five years on this path strewn with primulas, adopting all
the airs. I wrote my doctoral thesis in a Jacobean manor house at
Yarnton, minutes from Blenheim, the palace where Churchill was
born, and Bladon, the churchyard where he is buried. I swam in
the Thames; I went riding at Charlbury. I skied in Obergurgl and
sunned myself in Torremolinos. I saw Ordóñez gored by a bull in
Málaga and democracy skewered by army colonels in Athens. About
supporting dictators with my scholarship fortune I had little qualm.

We were part of a generation associated with rebellion. However, our rebellion was mild and modish. We modest radicals grew our locks and journeyed to London to have them cut at SMILE, hairdressers to the Beatles, just around the corner from Harrods. Vietnam was a dirty war somewhere far away. As earnestly as we debated issues of politics and war, the rivalries of croquet on the manicured lawns of our colleges took precedence.

Charybdis

THE IMPROVEMENT of German prospects in late 1917 and early 1918 radicalized political sentiment in Eastern Europe. What realistic alternatives were there to a German-dominated Baltic? The only possibility seemed to reside on the extreme left. Bolshevism, with its gospel of liberation, found growing support among Latvians. The Social Democratic movement had been strong in the Latvian provinces to begin with; the brutal reprisals that followed the 1905 revolution encouraged radicalism; the dislocation and destruction of the years 1915 through 1917 drove many toward the millennial solutions of Lenin's version of social democracy.

The Central Committee of the Latvian Social Democratic Party was controlled by the Bolshevik faction from August 1914 on, much earlier than in the Russian heartland. Among the Latvian refugees in Russia, Bolshevism found a keen response. Workers transplanted from Riga would play a key role in the two revolutions of 1917 in Russia, in the subsequent civil war, and in the victory of Bolshevism. John Reed, the American sympathizer and chronicler of the Russian Revolution, would be full of admiration for the Latvian Bolsheviks.[29]

Latvians, many have said, were Lenin's Praetorian Guard as well as hangmen.[30] Within a week of the October revolution Lenin brought in the Latvian riflemen's units, which had halted the German advance outside Mitau in 1915 and then defended Russian positions along the Dvina front, to protect his new government in Petrograd. Many of these *strēlnieki* were nationalists first and Bolsheviks second, but they fervently believed that both German imperialism and Russian tsarism had to be crushed if the Latvian idea was to blossom. Support for Bolshevism, this truly revolutionary movement, seemed the best way to promote such a development. After the November revolution all eight Latvian regiments went over to the Boksheviks. In July 1918 the Latvian regiments were used in Moscow to suppress the disturbances staged by Lenin's agrarian rivals, the Social Revolutionaries. Then in the Russian civil war, the Latvian units were deployed against Denikin's White forces in the south and against the feared Czech Legion on the Volga.

The firing squad that executed the tsar and his family in Ekaterinburg in the Urals in July is said to have been composed of seven Latvians and only four Russians. The military commander in the area, who gave the order for execution, was a Latvian, Reinholds Bērziņš. The commander in chief of the entire Red Army, after September 1918, was the Latvian servant's son Jukums Vācietis.[31]

Latvians figured prominently in the policing and administration of the Soviet state. The Latvian Jēkabs Peterss helped Feliks Dzerzhinsky set up the Soviet security police, the notorious Cheka. Reflecting on the roots of the gulag mentality and structures, Aleksandr Solzhenitsyn would write: "Back in the twenties all the jailers were Latvians, from the Latvian Red Army units and others, and the food was all handed out by strapping Latvian women."[32] Latvians were also represented disproportionately in the party hierarchy of the Soviet Union. Jānis Rudzutaks, Valērijs Mežlauks, and Dāvids Beika played important roles in economic planning. Jēkabs Alksnis commanded the Soviet air force from 1931 to 1937.[33]

But even in Livland and Kurland Bolshevism had a powerful appeal. In municipal elections in August 1917 the Bolsheviks won 41 percent of the popular vote in Riga, 64 and 70 percent, respectively, in the towns of Valmiera and Limbaži in the north. After the Bolshevik seizure of power, in the November elections for a Russian constituent assembly, the Latvian part of Livland that was still under Russian control gave 72 percent of its vote to Bolshevik candidates. By comparison, in Petrograd the Bolsheviks won only 45 percent, and in Russia as a whole only 24 percent.[34] In short, emotions ran high among Latvians. At a time when the United States was about to become directly involved in the Great War and a time when Woodrow Wilson was formulating his vision, in the Fourteen Points, of a new Europe and a new world, Bolshevism offered far more realistic possibilities for change in Eastern Europe than did American liberalism.

Fidelio

"In des Lebens Frühlingstagen ist das Glück von mir geflohen." Florestan's lament — "Happiness fled in the springtime of my life" — comes at the beginning of the second act of *Fidelio,* Beethoven's beautiful disquisition on love, humanity, and justice. Florestan's cry is of course one of sorrow. It is also the sigh of a martyr, unjustly imprisoned in a secret dungeon for his ideals. Florestan is the victim of a cruel despotism, the personification of violated humanity. Only through the devotion and imagination of his wife, Leonore, and then the intervention of higher political authority, is he saved.

I first saw *Fidelio* at the age of twenty-one, in 1965. I was on a circuitous route to Oxford and saw a production at the State Opera on Unter den Linden in East Berlin. The Wall had gone up four years earlier. I was staying with friends in West Berlin. On a Sunday in late September I crossed into the Soviet sector of the divided city at the Friedrichstrasse station. It was my first sortie behind the Iron Curtain. My Canadian passport stated that I had been born in Riga, Latvia, in 1943. That information meant that from a Soviet point of view, I was one of theirs, having been born in the wake of the absorption of the Baltic states into the Soviet Union in June 1940. My father had suggested I not venture into East Berlin. My hands trembled as I went through the checkpoint formalities.

I was much taken by the themes of the opera, most of whose music Beethoven had composed in the early days of Napoleon's imperial adventure, in 1803–4, after his initial admiration for the Corsican upstart had wilted. The composer had been outraged by news of Napoleon's coronation as emperor: "He's nothing but an ordinary mortal! Now he'll trample all human rights in the dust."

I remember little of the individual performances, Ludmila

Dvorakova as Leonore and Ernst Kozub as Florestan (a young Peter Schreier had a small solo part as another prisoner). But I remember well the moving prisoners' chorus, accompanied by inspired staging.

For this scene near the end of the first act, the set had been changed. High prison bars now divided the stage. The prisoners' side was in darkness. A few rays of light landed wistfully on the ground beyond the prison bars. Slowly, as the orchestra played its introductory theme, hands appeared, one after the other, pale, wizened, reaching through the bars to touch the sunlight. And then a gentle chorus of male voices rose magnificently from the darkness: "*O welche Lust in freier Luft / Den Athem einzuheben! / . . . O Himmel! Rettung! welch ein Glück. / O Freiheit, kehrest du zurück!*" (Oh, what pleasure, freely to breathe the air. Oh, heaven! Salvation! what fortune. Oh, freedom, may you return!)

On the initiative of Leonore, the prisoners are permitted a stroll in the prison courtyard, a pleasure cut short by the sudden return of the ruthless governor, Don Pizarro. I shivered through that scene. I wondered how the East German audience was reacting to the fate of the prisoners, the brutality of the governor, and the courage of Leonore. An intermission followed. I could have approached members of the audience. I did not dare.

Four years later, I witnessed official ceremonies celebrating the twentieth anniversary of the creation of the German Democratic Republic. I attended a gala evening in the same State Opera House. Tchaikovsky's Violin Concerto in D Major and Beethoven's Fifth Symphony were on the program. Between the two musical masterpieces were banal political speeches. One of those ended with lines of doggerel:

> In all of human history there have never been
> Two better friends than Moscow and Berleen.

You Can Go Home Again

AFTER THE GERMAN OCCUPATION of Riga in the late summer of 1917 and the Russian retreat, the Kurland refugees were informed that they could now go home. Jānis Vajeiks, with his wagons and horses that seemed to be multiplying in number, was suddenly in even greater demand. At this point when business was set to expand again, he made a decision: he would move back to the Kurland countryside.

Despite the business opportunities that Riga offered, the shortages and hardships of war in a large city made rural life appealing. With the collapse of tsarism, German military victory over Russia seemed assured, and the countryside offered a growing family greater security than the city.

So Jānis Vajeiks sold his carts and horses, at considerable profit — the severe shortage of horses had driven prices up — and closed down the little enterprise that had provided the family both a livelihood for the better part of a decade and a means of escape at a critical moment. He took his wife and four children off to the Kurland meadows he knew so well.

Seven kilometers upriver from Mitau was the hamlet of Tetelmünde (Tetele). Its principal property owner was Baron von Behr, whose estate encompassed 1,202 hectares, on which were to be found a palatial manor house and fifteen small farms that were either independently owned — acquired since the 1860s — or leased. The Behrs had owned the property since 1850. Looking for quarters, Jānis Vajeiks learned that the baron was prepared to let a house on his property where previously three servants had resided. Called Meiliņi, it stood, about a half hour's walk from the manor house, on the same Mitau–Kreuzburg railway line that Jānis had traveled regularly during his courtship of Paulīne. In the autumn of 1918, as the war was drawing to a close, the Vajeiks family moved to Meiliņi, on the Tetelmünde estate, unaware that that familiar railway line would soon bring terror instead of hope.

Good War

THE WORLD WAR II generation taught me. Many of my secondary school teachers had served in that war. Two of them, one short, one tall, had been, so it was mooted among the students, in a German prison camp together. They never spoke to each other. Three British "desert generals," of North Africa fame, crossed my path during my teenage years: Ritchie, Montgomery, O'Connor. Through a teacher's graces I met General Sir Neil Ritchie, by then a Toronto resident. As a student cadet, I was conscripted into a battalion honor guard to greet Field Marshal Montgomery on his visit to my school in the spring of 1960. And by happenstance, in the summer of 1961 I stayed in the home of General Sir Richard O'Connor, on Black Isle, near Inverness in Scotland. There, on successive evenings, I heard the story of his three escapes, the last of them successful, from Italian prisoner-of-war camps. The image O'Connor presented, through his personal story and its implications for the wider war, was that of escape from defeat, to victory. As his friend Arthur Bryant said of him, "Dick O'Connor took Time by the forelock."

The memorable encounter with O'Connor resulted from my participation in 1961 in the Commonwealth Youth Movement, the brainchild of a Canadian veteran of the Great War, Major Frederick Ney. Ney had served in the British army and, like so many others of his generation, never got over the front experience. The memory of the mud and horror of Flanders elicited for him values indispensable for the modern world: valor, commitment, service, camaraderie, and spirituality. For Ney, Ypres was a holy site, a shrine. In a gesture reminiscent of the ideals of Cecil Rhodes, Ney selected youths from the four corners of the old empire to gather annually, in what he called the "Quest," so as to renew their commitment to the values at the heart of British civilization. "God, who made thee mighty, make thee mightier yet," we sang in celebration of Britain's role as land of both hope and glory.

The climax of every Quest was an overnight vigil in a historic church. In 1961 the venue was St. George's Memorial Church in Ypres, whose foundation stone had been laid by Field Marshal Lord Plumer in 1927. Here, in half hour intervals throughout the night, Questors knelt in small groups before the altar and confronted their own souls in the context of British imperial history and the crisis of the twentieth century. Ney's aim was to have each youth come face to face with the ideals of commitment and service as the ghosts of the great conflict that was the First World War danced about in the clammy night air. "You will, I hope, sense something of a fellowship with them," he said of the dead, "for they were Questors too, and youthful."

Some of my fellows came away from this night of communion proclaiming that it was the most meaningful experience of their young lives. I approached my "watch" open to impression but also confused by the intricate weave of culture and slaughter.

Like British power in the world after Suez, the Commonwealth Youth Movement lasted for a few more years after my experience of it. Then it disappeared.

At university in Toronto all my mentors seemed to be war veterans: some had landed at Normandy, others had liberated Holland. In Oxford the warden of my college, F. W. D. "Bill" Deakin, had been a young aide to Churchill and then been parachuted into Yugoslavia to link up with Tito and his partisan forces. Deakin exuded leadership, compassion, and, like O'Connor, victory. Even the college's head scout, Fred Wheatley, regaled us with tales of his military exploits on the beaches of Italy. For us young people at St. Antony's, Bill Deakin and Fred Wheatley emitted the moral purpose of history: the cultivation of decency, common sense, good humor.

The kind of academic history we students were meant to write had to display similar characteristics. "I believe in clarity," declared the Regius Professor of Modern History at Oxford, Hugh Trevor-Roper. That clarity presupposed a law of causation — "x causes y in history," insisted Trevor-Roper.[35] History, in this world-view, was basically the story of leadership and power. History was about victory, about moral progress, about the march of law and justice. History was essentially about continuity — about clarity — not about catastrophe.

For all these men, good men, the world wars of our century had been good wars. Of that there was little doubt.

Peasant President

A NEIGHBOR IN TETELMÜNDE after the First World War was Kārlis Skalbe, a poet-politician renowned among Latvians for his fairy tales. The Vajeiks family would in fact buy property from him a few years later.

A little over a week after the Bolshevik coup d'état in early November 1917, a preliminary Latvian Assembly convened to discuss options. Only two days into the meetings, while Germans occupied the southern half of an imagined Latvia and Bolsheviks the northern part, Skalbe proposed that the assembly turn itself into a national council! For most Letts, let alone outsiders, Skalbe's goal of Latvian autonomy belonged to one of his children's stories.

Before 1914 no one had imagined the possible dimensions of future war. Nor had anyone envisaged the imminent and simultaneous collapse of empire, Romanov, Hapsburg, Hohenzollern, and Ottoman. The war brought about the improbable: it destroyed these dynasties and created a series of independent "successor states." Latvia was one. Over the course of 1917 previously rigid categories crumbled. Imagination of every bent — political, artistic, moral — was liberated. Everything seemed possible, even the impossible.

The abrupt collapse of authority in the Baltic produced a vacuum of power. A variety of interests scurried to seize the moment: Bolsheviks, Baltic-German defenders, and Baltic nationalists. A fierce brawl ensued. After dreadful violence it would end in 1920 with the victory of the local nationalists. Their victory would be due, however, less to their own strength than to the weakness of their opponents. The independent states of Latvia, Estonia, and Lithuania were the result of the sudden collapse, not simply the dismantling or restructuring, of empire. These states were created neither by the foresight of their own leaders nor by any vision of the victorious Western Allies. They were the product of ruin and disintegration, and only secondarily of positive effort. They were representative of what was to come in the century as a whole.

A Latvian National Council, successor to the earlier Latvian Assembly, proclaimed an independent Latvija on November 18, 1918. The provisional government was led by Kārlis Ulmanis, a politically minded farmer's son who had been born in 1877 not far from Mitau. He was exactly the same age as Paulīne Vajeiks. After secondary school in Mitau and then agricultural studies in East Prussia, Zürich, and Leipzig, Ulmanis had run afoul of the authorities in 1905 over a newspaper article he had authored. Following a term in prison he had emigrated first to Germany and then to the United States, where in 1909 he had taken a degree, again in agriculture, at the University of Nebraska. He had then worked for a dairy business in the American state, until an amnesty was declared in the Baltic in 1913. He promptly returned home and involved himself in the Latvian farmers' cooperative movement, and in May 1917 he founded and became leader of the Latvian Farmers' Union. This group played a notable role in the political discussions of 1917–18, and in view of his prominence and pleas for political compromise among Latvians, Ulmanis was chosen by the National Council to head the provisional government in November 1918.

In a land of nobles and knights, a peasant had taken control. By the old order he was derided for his looks and conceit. With his broad cheekbones and high forehead, he looked like a plebeian, they said. Such a man could possess none of the attributes of authority. "From the President on down — didn't they have names just like our former coachmen and servants?" asked a Baltic German. "And they looked just like that."[36]

The coachmen and servants had seized power. It was as if, in the guise of Kārlis Ulmanis, the carter Jānis Vajeiks, my grandfather, had come to political responsibility. Grieta's curse was echoing o'er pasture and orchard, o'er hill, steeple, and dale.

3

Baltic Battles

The tradition of all the dead generations weighs like a nightmare on the brain of the living.

KARL MARX

... the story of the peoples who live on the fringe of the Baltic
Sea is a tragedy that is having a happy ending.

OWEN RUTTER

Rolling Wars

WHEN THE VAJEIKS family left Riga and found quarters in the small
cottage at Meiliņi on the estate of Tetelmünde, they jumped, it
might be said, from the frying pan into the fire. Before they knew it,
they were at the very center of civil war, among Bolsheviks, Latvian
nationalists, White Russians, and German interests.

Despite their appeals for the self-determination of subject nationalities in Eastern and Central Europe, the Bolsheviks refused to
surrender the Baltic. In their political strategy the Baltic was a
bridgehead to world revolution, a foothold in the move toward
Germany and the West. Zinoviev saw the Baltic as "an ocean of
socialist revolution." Lenin, who earlier had professed the right
of the border nationalities to self-determination, was now outraged
by the declarations of Estonian and Latvian independence. "Cross
the frontier somewhere," he instructed, "even if only to a depth of
a kilometer, and hang 100–1,000 of their civil servants and rich
people."[1]

The Red Army took advantage of the lull and confusion following the November 1918 armistice to occupy the main cities of the Baltic provinces. The Latvian border they crossed on December 2, 1918; a month later, on January 3, they were in Riga.

As the Bolsheviks advanced into Latvia, the provisional government took flight. The Ulmanis cabinet abandoned Riga on January 2 and retreated first to Mitau, then to Libau (Liepāja), from where it sought desperately to organize a military counteroffensive. With communications in chaos and local loyalties sharply divided, that proved difficult. Bolshevism did not as yet mean terror and extermination; to many it suggested quite the contrary: peace and justice.

The Baltic-German response was also confused. Who was the enemy now? What was one trying to achieve? Dreams of some kind of affiliation of the Baltic area with metropolitan Germany — so tangible as late as the summer of 1918, when the German military offensive in the West was on the verge of success — had been dashed by the November armistice. To German landowners and merchants, Lenin was of course the Antichrist and Bolshevism his scourge. But Latvian independence was no solution either, and for many in the Baltic-German community, life in a Latvia run by Latvians would be little different from life under Russian communism. Both amounted to rule by rabble.

The option favored by most — some tie with Germany — was revived, oddly enough, as the confusion mounted. The threat of Bolshevism, as it grew, opened up all sorts of strange possibilities, including visions of a united front of Western civilization against the "Asiatic blight." Such a broad alliance would put Germany and her former enemies on the same side, and then anything was possible. On the very day the armistice was signed, the Baltic-German community established a militia for the Baltic provinces, the Baltische Landeswehr, to defend their interests.

Some of the Baltic Germans sided, however, with the White Russians. Prominent members of the Lieven, von der Pahlen, and Behr families, all of whom had a long tradition of cooperation with Russian interests, did so. Prince Anatol von Lieven, son of Paul and Natalie, formed a unit of White Russians. Count Alexis von der Pahlen was an adjutant, the Baron von Behr an officer in the unit.

The victorious Western Allies had in fact left room to maneuver. They were increasingly apprehensive about the Bolshevik threat; and while not prepared, perhaps not even able, to intervene to significant effect in the Russian situation, they sought other means of thwarting a Communist advance. If the sea could not be pushed back, a makeshift dike, using all manner of materials, had to be built. In view of this, Article 12 of the November armistice had stated: "All German troops at present in territories which before the war formed part of Russia must . . . return to within the frontiers of Germany . . . *as soon as the Allies shall think the moment suitable, having regard to the internal situation of these territories.*"[2] That same clause would be repeated in the peace treaty signed at Versailles at the end of June 1919. It did not require great subtlety to realize that the Allies were inviting Germany to take the lead in halting the advance of Bolshevism. They were asking Germany to do in 1918– 19 what Hitler set out to do after 1933. No wonder the response to Hitler would be ambiguous.

To explore on the ground the possibilities inherent in this situation, the socialist-republican government that had assumed power in Germany in the wake of revolutionary disturbances in early November appointed August Winnig as its plenipotentiary in the Baltic. Winnig was a strange bird whose romantic brand of socialism was closer to the later Nazi variety than to that of Marx. In the Hansa port of Riga, among German-built spires and merchant houses, Winnig sensed, in the chaos of late 1918, that the setting was right for a spot of legerdemain. In the extreme vulnerability of the Latvian provisional government and in the less obvious but perceivable vulnerability — especially on the issue of Bolshevism — of the Allies, Winnig felt there was room to achieve both guarantees for the Baltic Germans and leniency in Allied policy toward Germany.

In an agreement, of December 7, negotiated by Winnig with the Ulmanis government, Germany undertook to assist Latvia in the defense of its borders. Germany would provide assistance, primarily in the form of training and leadership, to the Baltische Landeswehr, and would also supply a military division. German officers would command both units. The division — to be known eventually as the Iron Division — would consist of volunteers from the German

Sixth Reserve Corps, still stationed in Latvia, and those sent by recruitment offices in Germany. The volunteers from Germany would
come as individuals or as whole units, Freikorps as the latter were
known. These military units, essentially private armies led by demobilized officers, mushroomed in the political and economic confusion of postwar Germany.

Of the thousands of German volunteers who flocked to the Baltic,
some joined up because they were promised land and booty; they
pictured themselves as Baltic-German landlords overseeing estates,
peasants, and even armies. Other volunteers were driven by ideals
comparable to those of their crusading Teutonic forbears in the
thirteenth century: they were to save civilization from the barbarians. Most, however, were simply adventurers spoiling for action.
Home, nation, and politics they derided as abstract, nonsensical notions. Erich Balla glorified these tough young mercenaries: "These
primitive men . . . have no nerves and no moral scruples . . . They
are just like nature — instinctively good and instinctively cruel."
Ernst von Salomon, a sixteen-year-old volunteer, reveled in the
freedom that this battle of the frontiers, in both a geographical and
psychological sense, offered: "We were cut off from the world of
bourgeois norms . . . The bonds were broken and we were free." His
unit, the Hamburg Freikorps, was representative of this riotous,
exuberant mood: they grew their hair long and refused to salute any
but their favorite officers.[3] The French military attaché in the Baltic,
Colonel du Parquet, called the whole crowd *"une armée de bandits."*[4] Colonel Alexander (later Earl Alexander of Tunis), who had
fought the Germans on the Western Front, at Ypres and the Somme,
commented that in Riga "the Germans are anything but the beaten
Hun as we knew him."[5]

The Baltic was forced on the attention of the central government in Berlin, but it also caught the interest of a fringe element in
Germany that was looking for some *deus ex machina* solution to
Germany's quandary. Among the wild plans articulated was one
whereby Germans would assist the White Russians in restoring
monarchy to Russia, and White Russians would in turn assist German monarchists in Germany. The two re-created Romanov and

Hohenzollern monarchies would then join hands against the Western Allies and force them to rescind the armistice terms. Russia and Germany, the two major defeated powers of the Great War, would emerge as victors. The axis for these developments would be the Baltic.

Wild dreams? Of course. But then the Great War had been a chrysalis from which all kinds of fantastic possibilities emerged. As Count Harry Kessler noted in his diary in early February 1919, life had become "too crazy for words."[6]

Next to the Russians and Germans, the British showed the greatest interest in the Baltic. They intervened less with manpower than with threats and supplies. As long as the involvement was not too costly, Britain wished, for economic and security reasons, to reestablish influence in the Baltic.[7] In March 1919 the soldier-diplomat Stephen Tallents was sent there from Warsaw, where he had been organizing food relief, to assess the situation. He later admitted that on receiving his orders he was completely ignorant of the lands to which he had to proceed: "I doubt if I should have questioned it if Paris had sent me with its telegram a supply of yen for my travelling expenses."[8] But within a month he was back in London to urge establishment of a British mission in the Baltic. The recommendation was accepted, and in late May Tallents, accompanied by Colonel Alexander, returned to the Baltic to set up the mission. The policy of a *cordon sanitaire*, to ward off diseases from the East and to keep a troubled foe, the German, weak and off balance, was taking shape.

High on the Hill

"HIGH ON THE HILL SHE STANDS, her tower a landmark clear." So began the school song. The words described a physical reality and suggested a figurative aspiration. This was the school of the Canadian establishment, a school of tradition, a crucible of values, like loyalty and service, that would pervade and rule the land. This was Upper Canada College.

The *War Book of Upper Canada College*, published in 1923, lists those who served and those who died in the Great War. It contains many familiar names, names of my classmates and school chums: Macdonald, McKay, McMurrich, McMurtry, McWhinney.[9] The entries reverberate with notions of duty and valor. Sidney Mercer McWhinney, for instance, was wounded at Hill 60 in front of Ypres; he died in University College Hospital, London, and is buried in Mount Pleasant Cemetery in Toronto. He must have died, as the imperial vernacular would have it, with a smile on his face. Among the veterans fortunate to come back, so many had names that would resonate into Canada's future: Beatty, Bond, Coleman, Cook, Eaton, Heintzman, Hyland, Jackson, Lash, Lister, MacKintosh, Massey, Matthews, Neville, Ross, Wright. I knew their scions well when I attended the college from 1956 to 1961.

The cadet battalion and the playing field were to imbue us with this tradition of collective esprit, noble purpose, and sacrifice. Mounting Cold War tensions — the Soviet invasion of Hungary and repeated crises over Berlin — suggested that these values might be needed again on a battlefield soon enough.

As cadets, we were dressed, fittingly, in black uniforms and armed with surplus 303s. Twice a year we assembled for a church parade. We marched from the college to St. Paul's Anglican Church, where we invariably sang "Jerusalem," "God of Our Fathers," and "Praise, My Soul, the King of Heaven." Along with William Blake we declaimed: "I will not cease from mental fight, till we have built Jerusalem in England's green and pleasant land." Rudyard Kipling's incantation "Lest we forget" we intoned along with his references to "lesser breeds without the law." If we cared to look at the memorial window of the church, which contains some six hundred pieces of glass from seventy European ruins, we could see a boy soldier depicted. Ourselves.

The ethos of the school was that of Sir Henry Newbolt's patriotic poetry, in which the empire is saved by the team spirit acquired on the playing fields of one's youth. "Play up! play up! and play the game!" Dressed in whites we played cricket. Baseball was considered a vulgarity equivalent to gum chewing. One master, F. J. "Freddy" Mallett, was a veritable icon: when he walked the halls he was greeted by a hush of veneration. He, we whispered to one another, had been gassed in the Great War. That he was a teacher of chemistry we found oddly appropriate. The suggestion was that had it not been for his sacrifice — and the supreme sacrifice of sixty thousand Canadians in the First World War and forty-two thousand in the Second — the German flag would be flying over Canada.

Red Ice

AFTER OCCUPYING RIGA on January 3, 1919, the Bolshevik forces fanned out. By January 8 Mitau and its environs came under their control. Within days, three quarters of Latvia was Red.

But enthusiasm for communism waned rapidly. Many peasants had assumed that the Bolsheviks would introduce land reform based on individual units; instead, they began full-scale collectivization. Overnight, food disappeared from markets. The shortages brought severe hunger to the cities.

Communist violence was haphazard but extensive. Between January 8 and March 18, when the Bolsheviks left Mitau, about seventy inhabitants of that city were shot. Many had been tortured.[10] A French observer, Joseph Chappey, was shown about forty bodies in the courtyard of Mitau prison, all Baltic Germans as far as he could tell, teachers, clergymen, landowners. As he looked around Mitau he was stunned by the evidence of massive violence and called the locales "these places of massacre and horror."[11] In retreating from Mitau in March, the Bolsheviks took with them a large number of hostages. Most of these they killed when the retreat had to speed up. Corpses of women, children, and old people dotted ditches along the road to Riga. A few of the hostages made it to Riga; they were later found dead in the city's Central Prison.

Riga saw even more executions than Mitau. The Communists arrested many prominent citizens, including most of the city's clergymen — usually seized in the act, as it were, standing at their pulpits — and executed these prisoners at a steady rate, usually without explanation; the pace of murder picked up, it was said, on days when news from the front was bad. The Latvian Bolshevik leader Pēteris Stučka later admitted that the Latvian bourgeoisie "did not live sweetly" during the Communist period.[12] August Winnig reported to the Berlin government on April 24, 1919, that by then six thousand inhabitants of Riga had been executed. "In all of Riga not a single coffin was to be found," wrote a survivor.[13]

Probably the most dangerous profession in the Baltic was that of clergyman. To the indigenous peasantry Baltic-German pastors, as visible leaders of the village community, represented authority and discipline in morality and education. Even more than the estate owners or administrative officials, they symbolized the status quo. In times of upheaval, such as 1905 and 1917–19, clerics bore the brunt of hostility. The Bolsheviks, with their adamant atheism, singled them out for eradication. In a letter of 1922, Lenin was to write: "The greater the number of representatives of the reactionary clergy and reactionary bourgeoisie we succeed in executing . . . the better."[14]

The Bolshevik goal, to eradicate the bourgeois order and replace it with a classless society, meant that all property, money, and other traces of wealth, like silver, fine furniture, and jewelry, had to be sequestered. Families in houses or flats had strangers billeted with them. As markets closed and food and firewood disappeared, soup kitchens serving thin gruel once a day became the only means of survival for city dwellers. Typhoid and diphtheria spread rapidly amidst the shortages and unsanitary conditions.

That the worst Bolshevik crimes were committed by Latvian women — *Flintenweiber*, as the Germans called them, or riflewomen — became a firmly established assumption among anti-Communist forces.[15] "In beastly massacres, in which the Latvian mob, and especially the dehumanized rifle-women, distinguished themselves," wrote the Baltic German Paul Rohrbach a few years later, "thousands of Germans were slain indiscriminately, men, women, and children. Intellectuals, clergymen, teachers, doctors, etc., along with the nobility, were the most frequently sought-out victims."[16]

Some evidence of atrocities committed by women exists, but the

facts were embellished by a warrior culture steeped in virile fantasies, male comradeship, and homoerotic violence. Working-class Latvian women were, according to this outlook, automatically whores,
butchers, castrators, and spies. The sexually voracious woman was
by definition a Bolshevik, and every Bolshevik woman was, by cor-
ollary, insatiable.[17]

In contrast, proper Baltic women were viewed as sexless. They
were mothers, strong and just, and sisters, tender and innocent, certainly not whores, ruthless and evil. The latter were strangers, foreigners, corrupted by an alien spirit. Eduard von Keyserling wrote
masterly descriptions of this world in which fortress walls, like
those of crusader castles, were built around women. Sensuality in
a woman was not permitted, not even in marriage. Should a modern idea or even a whim appear, should a cry for life resound, then
all lights would instantly be extinguished. "One cannot," as Ernst
Heilborn wrote of this world, "make compromises with the modern
spirit; one can only be destroyed by it."[18]

In such a world the *Flintenweiber* had to be not only destroyed
but, in a symbolic act of revenge, tortured and mutilated as well. In
one of his novels about the Freikorps experience in the Baltic, Edwin
Erich Dwinger had a character called Pahlen learn that his family —
father, mother, and sister — are being held by Latvians in Mitau.
Rumor has it that they have been tortured. Beside himself with rage,
Pahlen gives orders that a young Latvian rifle-woman, Marja, whom
his group has captured, be beaten to death, slowly, with a small
Cossack whip. Two of Pahlen's henchmen obey and Marja's body is
gradually reduced to an unrecognizable sodden mass. When, by the
next mail, Pahlen learns that his family is in fact still alive, he feels
no remorse, only joy.

In 1938 the French novelist Marguerite Yourcenar wrote a novella
inspired by her personal romantic agony, her love for "a man who
loves only men." As a setting for her story, which she composed in
the summer heat of Capri and Sorrento, she chose the Baltic during
its civil war twenty years earlier. In the story, the female protago-
nist, her passion unrequited by a man who loves not her but her
brother, joins the enemy in the civil war. She is captured and then

executed — executed by the man she loves. *Coup de grâce* is written
in a spare, taut prose befitting a theme about which one dare not
speak at length. But in this novella, whose mood Henri Hell called
"at once red-hot and ice-cold," Yourcenar instinctively touched on
many of the frightful motifs of the Baltic: the misogyny, the violence, and, worst of all, the cold, the emotional cold.[19]

Would you have been a rifle-woman, Grieta?

Masters

WHEN I WAS A STUDENT at Upper Canada College we were
taught not by ordinary "teachers" but, in the British manner, by
"masters." My classics master, Mr. Killip, was a Mr. Chips *après la
lettre*. We called him Fuzzy, presumably because of his bald pate.
Rumor — in this case completely false — had it that he had fought
with Gordon at Khartoum and that the nickname had Kiplingesque
associations with Sudanese warriors, the fuzzy-wuzzies. "His fate
was mingled with the frenzies of Empire and the doom of peoples,"
one might have said of him, echoing Lytton Strachey on Chinese
Gordon.[20] Killip, who had come out to Canada in the 1920s, oversaw
the scholarship and entrance examinations. The gentle chalk-chew-
ing man took me under his wing. The headmaster, Reverend Cedric
Sowby, another Englishman, who had arrived in 1948 to run the
school, also smiled on my efforts.

Partway through my second year, in the spring of 1958, the school
building that had been erected as recently as 1891 was condemned.
That building, said Messrs. Mathers and Haldenby, architects of
renown, was structurally unsound. A high wind or wet snowfall
might bring down the tower and roof. The school was immediately
evacuated. We students spent the better part of two years in portable
classrooms while the old building was torn down and its Georgian
substitute built.

In September 1960 the new edifice was officially opened by Vincent Massey, the former Canadian high commissioner in London
and the first Canadian-born governor general. In his address to the
college community assembled in the flagstoned quadrangle, Massey

praised the specifically English qualities of UCC, qualities that would endow students with the will and capacity to turn disaster into triumph. As an example of what he meant, he pointed to the British effort in the Second World War, which began with the debacle at Dunkirk and ended in victory.[21]

In the meantime, the duke of Edinburgh had visited the school and Field Marshal Montgomery had dedicated the new front doors. The library of the new school was named after Sir Edward Peacock, who had been a master at the college from 1895 to 1902 and had gone on to become a director of the Bank of England.

My world at UCC was shaped by a powerful tradition, a British imperial tradition that saw connectedness and continuity in the human drama. The goal of this tradition was understanding, a form of conquest. My own experience contradicted this tradition fundamentally, but who was I to argue at that stage of life?

The symbolism behind the demolition of the old school building was strong. The intellectual and moral underpinnings of empire, and of Anglo-Saxon preeminence in the world, were being questioned at the same time.

Springtime

IN MID-MARCH 1919, Mitau was "liberated" by the ragtag army of General Count Rüdiger von der Goltz, formed in the preceding weeks from the Baltic-German Landeswehr, former German army units, Freikorps elements, a few Latvian batallions, and some White Russian forces. Von der Goltz had arrived in the Baltic in early February with a reputation as a committed Bolshevik basher. He had been in Finland in 1918 to help repel the Communist assault there and had aided in the reorganization of the Finnish army. His purpose in the Baltic was similar. His initial successes were, once again, impressive.

That spring of 1919 was a memorable season, for its beauty as well as its horror. Many who have observed the sudden arrival of spring thaw in the Baltic have commented, as Elizabeth Rigby did, on "the rapture with which the dawning blessings of summer are hailed."[22] But while every spring in the Baltic inspires awe, that spring following the great European war was exceptional. One volunteer soldier, Siegfried Boström, seemed more taken by the weather than the campaign:

> On April 8 we gathered in Mitau for our departure. We crossed the bridge over the Aa and then turning sharply right we took the road to Tetelmünde. It was spring, early spring, such as I had never read about in any book and have never experienced since. The temperature was about 10–12°. The earth was so soft that you had to stay on the road. One wayward step and you were up to your calves . . . Standing guard was a real pleasure. You could follow constantly the flocks of birds in the sky. The sounds of cranes, geese, and swans could be heard inside too.[23]

Against the backdrop of this splendid spring, the massacres multiplied. German vengeance against the Bolsheviks and their collaborators knew no bounds. In the wake of "liberation," 500 Latvians were shot without trial in Mitau, 200 in Tuckum (Tukums), and 175 in Dünamünde (Daugavgrīva) on grounds that they were pro-Bolshevik.[24] Both sides seemed bent on exterminating each other.

On Ascension Day, May 22, 1919, Riga was freed. The government in Berlin had refused to sanction the attack, wary of negative repercussions on the peacemaking process in Paris — the Allied terms had been presented to the Germans on May 7, but von der Goltz went ahead anyway, claiming that the Landeswehr, the chief military force in the attack, was Latvian, not German, and that the Allies could therefore not object.[25] Leo Schlageter, who was to become Hitler's hero, held the bridgehead once the Lübeck Bridge over the Dvina had been crossed; Hans Baron von Manteuffel, of the renowned Baltic family, was hit in the head by a bullet while leading the assault on Riga's Central Prison to liberate prisoners and hostages there; Walter-Eberhard Freiherr von Medem, commander of an elite Freikorps unit, seized the Baltic standard and carried it to victory.

Riga, that German city, had been liberated by the Germans yet again. How could Latvians make any claims to it? On May 30 the head of the American mission in Riga, Warwick Greene, gave an interview. "The removal of German troops from Latvia would mean the sure and complete destruction of Latvia," he said.[26]

In the capital city, victory and martial law went hand in hand. Overnight, terror changed sides. The political cleansing that Mitau had experienced was repeated in Riga with even greater ferocity.[27] Summary executions went on for weeks. Corpses remained in the streets for days. The French military envoy Colonel du Parquet reported that fifty to sixty prisoners were executed every morning in Central Prison. He claimed that the prisoners had first to dig their own mass grave in the shape of a trench, were then lined up along it and shot,[28] a practice that had been used by the Bolsheviks during their occupation, would be repeated by them in 1940–41, and then again by the Germans after they once more drove out the Russians in 1941. The tranquil Biķernieki forest, on the outskirts of Riga, was the site of much of this horror, then and later.

Hate prevailed. In combat, prisoners were not taken — that was understood; in victory they were taken but then murdered, in a kind of ritual, to make the point about victory clear.

After capturing Riga, the Landeswehr moved north intending to take control of Estonia. By mid-June, however, the Latvian national army, though not nearly as strong in numbers as the combined forces of the Baltic Germans and Freikorps, had two divisions of determined fighters and, thanks to the British, a sizable cache of weapons. Moreover, Ulmanis was determined to take the initiative away from the Baltic Germans. On June 23 the Latvians, in league with the Estonians, surrounded the Germans at Wenden and, against all expectations, forced them to retreat.

With the Versailles deliberations at a crucial stage, the Allies had little time for the Baltic. Only the British took more than a passing glance at the situation. J. D. Gregory, who was on the Northern Department desk of the Foreign Office at the time, recalled later how hard it had been to get anyone to pay attention to what was going on in the Baltic. "It was uphill work, because it was exceedingly difficult in the stress of post-war troubles to get the Great and Good to attend to problems that to a large extent were of only academic importance to us."[29] Through the efforts of Stephen Tallents and the British military mission a ceasefire in the civil strife was achieved on

July 3. "It was a terrific struggle to get the different sides to agree,"
wrote Tallents's aide, Colonel Alexander.

> The whole proceedings were very dramatic. We all sat round a table in
> a bare room with candles flickering in the draught. On our side,
> Tallents, tremendously alert and businesslike; Victor Warrender of the
> Grenadiers, cool and correct; Harrison, our shorthand typist, rather
> journalistic; Colonel du Parquet, the Frenchman, obviously not un-
> derstanding a word of the discussion in English, but looking fright-
> fully formal and severe; Colonel Dawley, the American, making long-
> winded speeches entirely off the point, and getting rather snubbed by
> the Germans; the Estonian, frightfully suspicious and not at all anx-
> ious to sign an armistice but longing to get at the throats of the
> Germans.[30]

The German forces and their allies agreed to evacuate Riga. Ulmanis was returned to power, moving back to the capital from Libau.
Perhaps the most stunning development was that the Landeswehr
was put under temporary British command. Colonel Alexander, who
in the next war was to become a field marshal, then governor general of Canada, and finally minister of defense in a Churchill government, took charge of a company of Germans. He designed a
special uniform for himself, a combination of Russian and German
military dress: a soft peaked cap, a blouselike tunic, breeches, and
jackboots. On his shoulder straps this British officer wore the insig-
nia of the German army. Under his command, which was accepted
without question, the Baltic-German Landeswehr was sent to clean
out the last Bolshevik strongholds in the eastern Latvian province of
Latgale. Kipling must have been thinking of a situation like this
when he pointed to the intimate relationship between crisis and
comedy.

Toronto the Good

IN THE SUMMER of 1952 our family moved east, from Winnipeg to Toronto. A group of Latvians in Toronto had asked my
father to come and lead a Latvian church congregation.

At that time, less than a quarter of Toronto's population was anything other than British or French in background. In the province of Ontario as a whole, as late as 1941, about 95 percent of the population had been born in Canada, the United States, or Britain.[31] The names of the city's main streets — King, Queen, Victoria, Richmond, Wellington, Parliament, Adelaide, Church — signified both the British connection and the Victorian values of abstinence and respectability that Toronto celebrated. Before 1950 playgrounds were closed to children on the Sabbath: the city fathers padlocked gates and chained swings together. Spirits you could purchase only in government-run shops whose employees looked more like stern schoolmasters than purveyors of drink. The food on the shelves of grocery stores reflected similar Puritan instincts. What was called French stick bore no resemblance to bread, let alone a baguette, and the range of available condiments ran the gamut from catsup to ketchup.

As tenants in need of inexpensive housing, our existence in those first Toronto years was peripatetic. We moved from one peripheral part of the city to the next, from New Toronto to the Beaches. To keep us afloat financially, my father took an English-Canadian congregation as well as the Latvian one that had summoned him to the city. On Sundays he would preach three times, at eleven and seven o'clock in the Canadian church and at four in the Latvian one. During the week there were sundry meetings. He somehow also found time to edit two religious journals.

My mother found work as a clerical assistant at the University of Toronto library, where she prepared periodicals for binding. From colleagues there, many of whom stemmed from old Toronto families for whom librarianship was a form of philanthropy, she heard about a school of privilege and renown, Upper Canada College. She urged my father to make inquiries. He, poor beggar, kept putting the matter aside.

It was while we were living in the West End, in the vicinity of Toronto's abattoirs and major meat-processing facilities, whose smells choked us when the wind blew the wrong way, that my father finally screwed up his courage and visited UCC to ask about scholarships. One day early in 1956 I took the scholarship examinations and some time later found out that I had won entry. I began at the upper school at age twelve, in September 1956, a mere six and a half years after leaving the refugee camps of Europe.

That first year, I wondered if I carried the smell of Toronto's stockyards and slaughterhouses with me. I used to take the Rogers Road and St. Clair streetcars to school, getting off at the corner of St. Clair and Avenue Road. The daily morning walk up Avenue Road's arbored esplanade, past imposing Victorian red-brick homes and with the school towering in the distance, is a memory tinged still with excitement and dread. Despite my success at the school, despite the kindness of teachers, despite friendships established, I always felt an outsider, an interloper in an Anglo-Saxon bastion.

Within a few years those stately houses along Avenue Road would make room for Toronto's first generation of high-rises. The names of these high-rises — among them Algiers North and Algiers South — suggested what was happening to the city's ethnic homogeneity. About the same time, rye bread became available around the city.

Absurd Theater

IN THE BALTIC in the summer of 1919, the bizarre gave way to the preposterous. Intrigues swirled. A wild plot was hatched in Berlin, involving former Russian diplomats, Barons Rosen and Knorring, a society hostess, Countess Kleinmichel, and German industrialists, to create a separate west Russian state from a base in the eastern Baltic. Meanwhile, Count Konstantin von der Pahlen, whose family owned the huge estate at Gross-Eckau where the Vajeikses had worked, tried, from Mitau, to set up a Russo-German administrative structure for a proposed corridor in the Baltic provinces between Germany and Russia.

From his headquarters, in Mitau as well, General von der Goltz, sensing that he was about to be abandoned for good by his government in Berlin, called on the Iron Division and its Freikorps units to join a White Russian adventurer, Colonel Bermondt-Avalov. Purportedly a Cossack, Bermondt was fanatically opposed to communism, but in his quest for alliances he had been rebuffed by his White Russian military peers. Consequently he now turned to the Germans for help in organizing a "Russian Army of the West" to fight Bolshevism and reestablish Russian imperial power. In von der Goltz and Bermondt two dreamers joined forces.

Bermondt believed his fate was to destroy Bolshevism and to re-create a Russia fit for aristocrats like himself. Von der Goltz in turn thought that such a feat would be a first step toward liberating Germany from its present thralldom to socialism and pacifism. Most of the Freikorps units, though only some of the Baltic-German component of the Landeswehr, heeded the command of von der Goltz — in the process repudiating that of Berlin — and did join Bermondt. Of the fifty-two thousand troops Bermondt now commanded, about forty thousand were German. Because it contradicted orders from Berlin, the action of von der Goltz and his soldiers came to be called the Mitau mutiny. Ten thousand troops marched through Mitau in a torchlight parade on Sunday, August 24. Provocative speeches were made. "The die is cast — there is no going back," exhorted Major Bischoff, commander of the Iron Division. "We march on Riga."

The mood in Mitau that evening was charged with apocalyptic excitement. "Such enthusiasm has not been seen since August 1914," noted one seasoned participant.[32] To avoid legal complications, von der Goltz resigned his command and joined his division as a private soldier. Ernst von Salomon said of the formal rupture with the homeland: "Outcasts, exiles, homeless and beggars — we held our torches high . . . We rather sulkily drank vodka and learnt to swear in Russian. Since we had been discarded by Germany, we became Russians."[33] The next day, plunder and brutality began.

In his bearing and pretensions, Bermondt was a character out of Franz Lehar's operatic imagination, except that as would befit the violent land he now claimed his own, he too was monstrously violent. Everything about him was excessive. When Stephen Tallents went to see him in Mitau, Bermondt, though fully dressed, received him in bed, smoking cigarettes and eating apples as they talked. The conversation was civil and full of the requisite courtesies, but Tallents suspected that as soon as he had left, Bermondt had emptied his revolver into the ceiling.[34]

Bermondt's vision involved, as he put it, a "German-Russian comradeship in arms," which would lead the two peoples together "to a beautiful future." Germany and Russia would both shake off the shackles of socialism and military defeat, and the Baltic lands would once again return to the bosom of Mother Russia. "Here in the Baltic," Bermondt said, "the bond of friendship between Russia and Germany, that had been sundered by the war, was tied again." Kurland and Mitau were important to his plans because of their strategic location, a base for the imminent attacks of the Army of the West on Moscow and St. Petersburg, as he insisted on calling Petrograd. As a key railway junction between Russia and the West, and between Germany and the Baltic, Mitau had to be held.[35]

Cut off completely now from any official German support, blockaded by Allied sea power, and squeezed by growing diplomatic pressure, Bermondt tried — through the agency of Count von der Pahlen, among others — to raise money from German industrial circles, in vain. To pay his troops he began to print his own money in Mitau.

In this surrealistic realm, success and failure blurred. In conventional terms the Bermondt escapade turned out to be a total disaster. In Ernst von Salomon's categories, or those of the vitalistic ethic of modernism, however, the experience, beyond moral convention, was all-important, the result secondary. The adventure was the essence, and the ironies — the dance of death — made it all the more intriguing. It was the "dangerous strangeness" of the land and its "deceitful loveliness" that enticed him, said Ernst von Salomon: "Just to stand forever . . . on the treacherous bog-land was enough!"[36]

Ernst von Salomon's superior, a Lieutenant Kay, captured the absurdities of the situation: "We are German soldiers who theoretically are not German soldiers, and we are defending a German town which theoretically is not a German town. And out there are the Letts and the Estonians and the English and the Bolsheviks — and by the way, I like the Bolsheviks the best of all that crew — and farther south are the Poles and the Czechs, and then — well, you know it all as well as I do . . . Have you got a cigarette for me, youngster?"[37]

On September 4, the British insisted that all German mercenaries withdraw from Latvia. Bermondt paid no attention. On October 4, a second British note repeated the earlier demand. Bermondt now felt forced to take action. Retreat was not possible. He reached agreement with his German units, assuring them of land in the Baltic. He even granted their members, on his own authority, Russian citizenship, so as to be able to tell the Allies that he commanded Russians, not Germans. He then moved his contingent on Riga once again.

To the north, on the Narva front, General Yudenich, on hearing of Bermondt's move against Riga, was incensed. Since the summer the Allies had been trying to persuade Bermondt to join Yudenich. Prince Lieven's unit of White Russians had complied, but Bermondt had consistently refused, and Yudenich denounced Bermondt as a "traitor to Russia." On behalf of the civilian council attached to Bermondt's army, Count Konstantin von der Pahlen replied to Yudenich: "The council concludes that your designs against a Russian army which is fighting for the last strip of Russian coastline have been influenced by dark forces."[38] Dark forces are common characters in borderlands.

After bitter fighting in early November, the attack on Riga was repulsed by Latvian troops, with the help of a naval bombardment and material assistance from the British. Ernst von Salomon noted that all the dead Latvians he came across wore new uniforms and had British weapons and Sam Brownes.[39] Bermondt blamed Stephen Tallents in particular for the British intervention: "The highwayman and pirate," he said of Tallents, "became lawgiver and judge."[40]

After this setback, the Bermondt forces, disgruntled and dispirited, began to disintegrate. Discipline collapsed. For those German forces who remained, plunder and looting became the principal activity. Lured to the Baltic by the prospect of land if they drove out the Bolsheviks, the German volunteers now felt tricked and betrayed by their own spineless government in Berlin, by the treacherous Allies, and especially by the two-faced Latvian regime under Ulmanis. In a murderous frenzy they took out their frustration on the land they had come to rescue: "Somebody dragged out a man from under a broken cart, a tall old peasant who wailed for mercy. Before he was able even to stagger to his feet, the sledge-hammer came down on his head so that he crumpled up like a rag." What they couldn't murder, they stole. They stole anything that moved or rolled — horses, cattle, carts, farm implements — and burned or smashed anything that didn't.[41]

In early November a premature freeze set in, with snow and biting cold, further depressing the spirits of mercenaries, freebooters, and intruders. The Bermondt supply lines faltered. Food ran short. After earlier disagreements the Estonians now began reinforcing the Latvians, and the Lithuanians, too, declared war on the "West Russian government."

New Canadians

"THE TRUEST MEMORIAL to the sleeping victors of the struggle," one Canadian had written in the wake of the Great War of 1914–18, "is a nation homogeneous in character, united in purpose." At about the same time a Manitoba cleric had denounced the "alien foreigners" in his midst, "the strangers within our gates." Because of their purportedly inbred criminal inclinations, these aliens were much too expensive to "educate and christianize." They should simply be deported. They would be replaced by the wives and children of the "fallen heroes" of England, Ireland, and Scotland.[42] Such opinions had not disappeared in the wake of the next great war, that of 1939–45.

The principal architect of Canadian immigration policy toward the displaced persons of Europe after the Second World War was Arthur MacNamara, the deputy minister of labor. The first wave of postwar immigrants from the camps of Europe came to be known as "Mr. Mac's DPs." MacNamara was a careful technician, a numbers man. He had worked in the Manitoba branch of the Labour Department during the Depression. His first responsibility, he felt, was to those already residing in Canada, not those clamoring to get away from war-torn Europe. "We should not try to go too fast in the matter of encouraging immigration," he said. The Department of External Affairs had much the same attitude: "It is not likely," it advised the Canadian high commissioner in London in November 1945, "that any large scale movement of immigrants to this country will be authorized in the near future."[43]

When we arrived in Winnipeg in February 1949, we became the proverbial strangers within the gates, within the gates of a country where more than 80 percent of all Canadians were of British, Irish, or French descent. We were expected to embrace "the Canadian way."

My first school was King Edward Public School, a palace of a place on Selkirk Avenue. Its name bespoke the ethos of the land we had come to: the spiritual bond to Britain was strong and the DPs were thought to threaten it. To meet that threat, British immigration was encouraged. "As many continentals and foreigners are now being permitted to enter Canada," a Canadian agency in London had announced in June 1947, "we feel that it is essential that we maintain our present percentage of British stock."[44] For the British, the Assisted Passage Loan Scheme would be introduced. In the ten years after 1945, 350,000 British immigrants would come to Canada in the attempt to keep Canada British.

Not surprisingly, we "New Canadians" were not greeted with open arms. In public places we were sometimes told to "Speak English!" The Anglo-Saxon majority had a "little Englander" mindset that suspected anything exotic to be a carrier of some dangerous bacillus. Canadian doctors and dentists opposed the admission to Canada of their DP counterparts on grounds that their qualifications were unsatisfactory. The general secretary of the Engineering Institute of Canada stated in February 1951: "By far the best type of person for our work is the Britisher."[45]

Canadians were on the whole ignorant of Europe. A Lithuanian doctor commented later: "I never encountered any prejudice from Canadian doctors. But they were misinformed about the level of

European medicine and about European life in general. Out of one hundred perhaps one would really know something. A few had been to Vienna to study there for a few months; others had been, say, with the Canadian hockey team in Switzerland — that was about the extent of their understanding."[46] Professionals from Europe were profoundly shocked by this provincialism. If doctors, dentists, and engineers had difficulty reestablishing themselves in Canada, for lawyers, teachers, and civil servants their professions sank out of sight on arrival in this country. They had virtually no chance of reviving their careers. Even if language was not an insurmountable problem, their education and experience were not considered applicable in Canada.

The hostility to the newcomers combined with the strong cultural traditions among the DPs meant that the process of assimilation expected by immigration authorities did not take place.[47] The individual ethnic groups, be they Latvians, Lithuanians, Poles, or Ukrainians, established strong bases in their new land, with cultural centers, churches, and newspapers as beacons of the ethnic community. Multiculturalism as government policy in Canada would emerge more by default than by conscious political and social effort. It was to be the recognition of a reality, not the enunciation of an ideal.

The DP experience in America was different. The Anglo-Saxon — indeed Loyalist — stranglehold on Canada had no parallel south of the border. The more varied ethnic complexion of the United States, where religious and racial tensions were far stronger than ethnic differences, undermined more quickly the sense of cultural distinctiveness among immigrants.

And yet Canada was, by definition, a land of opportunity. Its constitutional freedoms, its democracy, its very size invited and rewarded individual effort, as did, paradoxically, the coldness of the climate, both real and spiritual.

The lineage and titles that some displaced Europeans brought with them to this new land meant nothing here. When Earl Alexander, the British hero of the Latvian civil war, arrived in Canada as governor general, he went looking for his old comrade-in-arms

Cemetery Street in Liepāja, where my father grew up.

My father, Rūdolfs Ekšteins, as a soldier in Latgale, winter of 1919–20.

German mercenaries
burning the palace
at Mitau, 1919.

Rūdolfs Ekšteins (front row, center) as a Baptist seminary student, 1925.

The house at Nightingales, built by my grandfather Jānis Vajeiks in 1924–25.

A picnic on the riverbank at Nightingales, June 1935. The main house
is partly hidden by the barn.

Rūdolfs and Biruta Ekšteins in Riga, shortly after their marriage in 1937.

Biruta Ekšteins with her daughter, Mudīte, at harvest in 1940.

Bodies being exhumed on the grounds of Riga's Central Prison, July 1941.

Kommando Arājs. Viktors Arājs is third from the left in the front row.

The Lielupe River at Nightingales. By late July 1944 the Soviets were on the far side of the river, the Germans on the near side. We were trapped between them.

On the right, the cold-cellar of the old Behr manor house, where we hid during the battle of late July and early August 1944.

The palace of the dukes of Kurland, at Jelgava, designed by Rastrelli.
It was destroyed in 1919 and again in 1944.

The front entrance of the Anhalter railway station, where we used
to hide from the bombs, as it appeared in 1989.

An overturned locomotive in a field that once was the Anhalter station
symbolizes the fate of nineteenth-century visions.

from the Baltic battles of 1919–20, Baron Cecil von Hahn. He had heard that the baron was working in a department store in Mont-real. Alexander looked him up one day, only to discover that this Baltic aristocrat was a "handyman" who "pushed mail order trucks around the basement."[48] For some the loss of social status magnified the seeming crudeness of the local culture. Others simply accepted the egalitarianism of the new world, where status was based more on wealth than on title.

Despite superficial setbacks and difficulties, this land, this "peace-ful kingdom," proved to be, for our family and for most immigrants, a haven of perfectly poetical nature, a shelter from a world of depri-vation and horror, a land of plenty, a country never occupied, never bombed from the air, a veritable Eden.

By 1952 Canada had accepted more than one hundred thou-sand DPs.[49]

Rage

IN MID-NOVEMBER 1919, the Latvian national army, now number-ing about thirty-six thousand, prepared to attack Bermondt's head-quarters in Mitau. In their assault Latvian units crossed the Aa at Garossen and Stalgen, just upriver from the village of Tetelmünde and the house at Meiliŋi where my grandfather had sheltered his family.[50] The Bermondt troops retreated and, in a crescendo of vio-lence, devastated the countryside. Ernst von Salomon was back on the Eckau River not far from Tetelmünde.

> We hunted the Letts across the fields like hares, set fire to every house, smashed every bridge to smithereens and broke every telegraph pole. We dropped the corpses into the wells and threw bombs after them. We killed anything that fell into our hands, we set fire to everything that would burn. We saw red; we lost every feeling of humanity. Where we had ravaged, the earth groaned under the destruction. Where we had charged, dust, ashes, and charred balks lay in place of houses like festering wounds in the open country. A great banner of

smoke marked our passage. We had kindled a fire and in it was burning all that was left of our hopes and longings and ideals.[51]

Fire became the symbol of rage. The writer Kārlis Skalbe, soon a
neighbor of the Vajeiks family, saw a wounded soldier who, lying in
his own blood, had been set on fire by the retreating Germans.[52]

Their fury was directed not just at Latvians and their property.
Baltic-German manor houses also were razed. It was as if this German-Russian tornado were out to eliminate all traces of a centuries-
old cultural influence in the Baltic.

As they retreated in armored cars along the railway line running
past Meiliņi, the Bermondt troops fired on anything that moved. As
the Vajeikses hid in terror, my mother, Biruta, a toddler of two, is
said to have exclaimed: "Uncles, bang-bang." After the mechanized
column had passed, a second contingent arrived on foot. They forced
the Vajeikses to evacuate their house, then set it ablaze. The same
fate befell other buildings on the Behr estate, including the magnificent manor house at river's edge. Jānis Vajeiks and his family
were left homeless again.

They were not alone. Owen Rutter, a British visitor at the time,
commented on the huge population losses and noted that many who
survived were "homeless and eked out a miserable existence in the
cellars of their former houses, in dug-outs or even in trenches which
they roofed with wood and earth."[53] One such survivor was Jānis's
father, Juris, who at age seventy set up house in a concrete bunker,
built by the Germans during the Great War, on the von der Pahlens'
Gross-Eckau estate. When he died three years later, in 1922, his last
words to the older of his two granddaughters were: "May you have
a better life. Mine didn't turn out that well."

Mitau was badly damaged. The Latvians fired on the city, and the
Germans destroyed the rest. They set fire to the Rastrelli palace,
with its fine furniture, tapestries, and other works of art, and even
had themselves photographed *in flagrante delicto*. In one photograph flames and smoke are leaping skyward as a group of soldiers
looks on.[54] To ensure destruction, the German soldiers had immobi-
lized Mitau's fire brigade. They also burned schools, including the

Peter Academy (Academia Petrina) with its library of more than forty-five thousand volumes.

"They rampaged through the palace in great swarms," wrote Edwin Erich Dwinger, "lying in the baronial beds . . . , using the baroness's rococo salons as lavatories, . . . and the Steinway grand as a table for their revels, feeding the fires with the contents of the old libraries."[55] Dwinger's account was purportedly of Bolshevik behavior during their occupation earlier in the year. However, it is more than likely that his description stemmed from his own experiences as a member of the Mannsfeld Freikorps. The political extremes of left and right are related in our century.

"Do you know," said Baron Krüdener, "it was a strange thing, one could go into a ballroom and find the windows broken, the pictures slashed, the furniture hacked to pieces, but all the mirrors untouched. It was an old superstition that whoever broke a mirror would die."[56] Narcissus, lover of mirrors and patron saint of modernism, would have acted in similar fashion.

As *la valse* became more frenzied, all categories collapsed. One of our century's most famous killers, Rudolf Höss, commandant for three and half years of the Auschwitz extermination camp during the Second World War, spent several months in the Baltic in 1919 with the Rossbach Freikorps. He fought alongside Leo Schlageter. From his cell in Cracow, Poland, in 1946–47, he reminisced about the horrors of the Baltic and suggested that that experience represented an important stage in his own development, moral and political.

> The battles in the Baltic were more wild and ferocious than any I have experienced either in the world war or in the battles for liberation afterwards. There was no real front; the enemy was everywhere. And when contact was made, the result was butchery, to the point of utter annihilation. The Letts were especially good at this. It was there that I first encountered atrocities against civilians. The Letts exacted a terrible revenge on those of their own people who had hidden or cared for German or White Russian soldiers, as the case may be. They burned their houses and left the inhabitants to burn as well. Countless times I saw horrible images of burned-out cottages along with the charred or smeared corpses of women and children. When I saw this for the

first time, I was turned to stone. I could not believe then that this mad
human desire for annihilation could be intensified in any way. Although later I had to face more horrible images repeatedly, I can today
still see, perfectly clearly, the scorched cottage with an entire family
dead inside, at forest's edge on the Dvina River. In those days I could
still pray and I did.[57]

Again, the symbol of fire, burnt flesh — on the edge of the forest, by
the river. More than a million Jews would die at Auschwitz while
Höss was its commandant — their gassed bodies burned in pits, on
the edge of the forest, by the river.[58]

By mid-December 1919, the German evacuation was complete.
In January 1920, the Latvian army and the Landeswehr, the latter
commanded by Colonel Alexander, moved against the remaining
Bolshevik footholds in the eastern province of Latgale. By the end of
the month the last Bolshevik units had fled.

Colonel Alexander had loved the whole adventure, despite the
freezing temperatures and hardships. "We are in a beautiful piece of
country here, the borders of Latvia and Russia," he wrote home on
February 2, 1920. "The country is quite hilly and dotted with fir
forests and lakes. I am going everywhere on skis . . . We are only
waiting for the moon to rise to go wolf-hunting. Sometimes I go to
Riga. The military mission gave a dance at the Ritterhaus. There was
an international crowd of people — Balts, Letts, Russians, Poles and
English. This sort of war is ideal. Fancy fighting a battle yesterday in
the snow, and next evening dancing in a brilliant gathering in Riga,
then back again to the front next day!" Walter Duranty of the *New
York Times* described Alexander as "the most charming and picturesque person I have ever met, and one of the two soldiers I have
known who derived a strong, positive and permanent exhilaration
from the worst of danger."[59] Like Ernst von Salomon and much of
the Freikorps crowd, Alexander reveled in the idea of the frontier:
"After this country, England seems like a garden, so small, compact
and beautifully cultivated." In several letters home he mentioned
the possibility of staying on in Latvia: "I love this country, and I
should like to live here." In March, just as he was about to give up
his command, he wrote to Lady Jane van Koughnet: "I think I am

going to try and buy an estate here. A couple of thousand pounds would get a place of several thousand acres and a nice house. I really think it is worthwhile, as the country is very rich, especially in timber."[60] Of his comrades-in-arms, the Landeswehr, Alexander said in his farewell address: "You are gentlemen and sportsmen. I am proud to have commanded an Army composed entirely of gentlemen."[61]

The events in Latvia were a symptom of what was happening throughout the Eastern European borderlands in the wake of the Great War and the collapse of empires. Kiev, capital of the Ukraine, changed hands sixteen times between the end of 1918 and August 1920. The Red Army, General Denikin's opposing White forces, Poles, Germans, and Ukrainians fought for control. Hungary, Rumania, Poland — all were in turmoil. Civil war threatened in Germany.

North End

OUR IMMIGRATION to Canada was sponsored by the Baptist Union of Western Canada. The head of its Social Services Committee was Reverend E. M. Checkland, minister of the Broadway–First Baptist Church in Winnipeg, one of the larger Baptist churches in Canada, with a membership of about nine hundred in 1947.[62] Checkland had led a vigorous program of refugee relief — nine tons of clothing were sent to Europe in 1947, for instance — with his own church acting as receiving depot and sponsor. The Baptist Union churches raised $6,000 for a "displaced persons rescue fund." Several families in that Winnipeg congregation showed us great warmth.

My father's first assignment for the Baptist Union was to travel the farmlands of the West, visiting local churches and talking about the situation in Europe in an attempt to find sponsors for refugees. He tried to persuade farmers to take on workers from the camps of Europe. In the better part of a year of effort he was able to find guarantors for just ten families. However, these guarantors wanted their workers right away, not several years hence. The difficulties and delays caused by the immigration process meant that not one of these "sponsored" families was actually placed in western Canada. My father's efforts were thus mostly in vain. In 1950 he was given his own church in Winnipeg, the West Kildonan Baptist Church, and what was left in the refugee fund was turned over to the Baptist World Alliance.[63]

The DPs were, of course, humbled by their experience and grateful to get away from Europe. Few were brazen enough to voice criticism of their new home. Officials, moreover, advised the newcomers to praise, not criticize. Yet the culture of this new world shocked profoundly. When among themselves, the DPs talked up a storm, beginning invariably with individual accounts of escape from the Russians, then about camp experiences in Germany, and in the end turning to comment on the strange values and even vulgarity of the country to which they had come. "In Germany everything was bombed," said one Lithuanian, "but somehow things were kept neater, a garden near the house, and flowers growing. Here we hardly ever saw any flowers, and it always looked strange to us that near those houses stood one or two cars. We said, why don't those people build better houses instead of buying expensive cars?"[64]

In the lumber camps and mines of the North, on the farms of the West, and even in the cities of the South near the American border, the sense of isolation, physical and cultural, was all-powerful. The architecture of this new land was for the most part either ugly or banal, the literature and music the preserve of a small elite, and a cosmopolitan life of the mind rarely felt. On Prime Minister William Lyon Mackenzie King *Time* magazine commented: "More perhaps than any living ruler, he is the embodiment of his country . . . A steady, colorless man with too much honor and intellect to be a demagogue, too little fire to be an orator, too little hair and too few mannerisms to be spectacular, King fits his country's mood and pattern."[65]

The DPs were particularly shocked by Canadian attitudes toward food, the profligacy and waste. When, as our invited guest, a prominent Winnipeg cleric dismissed the skin of our well-prepared chicken as inedible, we fat-deprived immigrants took umbrage. How dare he, thought my mother, just arrived from the refugee camps of Germany, not eat that fat-laden and hence delicious chicken skin! How could a man of God be so wasteful! Needless to say, nothing was said to our guest, but the incident was stored away in our otherwise pretty bare larder.[66]

We had rented from a Ukrainian a run-down house at 1019 Selkirk Avenue, in the North End of Winnipeg, for $25 a month. The house had no basement, just a dirt cellar. The North End was an immigrant and working-class neighborhood, also called "the foreign quarter" or "CPR town." Our house was right next to the Canadian Pacific Railway tracks and trembled whenever a train passed. We called the place "the Ukrainian's shack." We had a wood stove in the kitchen. This warmed the small house. Here we prepared and ate meals; here we bathed as well, in a small tub.

In the backyard was a chicken coop. Someone gave us fifty chicks, forty-nine hens and one rooster. Some of the chicks died, most survived. For some time the hens gave us eggs and Sunday dinner, prepared on the wood stove. The rooster, whom we called Ansis, survived the longest. When winter came we put him in the dirt cellar so he wouldn't freeze. He was not one of us passive DPs. He lost his cool. Whenever we opened the cellar door, he would attack, pecking fiercely. The only remedy was to have a last feast.

The first full winter we spent in Winnipeg, temperatures plummeted to minus 49 degrees Fahrenheit. It was said to be the coldest winter in seventy-five years. Snow reached the windows of the house. I was sent off to school bundled up with only my eyes showing. But the cold of Winnipeg was not only physical. The city had been especially hard hit by the Depression, the province beyond wracked by drought and rural poverty. The prairies suffered much more from the economic collapse than the East. Crops withered. Farms were foreclosed.

After grasshoppers and drought, refugees were merely another problem. A Polish immigrant remembered: "This word 'DP' was a terrible thing. Our cousins' daughter told us, when we got to Winnipeg, 'We don't want any DPs here.' She was fourteen years old."[67]

DPs were by definition disrupters. They would bring ideology, complexity, argument. They were not wanted.[68]

If that first winter in Canada was desperately cold, the spring brought more anxiety. When the endless snow finally melted, the Red River flooded. That disaster spared the North End but retained for us its suggestion of calamity.

Recognition

IN AUGUST 1920 in Riga, the Latvians and the Soviets signed a peace treaty patterned on agreements the Russians had signed with the Estonians in February and the Lithuanians in July. In these accords Soviet Russia relinquished all claims to the Baltic territories and recognized their independence in perpetuity.

Recognition from the international community was slow in coming. Despite the rhetoric of liberty, imperial powers were reluctant to subscribe to the dismantling of empire, even if that empire was tyrannical. Great Britain, France, and even the United States believed their agency should bring about integration rather than disintegration, consolidation rather than disruption. For all his talk about the self-determination of peoples, President Woodrow Wilson felt that "the dismemberment of empires" was, as he put it in August 1917, "childish and in the end worse than futile."[69] For David Lloyd George, the British prime minister, the Baltic provinces were comparable to Toulon and the Vendée during the French Revolution — trouble spots contradicting the drift of history. When Winston Churchill called for British recognition of the Baltic states, Lloyd George responded with visions of a post-Bolshevik Russia intent on regaining control of the Baltic provinces: "Are you, Mr. Churchill, prepared to go to war with perhaps an anti-Bolshevik Government of Russia to prevent that? If not, it would be a disgraceful piece of deception on our part to give any guarantee to those new Baltic States . . . You won't find another responsible person in the whole land who will take your view."[70]

Latvia and Estonia had to wait until January 1921 for *de jure* recognition from Britain and France. The recognition of Lithuania took even longer, until December 1922. The Polish-Lithuanian quarrel over Vilnius delayed matters there. Only in September 1921 were Estonia, Latvia, and Lithuania admitted to the League of Nations. And the United States did not recognize the Baltic states until July of the following year.

No one, however, intended to protect the new states. After Esmé Howard expressed sympathy for Latvia and Estonia at the Paris peace conference, Field Marshal Sir Henry Wilson, chief of the imperial general staff, took him aside, put his arm around his shoulder, and pointed to a map of the Russian empire on the wall. "Now, my boy," he said, "look at those two little plots on the map and look at all that enormous country beside them. How can they hope to avoid being gobbled up?"[71]

"They Are Taking Us to Siberia"

MANY WISHED TO COME TO CANADA. We came for lack of a better alternative. America was the dream. But America dallied. Sweden or Britain would have been fine, but they didn't want us. And so it was Canada, *faute de mieux*. For the year ending March 31, 1949, Canada admitted 3,331 Latvians. We were four of those.

We arrived on Pier 21 in Halifax harbor, the famous immigrant pier. Our sea voyage had taken almost two weeks. Other voyages lasted much longer. Some refugees took their fate into their own hands. Fearing that the Swedes might decide to repatriate all Balts in their country, 355 men, women, and children crammed aboard a rusty old trawler, the HMS *Walnut*, built to accommodate little more than several dozen crew. The families had pooled their money to buy the ship. They set sail from Gothenburg in November 1948, and four long weeks later, on December 13, they finally reached Halifax. After several months of detention the newcomers were permitted to stay.

To a world sinking into cold war, to a Europe threatened by Soviet tanks, Canada represented incomparable safety. "We were short of everything in Germany after the war," recalled a German immigrant, "food, and clothes, and jobs and places to live. Our country was divided, and we thought it had no future. We were afraid the Russians would move in. Canada seemed so big, so safe, so far away from our troubles."[72] So it was. A month after we arrived in Canada in February 1949, the Soviet deportation of Latvian farmers to Siberia reached its high point.

We knew as much about Canada as did the Schleswig-Holstein office of the central German bank. When the foreign assets of that regional branch of the Reichsbank were counted after the German surrender, they included, among forty different currencies, large sums of American dollars, British pounds, Swiss francs, and Greek drachmas. And then there was one Canadian dollar.[73]

Those denominations of money and their national origin had symbolic value for our family. My father had studied theology in Britain and America; because of its importance to biblical interpretation he knew ancient Greek; in 1937 my parents had spent part of their honeymoon in Switzerland. U.S. dollars, pounds sterling, francs, and drachmas played a role in their awareness of the world. But Canadian dollars? We weren't even familiar with Voltaire's famous dismissal of Canada as *"quelques arpents de neige"* (a few acres of snow).

The trip from Halifax to Winnipeg went on forever. My father jumped off the train at major stations in search of fresh fruit after our fortnight on the high seas. I was terrified that the train might depart without him. Fifty years later I still recall the magnificent scenery of the north shore of Lake Superior — the cliffs, the water, the primeval forest. A Russian Mennonite following the same route thought "the wilderness would never end. So much bush, so much empty space."[74] My parents must have had a wrenching feeling. They kept traveling farther, ever farther from home. Would the journey ever end?

The vast expanse of the land never failed to impress. Among the first batch of DP emigrants to Canada were laborers for the lumber industry. From forests devoid of permanent human habitation they wrote to friends back in the crowded camps of Europe to say that "they were dancing folk dances for the bears."[75] Mine workers fanned out across the country. Farm workers headed across the prairies. "It looked as though they were taking us to Siberia," said one. "No trees, no houses. You'd come to some little town — real shacks!"[76]

Our train finally pulled into Winnipeg's vast railway station, this Canadian junction between the big industrial cities of the East and the farmlands of the West. Winnipegers boasted that they had the largest rail yards in the world.

We arrived as innocents. We had no idea what to expect. We would become statistical evidence of the transition of Canada from an agrarian to an urban and from a bicultural to a multicultural landscape.

Skull

ONE DAY NOT LONG AFTER the fires at Meiliņi and Tetelmünde, the Vajeiks children were playing in the ruins of the old manor house. Sifting through the rubble, they came upon unusual treasure. A human skull. They took it home.

Various theories as to its provenance surfaced. The local forester suggested it might belong to one of the baron's sons. The young man had fallen in love with a local Latvian girl, but his father had forbidden marriage, and so the young man had shot himself.

Or it could be, others thought, the skull of a Latvian woman called Mausīte. She had managed the domestic staff at the manor house, but the baron, it was said, had grown tired of her. He arranged for her to leave. There was a grand farewell dinner, and afterward a red-haired gentleman arrived to take Mausīte away. Rumor had it that he was Mausīte's executioner.

That skull represented the legacy of empire, war, revolution, counterrevolution, and civil war. That skull symbolized the horrors at the heart of Baltic history. It spoke of a deed, a ghastly deed, in which victim and agent blended.

Crossing

WE SAILED THAT FEBRUARY, 1949, on the tenth, from Cuxhaven, on the Cunard liner SS *Samaria*. The ship had been launched in Liverpool in 1920, had served as both ocean liner and cruise ship between the wars, and then as a troopship until it was assigned in 1948 to the International Refugee Organization. It could carry well over a thousand passengers. The men, and boys over ten, were segregated from the women and younger children. They slept in metal bunk beds in the hold. Our crossing should have taken seven days; it took thirteen. We ran into a midwinter storm, and the ship tossed and heaved for days. Passengers were forbidden to go out on deck, but as the air in the cabins and assembly rooms was appalling our mother took my sister and me outside. The waves towered over the decks. During the storm the ship took on water. My father found his suitcase floating about; a pair of shoes he had left on the floor he never recovered.

On February 20 the sun reappeared and everyone on board was given an orange. On the twenty-second the winds finally died, and the next day we caught first sight of Canada's shores. We docked in a rainy Halifax. My sister had had the hardest crossing. She had eaten hardly a thing and could barely walk when we disembarked.

Churchyard

IN THE HOT SUMMER OF 1920, when Anatol von Lieven was back on his estate at Mesothen (Mežotne), he was visited by the American journalist Arthur Ruhl. Ruhl was much taken by the setting. He sensed a natural order in place: "It was beautiful there on the hill. Below us, drowsing in the lazy afternoon, lay fields and river, the tawny length of the manor house, the distant pine woods of what had once been a little principality all but sufficient unto itself. A little way upstream peasant girls were swimming. They laughed and splashed and chased each other over the grass, all that was peasant about them left with the clothes out of which their strong round bodies had hurried — white nymphs in an ancient paradise." He was taken across the river to the churchyard and the family cemetery, where ancestors were buried, including Princess Dorothea and Anatol von Lieven's father, Paul. A tomb to Prussian officers who had fought against the Russians in the Napoleonic Wars was also there. During the Great War the Germans had come again and left an inscription saluting their fallen comrades of a century earlier. The Bolsheviks had in turn despoiled the churchyard on their arrival in early 1919. As the American guest looked on this land heavy with history, a Lieven daughter spoke: "We used to wonder how war could ever have been here. It was so quiet and so far from the world. And that war should come here again . . . here . . ."[77]

4

Displaced

This is the night for murder: give us knives:
We have long sought for this.

EDGAR ALLAN POE

Brutality, violence, and inhumanity have an immense prestige
that schoolbooks hide from children, that grown men do not admit, but that everyone bows before.

SIMONE WEIL

The New Age

IN THEIR SEPARATE WAYS my uncle Artūrs Vajeiks and my father
represented the exuberance and ambition of the new Latvia. For
Artūrs, his responsibilities in the national home guard, the Aizsargi,
were especially important.

In the chaotic conditions in Latvia after the 1914–18 war, the
newly created Latvian army was too preoccupied with external
threats and too weak in numbers to assume responsibility for internal security. Consequently, as early as March 20, 1919, while Riga
and much of the country were still in the hands of Bolshevik insurgents, Minister President Kārlis Ulmanis, along with his minister of the interior, Miķelis Valters, called into being a civil defense
force, the Aizsargi, to be established in each district and based on
the compulsory service of all males between the ages of eighteen
and sixty.

When the Bolshevik menace subsided, the home guard was

turned, in 1921, into a voluntary association. Its organization and command structure followed the usual military practice but it also had a social and cultural dimension. Sports, theatrical, and musical activities made the Aizsargi a tangible force in society, particularly in rural communities, where each branch often had its own building and sports facilities. While the organization was supposed to be apolitical, a declaration of strong national sentiment was a requirement for membership. Artūrs Vajeiks fit in perfectly. He rose to the rank of sports leader of the Aizsargi group in Tetele.

Uniforms, banners, salutes, flowers, chants — all this was a standard part of the European landscape after the Great War, a ritual of collective affirmation that in fact masked extreme self-doubt: the greater the doubt, the more virulent and violent the affirmation. Nazism in Germany was born of military defeat in the war and carried to power by social and economic collapse. Fascism in Italy was spawned by similar social disorder and by what was perceived as a "mutilated victory" in the war. Bolshevism in Russia, especially its Stalinist form, had striking similarities to fascism, despite ideological pretense to the contrary. By some it was simply called Red fascism.

In Eastern Europe, in small states whose origins were clouded by confusion and whose existence was precarious, radical sentiment, especially of a fascist stripe, was widespread. Action was exalted, the uniform venerated. Patriotism and national pride easily shaded into xenophobia and hate.

The postwar Latvian governments, like those of all the successor states of Central and Eastern Europe, faced gargantuan difficulties: a massive outlay of funds was required to build an economic and administrative infrastructure, and this government spending brought in its wake inflation, spiraling prices, and wages that could not keep pace with the cost of living. Confronted with these huge practical problems, the idealism and enthusiasm that had been spurred by patriotism and the providential nature of independence degenerated into partisan bickering and accusation. Within a few short years of independence, in this country of fewer than two million people, almost thirty political parties were operating.

Economic issues threatened to overwhelm the politicians. Larger

territorially than Switzerland, Denmark, or Belgium, Latvia had
at the end of the civil strife only six locomotives left in the entire country. The ports were dead, factories silent. Whole provinces
were denuded of people and resources. Ventpils's (Windau's) prewar
population of thirty-five thousand had dropped to three thousand.
One out of four buildings in the country had been destroyed or
damaged.

It was clear to all that in order to survive Latvia had to export, and
to do so it had to develop its agricultural and forest production. For
purely economic reasons land reform was essential. Political and
social considerations added urgency to the matter: the Bolshevik
appeal to the landless had to be countered. But in the end it was
the resentment against the Baltic Germans that energized the re-
formers.

Of the three Baltic states, Latvia, where 162 noble families owned
77 percent of the land, instituted the most radical land reforms.
These were passed into law in September 1920. Thirteen hundred
estates were seized; former large landowners were allowed to retain
less than 2 percent of their property. In Latvia, in contrast with
Estonia and Lithuania, no compensation was granted, a decision that
attracted criticism in Western Europe where in conservative quarters the Latvian reforms were equated with Bolshevism. Most of the
large estates and existing government-owned land were pooled to
form a reserve from which lots could be purchased by citizens who
wished to farm. First priority was accorded to military veterans of
the struggle for independence. The next category consisted of agricultural laborers and farm tenants with families. As a result of the
land reform, the number of farming units increased from 150,000
in 1913 to 237,500 in 1935.[1]

After land reform Latvia became a country of small farmers.[2]
Agriculture became the backbone of the economy, representing
roughly 40 percent of the national income. Timber, flax, meat, and
dairy products were the main exports. In turn, politics in the new
Latvia revolved around the interests of farmers.

The Lievens, von der Pahlens, and Behrs all lost their huge estates.
After the forfeiture of their land in Russia, to the Bolshevik regime,

the Baltic Germans found these measures even more painful. The Baltic lands invariably included the family seat. Its loss signaled the end of a world. Most Baltic Germans looked with scorn at the new states that had emerged. "An independent Latvian or Estonian culture," wrote Paul Rohrbach, "is not possible; it is more a question, here and there, of choosing between dependence on Russian or German culture. Both history and the present are proof of that."[3]

A few Baltic Germans, like Anatol von Lieven, remained on a rump of their former domains. Some moved to Riga or to other towns to seek a livelihood. Many went back to Germany. Those who left — among them the von der Pahlens and the Medems — harbored great bitterness. They felt betrayed by Allied statesmen, German politicians, and Latvian parvenus, all of whom had used and manipulated them as long as the Bolshevik threat was real but had then dropped them. They felt that the postwar German governments in particular had let them down, and that these governments were the agents of insidious internationalist forces — Jews, socialists, pacifists, and other "parasites" — that had complicated and at the same time degraded life. As émigrés in Germany, the Baltic Germans lived in a dank right-wing fog that would spawn illusion and violence. The traditional conservative right offered no acceptable remedies; only the "revolutionary right" presented options where the action befit the mood. "The earth wants severity, the earth wants clarity, the earth wants order," says a Baltic baron called Pahlen in the second of Edwin Erich Dwinger's Freikorps novels, *Auf halbem Wege*.[4]

National Character

IN THE 1920s, 1,230,202 immigrants had arrived in Canada. In the following decade only 158,562 settlers came. In 1936, at the height of the economic depression, Prime Minister Mackenzie King eliminated the Department of Immigration and Colonization, putting immigration matters in the hands of the Department of Mines and Resources, where they were to remain until 1951. For Mackenzie King and most Canadians, immigration policy had to be linked to economic development.[5]

After the First World War Canada had experienced a recession and considerable social unrest. That, it was felt in 1945, must not be repeated. "Discontented youth formed the vanguard of revolutionary movements abroad after the last war," the Canadian Youth Commission stated in 1945. "They might well play a similar role here should prolonged unemployment destroy their faith in democratic institutions."[6] A million Canadian men and women who had worked in war industries had to be relocated, and almost as many veterans had to be absorbed into the labor force, before immigrants could be allowed in. Moreover, forty-eight thousand Canadian servicemen had married overseas. Their wives and their twenty-two thousand children demanded priority treatment, ahead of any malodorous DPs, no matter how hard the latter were willing to work. A country with a population of only twelve million could not be asked to absorb large numbers of "foreigners" without risk of disastrous consequences. That there was lots of room — fewer than three people per square mile — was not the issue. Jobs mattered most.

An opinion poll in April 1946 revealed widespread hostility to immigration: only 37 percent of Canadians were willing to accept even large-scale British immigration. Northern Europeans, too, might be tolerated by some, but there was overwhelming opposition to Eastern and Southern Europeans, let alone Jews, Asians, and blacks. In May 1947 Mackenzie King told parliament: "The people of Canada do not wish, as a result of mass immigration, to make a fundamental alteration in the character of our population . . . I wish to make it quite clear that Canada is perfectly within her rights in selecting the persons whom we regard as desirable citizens. It is not a 'fundamental human right' of an alien to enter Canada. It is a privilege."[7]

However, as postwar economies stabilized and as the need for labor grew, the tempo of resettlement picked up speed. By 1947–48 a labor shortage, not a surplus, was feared. Political considerations had also appeared. DPs had become an issue in the Cold War.

Nightingales

NO POLITICAL ACT in the newly independent Latvia was more
replete with emotion and history than the land-reform measures
of 1920.

Stephen Tallents knew how important nature was to the Latvian
soul. Like his colleague Colonel Alexander, he could rarely comment
on any issue pertaining to Latvia without some reference to the
natural setting. Writing of the Baltic countryside more than two
decades after his first encounter with it, he recalled "its dun stubbles,
pale grasses and gray willows; its grey-green corn touched delicately
by the passing wind as by the shadows of flying smoke; the airy
lightness of its birch-trees, standing among dark pines." Like many
visitors before him, Tallents remembered the birds: "Magpies ahunt
the copses by the roadside and . . . jays in the forests. Larks and
nightingales abound: I never heard such a chorus of nightingales as
once by a stream of Livonia."[8]

It was by such a stream and among such a chorus that my grandfather Jānis Vajeiks acquired his own plot of land. He had not been a
soldier in the war for independence, and thus did not have first
entitlement to land as it became available in the wake of the reforms.
He had lived now for many years in the neighborhood of Jelgava
(Mitau) and did not wish to stray too far from his accustomed
haunts. The land expropriated from the baronial Behr family of
Tetele (Tetelmünde) had been parceled out, and one large section
had been accorded to Kārlis Skalbe, the poet and author, in recognition of his efforts during the struggle for independence. Skalbe used
the land only as a summer retreat, and several years later, in 1924,
concluding that he had no need of a large estate, he sold off some
hectares. My grandfather acquired fifteen of these, right on the river
Lielupe (Aa). With his own hands he built his house, a simple
two-story rectangular brick, stone, and mortar structure overlook-
ing the river. He called his new home, the first land he had ever
owned, Lakstīgalas, or Nightingales.

Here the river was of exceptional beauty, curving gently on its run from Bauska and Mežotne, past Stalģene and Jelgava, to Riga and the sea. A ferry stopped conveniently nearby: the trip from Tetele to Jelgava was but a few minutes. The river was clean and swimmable, a boon to commerce and a pleasure of the area.

While the soil was rich, the acreage at Nightingales was too small to produce a commercially profitable yield. My grandfather grew beets, some of which he did sell to the new sugar factory downriver at Jelgava, but the grain and the vegetables he cultivated were consumed by family and animals. His situation was duplicated by thousands of other small farmers in the country.

If prospects of growth and fortune were minimal, the ability to survive through one's own labor produced a fiercely proud and independent caste of small landholders, the veritable backbone of both the economy and the culture. At the same time, given the history of the area, its ethnic diversity and strife, the peasant farmer also displayed a good measure of suspicion toward outsiders and intruders.

Good Beef?

AS IMMIGRATION POLICY, set almost everywhere in the West by departments of labor, began to change in 1947, it was young unskilled workers who were given the first nod. Brawn was preferred over brains. Doctors, lawyers, and teachers were not wanted. My father, born in 1899, a minister of religion and student of classics, lost out on all counts. He was too old and too intellectual. No country needed him. In the British zone of Germany, one military official suggested dividing all DPs into three categories: "resettlers," "substandards," and "hard core." "Hard core" were those requiring institutional care — the chronically ill, the blind, the mentally defective — and "persons over fifty unfit for employment."[9] My father was verging on "hard core."

In this situation many lied about their past and did their utmost to produce calloused hands or mighty muscles. A directive of February 1948 from the Canadian Department of Labour to its employees

in Europe stated: "Apparently, many girls we are passing fail to disclose the fact that they have higher education. While it is agreed that
we will pass up to 10% who disclose having superior education,
wherever it is suspected that any girls possess such qualifications,
but are concealing them, please reject."[10]

Immigration teams from potential host countries toured the DP
camps recruiting candidates for placement — to work in the hospitals of England, the lumber camps or mines of northern Ontario, the
farms of Australia. At the peak of recruitment, some fifty national
missions sought immigrants from the camps. After selection at this
stage, extensive medical examinations ensued: chest x-rays, blood
and urine tests, and a general assessment of health. Those destined
for physical labor had to display their fitness for the task ahead.
Immigrants were selected, said one critic, "like good beef cattle."[11]
Some refugees were refused because they were underweight. An
inadequate result or an error in recordkeeping could shatter dreams.
Bribery of officials, abuse of applicants, and kindhearted oversights
of negative results were far too common aspects of this process
involving all-powerful officials and woefully weak supplicants.

The International Refugee Organization paid the passage of DPs
to the port of entry of the country of destination. The sponsor
paid passage from the port of entry to the new place of residence.
According to IRO estimates, the cost of the first stage of the journey was on average $160 per person, of the second stage around
$60. By December 31, 1948, in eighteen months of operation, the
IRO had resettled 354,286 people. We were not among those. We
were terrified of being left behind. But finally, late in 1948, positive news came: the Baptist Union of Western Canada was willing
to sponsor us.

A few weeks later we had passed the first stage of approval for
emigration, the screening process and the initial medical examination administered by IRO personnel. On December 18 we were sent
from our quarters in Lübeck to Fallingbostel, a transit camp that had
formerly been a camp for prisoners of war, for the next stage, the
medical tests by doctors of the host country. Our room there was
unheated. My father, who was always a closet hypochondriac, was

terrified that he might fall ill and fail the family at this crucial stage. My sister, too, had suffered one illness after another in the camps and had been hospitalized in the autumn of 1947. She was underweight and fragile. The cold gnawed at her.

In his diary entries my father's pen dried as his emotion mounted. The more deeply he was moved, the less loquacious he became. On January 13, 1949, he entered one line: "Today at two o'clock we had the examination by a Canadian doctor." The next day, the entry was a little longer: "At 4 P.M. we heard the famous word 'O.K.' from the Canadian consul; that means we can look on ourselves as worthy emigrants to Canada." His next comment was on January 30: "Embarkation papers and passport are in hand. There is talk that we depart on February 4."

Whether the Canadian consul actually used the term "worthy" to describe us is not clear from the diary. The adjective may have been my father's inspiration. Still, the cautious and protective nature of Canadian immigration policy suggests that the term belonged to the vocabulary of Canadian officialdom. It is the language of the roll of honor: "They served and were found worthy." It is the language also of the exclusive club, membership in which is open only to those capable of fitting in, to those found "worthy." In his address to parliament on immigration policy on May 1, 1947, Mackenzie King had stated repeatedly that his government would take special care in its selection of immigrants — "on a basis of suitability." "The government is seeking to ensure that the displaced persons admitted to Canada are of a type likely to make good citizens."[12]

Unbeknownst to us, the Canadian high commissioner in London, Vincent Massey, had, a couple of years earlier, found our sort worthy. He had done an inspection tour of the DP camps in Germany. If Canada, he had concluded, had to take new settlers from these camps, the Balts — and especially the Latvians — might be the best of the lot. In one camp he had visited "there were about 1,500 Balts of all ages and of both sexes, most of them from Latvia. I am deeply impressed," Massey wrote, "by the quality of these people who appeared to be industrious, clean, resourceful and well-mannered. The camp itself was a model of self-help, and I could not help feeling that of all the Europeans I have seen these Balts would make the most admirable settlers." Another official called our type "excellent citizen material."[13]

Massey was less gracious about the Poles. When three Poles got together, he boldly told a meeting of high commissioners in London in April 1946, a political party and a newspaper invariably emerged. Consequently, "one did not want too many of them about." A major in the Canadian Eighth Army Corps in Germany pointed out that if Canada let Poles in, "they will be unemployed or in jail, and in either case quite happy." He had little time for Lithuanians either — "as bad as the Poles" — but Latvians and Estonians he appreciated. They were "honest, ingenious and good workers. They would make good immigrants."[14]

The IRO had chartered a fleet of twenty-five ships. Each was refurbished so as to carry thousands of passengers. In 1948–49 they moved without cease across the seven seas.

Emergency, 1934

IN THE CRISIS OF SOCIETY, economy, and mind that seemed to overwhelm the West after 1918, decisive action, not parliamentary debate and constitutional niceties, offered the most enticing prospects. Mussolini and his Fascists took command of Italian politics in 1922. Pilsudski seized power in Poland in 1926. Lithuania followed in December of 1926 with an army-led coup against a socialist-populist coalition government. When Hitler took office in Germany, the heartland of Europe, in early 1933, vowing to destroy the putrid, festering corpse that was the Weimar republic, democracy — the great ideal after the Great War — suffered its most debilitating blow.

In 1934 Estonia and Latvia followed the road to authoritarian government. In Estonia Konstantin Päts, the prime minister, declared martial law on March 12, on grounds that an extremist veterans' group was about to launch a coup attempt. Three days later the pattern was repeated in Latvia, as Kārlis Ulmanis, who had headed five out of a total of sixteen governments since independence, suspended parliament and forbade party activity, his reason being that Thunder Cross (Pērkonkrusts), a genuinely fascistic movement, was planning radical action. Both Päts and Ulmanis, founding fathers of their respective states, claimed they were defending democracy, not destroying it. Democracy, said Ulmanis, had not been functioning properly; the constitution had to be revised; in the meantime the country needed a period of stability, to forget about divisions and differences of opinion and to work out its economic and international problems. Päts spoke of "guided democracy," Ulmanis of his commitment to the welfare of all Latvians and hence to a democratic spirit that transcended factionalism.

Homiletics aside, authoritarian rule was in place in all three Baltic states by the mid-1930s. Civil liberties and press freedoms were suspended, outspoken critics imprisoned, and ethnic-minority rights restricted. Nationalist rhetoric intensified. Latvianization of the economy accelerated. Ulmanis had the support of the army and of the home guard. He had the support of Artūrs Vajeiks.

Whether the Ulmanis regime in Latvia after 1934 was, strictly speaking, fascist is a moot point. That it borrowed ideas from abroad and that it was greatly influenced by the stunning developments in Germany in 1933, when Hitler took power, is clear. That its implementation of those borrowed ideas was less intense and less abrasive is also clear. Ulmanis did not control the entire right side of the political spectrum. Elements far more radical and violent stood to his right.

One such organization was Thunder Cross, a paramilitary movement of mostly young intellectuals. Its roots went back to 1922, the year Mussolini took power in Italy. Originally called Defender of the Fatherland (Tēvijas Sargs), it was banned in 1927 by a government led by Social Democrats, only to reappear in 1930 under its new name. Members wore gray shirts and black berets and adopted a Nazi-style salute accompanied by the greeting "Hail struggle!" The movement's slogan was "Latvia for Latvians." The Ulmanis coup of 1934 led once again to its proscription, to the arrest of about a hundred of its members, and to the exile to Germany of its leader, Gustavs Celmiņš.

The movement claimed eventually to have a membership of fifteen thousand; in reality the numbers were smaller, at most probably around five or six thousand, mainly university graduates associated with student fraternities. The movement had almost no support on the land, even though one of its cardinal platforms was the promise to maintain an agricultural economy in Latvia. Thunder Cross was as hostile to Germans as it was to Jews and Russians. "We will eradicate with sword and fire every German, Jew, Pole, and even Latvian who threatens Latvian independence and welfare."[15] And, on the "German question": "We will deal with you using the same methods you used against us, with the small difference that Thunder Cross will be more consistent and will complete its task."[16]

Soviet Reform

WHEN THEY OCCUPIED LATVIA yet again in 1944, Russian soldiers had a tradition to follow. Plunder — of watches and wedding rings — was standard, rape frequent. Mass executions were reported in the area between Jelgava and Tukums. Members of the home guard, the Latvian Legion, and other collaborators were summarily shot. Yet despite all the evidence, past and present, the British Foreign Office remained skeptical about the news reaching the West. "This is the usual tale of woe, and hatred of Russia," commented John E. Galsworthy, an official in the Northern Department, on December 18, 1944, ". . . and we can expect more for as long as even a trickle of refugees is getting out of the Baltic States. The main flow has, of course, now ceased."[17]

The professional classes, for the most part, had either been eliminated in 1940–41 or fled the Russian advance in 1944. They did not represent much of a threat. Still, those who remained were rounded up and marched off to the Russian interior. Since transportation was lacking, they were forced to go on foot.

It was now the turn of the Baltic farmers, the backbone of the culture. Any landowner of note who had stayed was arrested. A great number of peasant families were deported even before the war had ended. Protestations to the Allied governments met with silence. "Do not acknowledge . . . We can do nothing about this . . ." were examples of the marginalia scribbled by British Foreign Office staff on these protest notes with their increasingly frantic messages about national annihilation.[18]

Soviet functionaries flooded the countryside to prepare for collectivization. The wrenching Soviet experience of the 1930s was now repeated in the Baltic states. The first postwar *kolkhoz* (collective farm) in Latvia was set up in November 1946. In May 1947, the Moscow Politburo called for the beginning of thorough collectivization; by early 1949, against the backdrop of a massive deportation of recalcitrants (perhaps one out of every ten farmers in Estonia and Latvia, along with their families) and confiscatory taxation, the move to collective farms became a stampede. Entire villages and townships joined. By the end of 1950, 226,900 farms had been organized into 11,776 collectives, an average of 127.7 farms per *kolkhoz*. By Stalin's death in 1953 the process was complete.[19]

The postwar years saw a massive influx of Russians into the Baltic, particularly Latvia. Some 400,000 Russians and 100,000 people of other nationalities arrived in Latvia between 1945 and 1959. By 1953 Latvians, who had constituted 83 percent of the population in 1945, numbered only 60 percent. That proportion would continue to drop, though more slowly, in the years that followed until it reached almost 50 percent. By the late 1970s Latvians were a minority in their own capital city, Riga, and their majority was precarious in Jelgava and Liepāja. "Ethnicide" appeared as a word to describe the long-term Soviet project in the Baltic.

The renewed subjugation of Latvians did meet with some resistance. Anti-Communist groups fled to the forests and marshes of the Baltic and harried the Soviet regime for years, well into the 1950s. An estimated twelve thousand armed men, organized into 702 different groups, mounted some three thousand attacks on the forces occupying Latvia. More than fifteen hundred Soviet workers died, but the toll on the attackers was even greater.[20]

"The Less Said the Better"

THE AUTHORITARIAN turn in European politics between the wars threatened not only individual liberties but the security of the small states. Rhetoric of the Baltic leadership aside, the loss of freedom within augured ill for the preservation of freedom without. In Britain there was moral concern. "Coups and adventures are not either to our public or diplomatic liking," J. D. Gregory pointed out.[21] The pitch to the right of Estonia and Latvia in 1934 fueled the security concerns of the Kremlin. In discussions between the Kremlin and Anglo-French representatives in early 1939, the Soviets, ironically, wanted a guarantee from the British and French that they would protect the independence of the Baltic states. The Western statesmen refused, as always, to make such a commitment.

As European tensions increased, with Germany once again the main motor of crisis, the small states of Europe became the pawns of great-power intentions. In March 1938, Hitler annexed Austria. At the end of September, the Munich agreement dismembered Czechoslovakia. The following March, 1939, the rest of Czechoslovakia was occupied. Within days of that coup, Hitler sailed toward Lithuania aboard the ship *Deutschland* to demand the return of Memel (Klaipeda) to Germany. Lithuania's appeals for assistance fell on deaf ears. On March 23, Hitler entered Memel, through which most of Lithuania's foreign trade passed, and welcomed the inhabitants back "into an even mightier Germany." To Moscow the German foothold in the Baltic was unacceptable. Leningrad and the whole Russian interior were now threatened. In 1936 Zhdanov, the secretary of the Communist Party of the Soviet Union, had declared: "We wish to live in peace with the Baltic countries, but if these tiny peoples allow big adventurers to use their territories for big adventures, we shall widen our little window on to Europe with the help of the Red Army."[22]

In the foreign ministries of the Allies Hitler's action against Memel elicited little more than a murmur of protest. Alexander Cadogan, permanent undersecretary at the Foreign Office, said: "It would be useless to protest at the German seizure unless Great Britain was going to fight . . . If not, then the less said about the district the better."[23] The Baltic states were the product of happenstance, the unexpected upshot of collapse and confusion. They were the product not of policy but of its ruin. They were nothing to be proud of and as a result not worth defending.

As tension rose over Poland during the summer of 1939, the French and the British, in their attempt to secure an agreement with Stalin, seemed quite prepared to give him a free hand in the Baltic but would not permit him to touch Poland. At this point Hitler outflanked the Allies. He was prepared to deal with Stalin on both Poland and the Baltic.

On August 2 Ribbentrop told the counselor in the Soviet embassy in Berlin, Georgi Astakhov: "There is room for the two of us on the Baltic. Russian interests there by no means need to clash with ours."[24] To the Soviets, who had regarded the loss of the Baltic as a security disaster, these were irenic words. A few days later Ribbentrop indicated that Germany was prepared to agree to spheres of interest.[25] From this point on, events moved at a remarkable pace toward a non-aggression pact between Hitler and Stalin. The dreams of Pavel Bermondt-Avalov, August Winnig, and Rüdiger von der Goltz, of Russo-German cooperation and mutual affirmation, suddenly materialized. Doctoring reality as always, Joseph Goebbels had his Berlin newspaper, *Der Angriff,* describe the "mutual understanding" between Germany and Russia as the product of "a long and traditional friendship." In keeping with the new cabaret spirit, Stalin's coterie in turn had all mention of the victory of Alexander Nevsky in 1242 over the Teutonic Knights on the ice of Lake Peipus removed from schoolbooks. The word "fascism" disappeared from the Soviet press.[26] Of the surprise pact Albert Speer was to say: "To see the names of Hitler and Stalin linked in friendship on a piece of paper was the most staggering, the most exciting turn of events I could possibly have imagined."[27] In Latvia, the Baltic German Jürgen Kroeger called the agreement "simply fantastic. No one would have expected anything like this."[28]

On August 23 Ribbentrop arrived in Moscow to negotiate the secret protocol of the non-aggression pact. The swastika flags that flew beside the Soviet hammer and sickle on his arrival had been obtained from a Moscow film studio where they were being used as props in anti-Nazi films.[29] The understanding reached late that night was that Lithuania would fall into a German sphere of interest while Finland, Estonia, and Latvia would come under Russian control. Stalin was especially keen on the Latvian ports of Ventspils and Liepāja. Poland would experience a fourth partition and be divided into German and Soviet spheres of interest, with the rivers Narew, Weichsel, and San dividing the spheres. The city of Vilnius, the "eternal capital" of the Lithuanians which had been seized by Poland after the last war, was to be returned to Lithuania.[30]

In late August the summer's heat became unbearable. Every evening the sun set like a huge and ominous ball of fire. An old Latvian woman who used to bring Jürgen Kroeger wild berries remarked: "It's not good, the red sun. It was like that in 1914, when the Great War came."[31]

On September 1, Hitler attacked Poland. This time the Western Allies did not back down. They declared war on Germany, but only on Germany, not on the Soviet Union. On September 17, the Soviets, claiming that in the chaotic situation they had to protect their Ukrainian and Belorussian comrades, occupied their half of Poland with impunity. On September 28, Ribbentrop journeyed once again to Moscow and signed with Molotov a German-Soviet "border and friendship treaty," formalizing the frontier through Poland and dividing their interests. At the same time, an addendum to their month-old non-aggression pact assigned Lithuania to Soviet control. The eastern Baltic was now, to all intents and purposes, in Soviet hands. The Allies were not aware of the secret protocols. That, their statesmen and diplomats would argue, was why they treated Hitler and Stalin differently. But previous Allied policy suggests that even had they known the contents of the secret agreements, their statesmen would not have acted differently. Toward the Baltic, the Nazi-Soviet pact of August 23 did little that the French and British were not prepared to do.

Still, the Second World War, which would involve sixty-one states and four fifths of the world's population, had begun.

Human Rubble, 1945

IN THE CHAOS OF POSTWAR GERMANY, refugees were looked on as part of the rubble of war. Like the debris in the streets, the authorities wanted to get rid of this "human rubble" as quickly as possible. The mayor of Lübeck, Otto Passarge, called the refugees "disagreeable guests."[32] Reporting on public opinion in the occupation zone of Germany in August 1945, the British military described the DPs as a "black spot" in an otherwise promising situation — "Mil[itary] Gov[ernment] will be no less glad than the Germans to see the last of them."[33] "Quite honestly," said an exasperated British officer to a journalist, "the DPs give us a lot more trouble than the Germans."[34] One British official was to call the DPs "the scum of Europe."[35]

The average British Tommy or American GI simply lacked the patience and training to deal with masses of uprooted, desperate people. The U.S. War Department acknowledged that it might be asking too much of its young soldiers "to understand and like people who pushed, screamed, clawed for food, smelled bad, who couldn't and didn't want to obey orders, who sat with dull faces and vacant staring eyes in a cellar, or concentration camp barrack, or within a primitive cave, and refused to come out at their command."[36]

For convenience the Allies decided to divide the uprooted peoples they found in Central Europe into two categories. Slave labor and concentration camp survivors were called displaced persons. These were human beings who were, literally, displaced. The assumption was that most of these people would wish to return home. But the term "DP" was also applied to those non-Germans, like my family, who had fled the Soviet advance and ended up in Germany. Ira Hirschmann did not like the sound of the word "displaced" — "a smooth, diplomatic term which, particularly for the Jews, ridiculously failed to express the utter tragedy it encompassed."[37] To facilitate and coordinate their return home, the DPs were brought together in "assembly centers," set up when possible according to nationality.

The term "refugee" was initially reserved specifically for Germans who had fled the Soviet advance or were subsequently driven from their homes in Eastern Europe in the massive expulsions that followed the Potsdam accords of August 1945. The distinction between refugee and DP was belabored and inadequate. It led to considerable confusion, then and later. In fact those DPs who did not wish, for political and moral reasons, to return to a Soviet-occupied homeland were more likely to fit the category of refugee than the German expellees from the East who were forcibly "displaced." Regardless of definitions, the scale of human tragedy was horrendous. A state deputy in Lower Saxony, Heinrich Albertz, called the whole refugee issue "the greatest social problem facing the West."[38]

Everyone assumed that the postwar refugees, these uprooted human beings, were bearers of disease — "chronic carriers of plague."[39] Typhus, the great illness of war, which had devastated the Napoleonic Grand Army in 1812 and had swept through Eastern Europe during and after the Great War, did show signs of epidemic potential in 1945. It ravaged the concentration camps and was expected to ravage the malnourished and dirty refugee population. Tuberculosis, diphtheria, and influenza epidemics were also thought likely. To combat the dreaded lice that carried typhus, the Americans introduced the insecticide DDT and dusted everyone, with, it was thought, remarkably beneficial effect.[40] "I saw some official put a duster gun, a flea powder dispenser, up my fifteen-year-old sister's skirt, and down her blouse," recalled one young refugee.[41]

In June 1945, my sister became seriously ill. At the time we, along with about seventy-five hundred other "foreigners," were in Flensburg, living in a basement on the Südergraben. My parents took their daughter across the street to see Dr. Fritz Callies. He was a seventy-one-year-old notable who had practiced family medicine in Flensburg since 1915. He examined my sister and then produced this diagnosis: "In the patient Mudite Eckstein [*sic*] I am able to determine no scarlet fever nor any other infectious disease." That my parents saved the slip on which he wrote these words indicates how important it was for refugees to be able to prove they were not carrying a deadly disease. Unless you could prove otherwise, you were considered a carrier of the plague — *ein Bazillenträger.*[42] In September 1945, General George Patton likened the DPs of Europe to "locusts"; they had to be controlled; he suggested they be put behind barbed wire.[43]

Despite alarms, when schools, theaters, swimming pools, and other public facilities were closed — Lübeck had a scare in the summer of 1948 when typhus was confirmed in 345 cases — the epidemics everyone feared and expected did not happen.

Annexation

A MONTH AFTER the 1939 German invasion of Poland, the Kremlin forced first Estonia and then Latvia and Lithuania to sign mutual assistance pacts, on grounds that the Baltic had to be defended jointly against the threat of incursion. These pacts gave the Soviet Union the right to establish military bases in the three countries, to station soldiers, and to use airfields and naval facilities. The local population was to be evacuated from the vicinity of the various bases. Of these "agreements" the Latvian Communist newspaper *Cīņa* (Struggle) said that they had "released the revolutionary forces of the people that had been held in check for twenty years. These forces have started moving and there is nothing that can stop them anymore."[44]

The Russo-German "friendship treaty" of September 28 had included an agreement on the movement of peoples from the respective spheres of interest. Germany decided to evacuate sixty thousand Baltic Germans (Baltendeutsche) from Estonia and Latvia. This was called the Heim-ins-Reich-Aktion — the Home-to-the-Reich Action, the apparent conclusion of eight centuries of German expansion eastward. "The Führer calls!" — that was the simple explanation for the repatriation. News of the accord produced a mood of panic in the local populations. The Germans had never been loved in the Baltic, but their imminent departure now could scarcely be interpreted as anything but an omen of disasters to come.

The seventy-eight-year-old Lucy Addison, matriarch of the small English community in Riga, observed the events with a different kind of anxiety. She had gone out to Riga as a young girl to marry her husband, Ganf, who was there in the timber business. Lucy seemed frightened of boredom more than anything else: "The harbour is full of Hun ships waiting to take almost the entire Balt population off . . . We lose 123 doctors and surgeons including Faust and Kreisler! Eighty chemists from Riga — Hartmann (the second police chief), all those serving in the Army and even the criminals out of the prisons!!! . . . Nothing like this has happened in the world since the Israelites migrated from Egypt."[45]

After their difficult winter war with Finland — the Finns resisted and a Russian breakthrough came only in February — and after Hitler had launched his spring offensive in the West, the Soviets began to pressure the Baltic states in late May 1940. The Soviets wanted friendly governments in place so that there would be no repeat of the Finnish fiasco. In all three Baltic states Communists crawled out of hiding — several hundred members in Lithuania and Latvia, and 133 in Estonia.

In mid-May, fearing the worst, the Latvian government gave its minister in Britain, Kārlis Zariņš, plenipotentiary powers over all Latvian resources and representatives abroad, in case contact with Riga should suddenly cease.

In mid-June the bell tolled. Soviet pressure became irresistible.[46] Existing governments withdrew, and the Soviets set up puppet regimes backed by guns. In Moscow, Molotov told the Lithuanian foreign minister that small nations had become an anomaly. "Your Lithuania," he said, "along with the other Baltic nations, including Finland, will have to join the glorious family of the Soviet Union."[47] On June 17, around noon, Soviet tanks began to roll into Riga. They continued to arrive through the afternoon, evening, and most of the night. In the West few noticed. Attention was focused on Hitler's great victory against France as German troops entered Paris.

A correspondent for the *Chicago Tribune*, Donald Day, witnessed the appearance of Soviet troops in Riga: "On June 17 there was a mob at the railway station, waving red rags and screaming in hysterical joy about the arrival of the Russians. The Latvian language could not be heard. The speeches, the shouts, the screams were all in Russian or Yiddish."[48]

In July elections were rigged. Only candidates sanctioned by the Soviet occupiers were permitted, and all citizens had to vote — identity cards were stamped at the polling booth. In Latvia, 94.7 percent of the population voted; 97.6 percent of the votes went to the Communist slate. Former leaders were arrested and deported to central Russia and Siberia, where most of them died. Some were shot. Others succumbed to maltreatment and the harsh conditions. In early August the "people's parliaments" in the three Baltic states sent delegations to the Supreme Soviet in Moscow to apply for acceptance as Soviet republics.

The classic Soviet takeover had been put into play, a pattern that would be followed again and again in the next half century. Any cosmopolitanism and variety disappeared, replaced by, as George Kennan would put it, "the gray, dead shabbiness of isolation behind the impenetrable walls of Stalin's Russia."[49]

From the Western Allies no response came on the Baltic question. War had been declared against Germany for its attack on Poland, but not on Russia for its attacks on Poland, Finland, and the Baltic states.

Just before the summer solstice celebrations in June 1940 the Soviet state prosecutor Andrei Vishinsky announced that there would be no scores to settle in Latvia because there had been no armed resistance to the Soviet arrival. Speaking in Russian from a balcony of the Soviet legation in Riga, Vishinsky, who had been the chief state prosecutor during the purge trials in the Soviet Union, finished with a greeting in Latvian: "Long live free Latvia! Long live the unbreakable friendship between free Latvia and the Soviet Union!"[50] It was also Andrei Vishinsky who oversaw the ruthless sovietization that followed. He was later to become deputy foreign minister of the Soviet Union and the Soviet delegate to the General Assembly of the United Nations in 1946. In 1948 he would sign, on behalf of the Soviet Union, the Universal Declaration of Human Rights.

On June 23, 1940, the new minister of the interior, Vilis Lācis, declared in a radio broadcast that private property and individual rights would be respected. But bourgeois norms vanished quickly. By the end of July even the Boy Scouts had been banned. Latvia became "a socialist state of workers and peasants." The Latvian Social Democrats had offered to cooperate but were rejected and then subjected to persecution and reprisals. In the spring of 1941, 250,000 Soviet troops were stationed in the Baltic; by the summer of that year the contingent had ballooned to 650,000.

As in the First World War, warehouses were emptied, machinery and rolling stock removed, pharmaceutical goods and hospital supplies seized. Everything was shipped off to Russia, including President Ulmanis. Prices skyrocketed; clothing became unaffordable, food scarce. Hours of work were extended and the social legislation of the Latvian republic suspended. The working conditions and laws of the Soviet Union now applied. All savings in excess of 1,000 lats ($120) were confiscated. Nationalist organizations, the bourgeois intelligentsia, and leadership cadres were targeted for elimination.

My father, my mother, and my sister — Mudīte had been born that April, just two months before the Soviet arrival — took refuge with my father's mentor, Jānis Freijs, and his wife, who lived in retirement and seclusion in the quiet residential district of Meža-parks (Forest Park, or Kaiserwald as the Germans called it). The Baptist seminary where my father taught was turned into a Communist people's theater. Other churches were transformed into movie theaters, bowling alleys, and Red Army clubs. One church in Liepāja was turned into a circus. Religious instruction was eliminated from schools and the theology faculty at the university closed. Street names bearing a religious connotation were changed. Church of Jesus Street became Atheist Street, Bishop Street became Darwin Street. An attempt to prevent the celebration of Christmas in 1940 was abandoned, but in 1941 Easter celebrations were forbidden. In the nine months of Bolshevik rule, forty-one clergymen disappeared, including four Baptist ministers and the music director of the seminary, Kārlis Līdaks.

My grandfather lost his farm in the wholesale expropriation of private property. He was permitted to stay on the land, since his parcel was less than thirty hectares, but the property that he had worked so hard to acquire was no longer his to bequeath, sell, or even give away. While collectivization of agriculture was not rushed, for fear of inducing a repeat of the chaos that befell Russia in the 1930s, what the future held in store for the farming community was clear. Frightened of being labeled kulaks or rich landlords by the new regime, some peasants began slaughtering their animals.

Arrests came at night. Prisoners were crammed into cells. Interrogations were brutal affairs. The only options allowed a prisoner were, as one survivor put it, "admit or confess."[51] In an article published during the strife after the First World War, a Latvian Communist had given advice for interrogation: "Do not ask for incriminating evidence to prove that the prisoner opposed the Soviet either by arms or by word. Your first duty is to ask him what class he belongs to, what were his origin, education, and occupation. These questions should decide the fate of the prisoner. This is the meaning and essence of Red Terror."[52] Those arrested were of every political stripe and every ethnic group. Menachem Begin, the future prime minister of Israel, was arrested in Vilnius and sent to a labor camp in the Russian tundra where he experienced "white nights." When he arrived, the camp veterans insisted that the climate was ideal: "The winter only lasts nine months and after that you have summer to your heart's content."[53]

In August 1940, after all three Baltic states had been incorporated into the Soviet Union, the German ambassador in Riga visited his Soviet counterpart. Of this meeting Ulrich von Kotze reported: "I began by expressing my congratulations on the satisfactory completion of the annexation process . . . , and I added that as a nation friendly to Russia we too had just cause to rejoice. The envoy thanked me in a lively manner and assured me that he would work, in whatever capacity, for the improvement and perfection of friendly relations between the Soviet Union and Germany.[54]

Criminals

IF ALLIED SOLDIERS in post-Hitler Europe were not fond of
the DPs and had no sympathy for the German refugees and expellees, most locals in Germany despised the former and berated the
latter.[55]

The DPs, the "foreigners," were insufferable. They swarmed like
Patton's locusts over all available housing; they snatched like rats
anything resembling food; and, given half a chance, they would
carry away anything that wasn't nailed down. They stole money
and ration coupons from the elderly; they beat up innocent citizens
for fun; they slaughtered farm animals in the dark of night and
spirited the carcasses away; they engaged in firefights with the police; they lived like monstrous beasts, filthy and licentious. In the
transit camps in winter anything made of wood — beds, tables, window frames, even floorboards — was burned. And so it went. Incident after incident. Such was the popular image of the DPs.[56]

The camps in which the DPs were housed were under military
jurisdiction. That made them off limits for Germans, including the
German police. And indeed some DPs abused that situation, using
the camps as safe havens from which to launch criminal activity. For
their fate all DPs were inclined to blame the Germans collectively;
those DPs who had been subjected to life in a concentration camp or
to a brutal regime of forced labor often had no moral qualms about
stealing from the Germans, young or old. A bruised German psyche
found such behavior maddeningly objectionable and insulting. "Insecurity," the *Lübecker Nachrichten* concluded in an editorial, "is
the greatest enemy of all progress toward the peace that everyone
craves."[57] The DPs, in this view, were a threat to the whole cause of
postwar recovery.

Of all the various ethnic groups of DPs, the Poles had the worst
reputation. In the northern state of Schleswig-Holstein where we
lived, the Churchill Barracks in Lübeck were seen as the den of all
DP iniquity. That a haven of crime should have been associated in
name with the British war leader was a delicious irony for many

Germans, for more than anyone else, Churchill was blamed for the blanket bombing of German cities.

No one and nothing seemed safe from the Poles. Next to our camp was a cemetery, the Vorwerker Friedhof, supposedly a place of rest and contemplation. It became infamous for Polish criminal activity. Even funeral parties were attacked and robbed.[58] "Due to the villainy of a few bandits all Poles will come to be hated by the German population," the *Lübecker Nachrichten* predicted.[59] A Lübeck doctor, writing to the local physicians' organization, referred to the "boundless bestiality of these subhumans."[60]

While the Poles may have been singled out for special disdain, Germans blamed the DPs as a whole, and also the moral laxity and *Schadenfreude* of the occupation forces, for the supposed breakdown of their beloved law and order. A lawyer in Munich told his American interlocutor that he was obsessed by two fears: a Russian takeover of the American zone of occupation and armed DPs. In his mind, the two threats carried equal danger.[61] When German police were finally given access to the DP camps and when in August 1947 they raided the notorious Churchill Barracks, a crowd of German spectators stood beyond the main gates and cheered.[62]

Artūrs

BUTTONS. A handful of them. The small suitcase, when it was returned in May 1941, contained his pullover, boots, and those buttons.

Trouser buttons they were. The chekists used to snip off the buttons from a prisoner's trousers so that he couldn't run — if he tried, his pants would drop. If he hadn't been able to run, and the suitcase was returned, there was no hope.

The family found a trace of comfort in the thought that he had been deported, to the Russian tundra, in such haste that he had been unable to take his belongings. The prison had been so warm, they told themselves, that he hadn't needed his pullover or boots. But the buttons betrayed the hope.

Why had those buttons been put back in his suitcase? To offer a wisp of hope? To suggest the return of better days — of movement and freedom? The buttons both put the questions and answered them. They spoke of power and humiliation.

Artūrs Vajeiks, son of Jānis, grandson of Grieta, had known that he should get rid of his little arsenal, the pistol, the rifle, the truncheon, and the machine gun. Those orders were clear and widely circulated after the Russians moved into Latvia, yet again, on June 17, 1940. The Aizsargi, the home guard to which Artūrs belonged, were given emphatic instructions to surrender all weapons. But those few arms were important to Artūrs. The machine gun, which belonged to the Aizsargi, he had hidden in the well, the other pieces here and there. The rifle, however — his rifle — he had kept close at hand, in the attic. He couldn't have fought a private war with these weapons; even armed resistance against the invader at some point in the future was sheer fantasy. Those weapons were symbols. If Artūrs had given them up, he would have been surrendering his own identity and that of his generation.

For a long time Artūrs Vajeiks wasn't even an official statistic. We did not know where his body lay. He was part of an estimate. He was thirty years old when he was taken away on February 19, 1941. His date of birth is known. His death was for the longest time a matter of speculation. To his family and friends he simply disappeared. In an age when soldiers no longer necessarily wore uniforms, he went missing in action.

He was part of a generation that got caught up in a maelstrom of violence, driven by a vague vision of emancipation and power but even more by whim. In his daydreams he wished to be a hero in a free Latvia, but in the end he was prompted by rather more trite considerations. He liked the smart uniform, the camaraderie, the admiration of the girls, and he was terrified by the void that accompanied inactivity.

Some said he was a wild youth. Others merely called him spirited. He never finished school. He took off several times for tours around Europe on his motorcycle. That added to his bravado. In the rural setting he was quite the Don Juan. His temperament seemed to match the age and territory in which he lived, full of contradictions, ambiguities, energy.

On that Wednesday, February 19, Artūrs Vajeiks was planning to take a load of timber to Jelgava for cutting at the mill. Instead, he was arrested early while breakfasting with his wife, Valija. They had married less than two years earlier, in 1939. Members of the railway police, an auxiliary force, came for him. The charges against him were that he had "assisted the international bourgeoisie, belonged to a counterrevolutionary organization, and stashed weapons illegally." The weapons charge was the most serious.

Artūrs had already been questioned once, some weeks earlier. He had been called into Jelgava for interrogation. After that experience he told his father that it was time to go into hiding. But out of concern for the safety of his wife and newborn child, a son born the previous October, he never did. His best friend, also called Artūrs, worked for the railway and was, befitting the polarities of the time, a Communist. After the first interrogation, the friend told my uncle never to sign anything put before him by Communist officials, and by all means immediately to dispose of the weapons. It was the rifle they found.

After his arrest he was first taken to Jelgava, then transported to Riga and held there in the Central Prison, whose dumb walls had witnessed so much horror. One of his two sisters, Leontīne, went regularly to the prison to bring food and seek information. She stood in long lines to speak briefly to brusque, uncommunicative apparatchiks who perused lists and said nothing. Until May her food parcels were accepted. Then one day in May she was turned away, told to take her parcel with her and not bother to return. That spring an American official in Moscow noted, after visiting Lithuania: "People have no opportunity of seeing their relatives once they have been arrested and only know if they are alive if the prison authorities continue to accept clothing and food for those in prison."[63]

The family could now do nothing more than hope for the best and assume that Artūrs had been deported to Siberia. When the Germans arrived in early July and found hastily dug mass graves on the grounds of Central Prison and on the outskirts of Riga, they invited citizens to come and identify corpses. Artūrs's family did not attend, ostensibly because they wanted to believe he had been evacuated east. Even when the family retrieved his suitcase, the charade continued.

As the years went by, the war years and then the postwar tribulations, the hope that Artūrs might still be alive gradually evaporated. All in the immediate family except for his parents, Jānis and Paulīne, fled Latvia in 1944. Artūrs's wife remarried in the Latvian diaspora. We now assumed that Artūrs had been shot in Central Prison in May 1941.

When Latvia regained its independence fifty years later, in 1991, and archive doors opened, a goddaughter of Artūrs Vajeiks who had remained in Latvia discovered, to the considerable surprise of the remaining family abroad, that Artūrs had indeed been shipped east at some point in May or June 1941, to Astrakhan, in the Stalingrad district, and had been held there, in Prison Number 2, for many months. On February 11, 1942, almost a year after his arrest, he had been found guilty under the criminal statutes of the Soviet Union and sentenced to death. The sentence was carried out on the prison grounds a month later, on March 14.

In August 1995 the Republic of Latvia "rehabilitated" Artūrs Vajeiks.

Youth, Soldier, Churchman

FOR MY FATHER, 1940 was also a fateful year. Artūrs Vajeiks was arrested because he was prepared to fight the Bolsheviks. My father, Rūdolfs Ekšteins, was not arrested, even though he had fought the Bolsheviks, militarily and spiritually. He had taken part in the last military sweep against them through the province of Latgale, and later he had become a churchman, a pursuit anathema to the Communists. His survival in 1940 he found perplexing, then and thereafter.

Born in Liepāja in 1899, he was a fishmonger's son who never spoke to us about his family and his youth. In fact, he seemed to want to negate his origins. He refused to eat pickled herring. He could not abide its smell. His father and mother had sold herring along the docks and at the central market of Liepāja.

He, his sister, and his parents lived in a tiny row house, consisting of one room and a kitchen, on Cemetery Street (Kapsētas iela) in a working-class district near the dockyards. Though its origins as a fishing village went back to the Middle Ages, Liepāja was essentially a nineteenth-century town whose modern development was encouraged by the final partition of Poland in 1795, when Kurland was annexed by Russia. Ice free throughout the year, the port became an important Russian naval facility. The construction of a railway line in the 1870s linking the city to the hinterland turned Liepāja into a major trading center. The economic vitality was accompanied by the usual extremes of early capitalist growth. With its beautiful beach, rivaling the brilliant sands of Jūrmala, near Riga, Liepāja developed by the end of the nineteenth century into a smart resort city, preferred by Russian high society. At the same time, the city's sizable proletariat acquired a reputation for radicalism.

My father's schooling, which coincided with the push to Russify the Baltic provinces, had been for the most part in Russian. To the end of his life he spoke the language well. He later recalled Russian soldiers going from house to house on his street in 1905 looking for revolutionaries. They searched his small house too, poking bayonets into mattresses. And in 1912, for the three hundredth anniversary of the Romanov dynasty, his entire school class had to watch an imperial procession and bellow "Long live the tsar!"

During most of the Great War Liepāja was occupied by the Germans. The port was a supply nexus for the German army on the eastern front. His schooling interrupted, my father spent several years as a young dockworker, unloading coal and war materiel from German ships. At the end of the war, when the Bolsheviks invaded, the Ulmanis government fled from Riga to Jelgava and then to Liepāja. The port city appeared for a time to be the last bastion of hopes for Latvian independence and freedom. My father, age nineteen, volunteered for the national army and was eventually assigned to a newly established unit, the Eleventh Dobele Infantry Regiment. In the autumn of 1919 his unit was sent to Daugavpils (Dünaburg), in the eastern part of the country, and joined in the fighting there that finally drove the Bolsheviks out of Latvia.

He had grown up in a devoutly religious atmosphere. His parents were members of a Baptist church in Liepāja. The Baptists were a small sect in Latvia and in continental Europe as a whole. Their roots in the Baltic were not deep, going back only to the mid-nineteenth century. In the 1890s the mantle of Baptist leadership in Latvia had passed to Jānis Freijs, an energetic young entrepreneur, then in his thirties, who had training in mechanical engineering as well as theology. He displayed both a beguiling practicality and a firm religiosity. This combination attracted much attention. He ran his own printing businesses, which published hymn books, religious calendars, and tracts. He traveled to Palestine, Turkey, Greece, and Italy to observe at first hand the lands where Christianity originated. Entranced by the modern, he cycled from Riga to Paris and back in 1900. He loved machines, whether they were printing presses or automobiles. He would be one of the first in Latvia to own a motorcar. Convinced that religion was a matter of this world, not some imagined Nirvana, he ran in 1909 for elected office, as a candidate for the Riga city council, and won.

He had been introduced to Natalie Princess von Lieven through the evangelist F. W. Baedeker, an associate of Lord Radstock's; he had impressed her with his dedication and missionary zeal and had received from her considerable financial support for his work.

In October 1915, more than a year after the outbreak of war, Freijs was exiled to Siberia. No official reason was given, but by the tsar's officials Baptists were regarded as disrupters and potential insurrectionists and also, perhaps because of their origins in Reformation Germany, as friends of the German cause. A number of other Baptist ministers in the Latvian-speaking provinces of Russia were banished, their churches, forty in number, closed. Five churches were totally destroyed, seventeen damaged.

In April 1917, however, after the first revolution that year in Russia, the deportation order against Freijs was lifted by the provi-

sional Russian government, and in August he returned to Riga. His
trials were not over, though. When the Bolsheviks occupied Riga in
January 1919, he was again imprisoned; he spent the better part of
five months in various jails, in sordid conditions, and was one of the
few prisoners who survived the brutality, executions, and typhus
epidemics. Owing to the intervention of a young Latvian Bolshevik
who had once heard him preach, Freijs was released a mere three
days before the slaughter of prisoners that accompanied the liberation of Riga on May 22. Thus the attacks against this churchman
came from all sides, from within and without, from right and left.
His influence on my father was to be immense.

In 1920–21 Freijs visited England and North America. There he
garnered substantial aid for Latvian victims and for the needy.
Clothing, blankets, and shoes were sent and distributed to some five
thousand children and adults. But Freijs also managed to convince
British, American, and Canadian Baptists of the need to help establish a Baptist seminary in Riga that would educate future Latvian
churchmen. Only such an establishment, he argued, would allow the
denomination to flourish in a state where Lutheranism was dominant. The Riga seminary opened its doors in January 1922, in temporary quarters in the Baltic-German Baptist church on Vīlandes
Street.

Released from the army, my father applied to the seminary in the
spring of 1923 and was accepted. He flourished under the tutelage
of Freijs, and in 1925 went off to study for three years as a scholarship student at the Baptist College in Bristol, England. (The college
is now part of Bristol University.) Founded in 1679, this college,
along with Regent's Park, Oxford, became the most distinguished
Baptist educational establishment in Europe. Bristol itself, with
twenty-three Baptist churches, was a stronghold of religious non-
conformism in England.

On his return to Riga in 1928, my father was appointed teacher in
the seminary and assistant minister in the seminary church. He
became the representative of Latvian Baptists in Europe, traveling to
Tallinn, Rome, and Prague to attend congresses and to speak. In 1933
he won a scholarship for further study, this time at Colgate Divin-

ity School in Rochester, New York. After a year there, followed by travels through Depression-ridden America, he returned once more to the seminary in Riga. By now the seminary had its own building, a new construction at 37 Lačplēša Street, opened in 1934. It had classrooms, a library, a church auditorium, and apartments for its ministerial and teaching staff. My father moved into apartment 3. Two years later a pretty young girl from Jelgava began attending the Sunday services and youth program at the seminary church. Her smile was radiant. My father was smitten. On July 18, 1937, he married Biruta Vajeiks, and she joined him in the small apartment. He was thirty-eight, she nineteen.

All Latvian veterans of the war of independence were entitled to free higher education if they qualified academically. On his return from America, my father had enrolled in a part-time postgraduate program in classics at the Latvian University in Riga. His responsibilities in the church were considerable, and since his studies were free and the time he could devote to them limited, he was still in midstream in his doctoral work when the Bolsheviks arrived in 1940.

The new seminary building was Freijs's last great achievement, even though Freijs was no longer active when the new edifice arose. By 1928 he was having occasional difficulty speaking, and some time later he was diagnosed with Parkinson's disease. In 1930 he withdrew from all responsibilities. Ill and bedridden, he would nevertheless survive the horrors to come, living until 1950.

On June 13, 1941, the cattle cars arrived in train stations throughout Latvia. That night whole families were arrested, stuffed into those cars, and shipped east. Teachers, students, clergymen, civil servants, military officers — all "antisocial" and "counterrevolutionary" citizens were to be resettled, the Politburo had decided in May. These hostile elements included members of Rotary clubs and Esperanto societies, amateur radio operators and stamp collectors — and the head of the Latvian Boy Scouts. Some fifteen thousand arrests in one night. These victims, too, disappeared, for the most part without trace into the vast expanse of Siberia and of the Arctic tundra. "Clergymen" was one of the categories slated for deportation. My father had taken a job as a library clerk. He never thought his "reassignment" would work. He expected arrest. That he had fought against the Bolsheviks in the civil war two decades earlier would be another serious charge against him. Yet that night they didn't come for him. He wondered why.

In November 1995 the Commission for the Rehabilitation of the Victims of Political Repression, chaired by Alexander Yakovlev, presented a report that concluded that all told, two hundred thousand clergy had been slain under Soviet rule. "Documents relate," stated Yakovlev, "how clergymen, monks, and nuns were crucified on royal gates and shot in the basements of the Cheka, scalped, strangled, drowned, and submitted to other bestial tortures." Of forty-eight thousand churches in Russia before the Bolshevik revolution, seven thousand remained by 1969.[64]

Between thirty-five and forty thousand Latvians were murdered or deported by the Soviets during the occupation of 1940–41, most of them on June 14, 1941. Around four thousand of the victims were children or adolescents under the age of sixteen. Plans were under way for more deportations in July. Our family may have figured in the new lists. These plans were aborted by the German invasion.[65]

Enterprise

THE MILITARY was flummoxed by the DP question. In the district of Celle, in Lower Saxony, the British commanding officer thought a major military offensive might be necessary in the summer of 1945 to bring the DPs to their senses. They seemed to be slaughtering all the animals in the land.[66] An official of the United Nations Relief and Rehabilitation Administration (UNRRA) suggested the creation of a "special Camp" for what he called "unmanageable DPs." "This would be something in the nature of a police or prison Camp, under the control and care of the Army."[67]

Our own barracks in Lübeck, the Artillerie Kaserne, was the center of one of the most sensational black-market operations of the occupation era. A week before Christmas in 1947, fifty local policemen and thirty detectives raided the complex. They were backed up by a contingent of British troops who guarded the perimeter of the camp to prevent escape. The senior public safety officer, Lieutenant Colonel Berry, was present for the raid. To everyone's astonishment, that of both outsiders and most insiders, the police found 109 mature live pigs hidden in the camp, in three separate locations, an abandoned air-raid bunker, the basement ruins of two decrepit buildings, and a former garage. And in a thorough search of the barracks, the police uncovered from under floorboards a huge stash of corn, wheat, barley, oats, bacon, meat, and other provisions. The confiscated foodstuffs filled the back of a large truck, the pigs that of a huge cattle van. One German reporter, salivating profusely, noted that the edible meat equaled the standard weekly meat ration for 90,900 people, or a year's meat allotment for 1,748 persons.[68] In the wake of the raid sixty-seven Latvians and Lithuanians were charged with "unlawful possession of pigs." In May 1948 a lower court of the Allied Control Commission in Lübeck gave sixty of them six-month suspended sentences.

A few days after that operation at our camp, the Lohmühle camp for Polish DPs was raided. An intricate underground network of tunnels was discovered together with a huge cache, roughly four thousand kilos of high-quality leather — enough for the soles of ten thousand pairs of shoes — and more than two thousand kilos of skins. The total haul had a black-market value of 2.5 million marks. Even more curious was another find here: 415,000 phonograph needles.[69]

The DPs, in other words, were not doing things by half measures. This wholesale hoarding irked the local Germans enormously. The Balts and the Poles, whom the Germans had colonized over the centuries, had returned to the metropolitan roost with a vengeance.[70]

Barbarossa

AT DAWN ON JUNE 22, 1941, Operation Barbarossa commenced. The largest military force ever assembled moved toward Russia:

more than three million men in 148 divisions, with 600,000 trucks, 750,000 horses, 3,580 tanks and armored vehicles, 7,184 pieces of artillery, and 1,830 aircraft. Hitler rightly called it "the biggest front line in history."[71]

In 1967 Harrison Salisbury had his last meeting, in Moscow, with Ivan Maisky, the longstanding Soviet ambassador between the wars to the Court of St. James's. Maisky had sent Stalin repeated warnings that Hitler was planning to attack Russia. Stalin had ignored them all. "Stalin distrusted everyone," Maisky told Salisbury. "The only man he trusted was Hitler."[72]

5

Bear Slayer Street

How incredible to start torturing the Jews again in Paris,
Berlin, Spain and Hamburg — I thought such things belonged to the Middle Ages.

LADY COWPER TO PRINCESS LIEVEN, 1835

Comrade Stalin is the father of the world.

OTTO GROTEWOHL, 1947

Riga Rejoice!

HATED AS OPPRESSORS in 1905, reviled as colonizers in 1918, the
Germans returned to Latvia as liberators in 1941. Operation Barbarossa moved eastward with resolve and fury. The Soviet army was
unprepared and poorly deployed. Kaunas and Vilnius in Lithuania
were reached in two days, Riga in little more than a week.

The Germans crossed the river Niemen on almost the same day of
the year as Napoleon had. On June 29 and 30, Riga came under German artillery bombardment. Among the casualties was the famous
wooden tower of St. Peter's Church, the second-tallest church tower
in Europe. For two days the streets were quiet. Then on July 1 German troops entered the Latvian capital. They were greeted as lost
friends. Riga rejoiced.

"Bolshevism was threatening all Europe," the invader told the
invaded. "It was on the march to attack Germany, and it has also inflicted terrible wounds on you. If this world enemy had been rampant among you for a few more years, nothing would have been left

to you of your property and people. The Bolshevik leaders would have carried you off to Siberia, robbed, and murdered you."[1] If one accepted that German argument, as most Latvians did, then the next point had to be swallowed too: "At the cost of their blood the armed forces of the German people have overthrown the Bolshevik universal enemy; and so everyone will understand that this German people has now assumed the duty and the right to make such arrangements that never again will a similar danger threaten the traditions of the people of Europe, and indeed their very existence." Without the Germans, Bolshevism could not have been ousted. If in 1919 the Latvians had refused to accept that truth, now, in 1941, they bowed to it without difficulty.

The Germans returned as a latter-day reincarnation of the Teutonic warlords. The SS in particular nurtured that image: they trained in medieval castles, brandished prehistoric symbols, and practiced ancient rituals.

"We conquer, conquer, conquer," wrote Ruth Andreas-Friedrich in her diary. "And every victory makes Hitler more arrogant. Goebbels is already calling him 'the most gifted commander of all time.' The deification is taking on a frightening form." A friend of the diarist remarked: "After such success, Hitler can permit himself anything."[2]

Liberation? By the Wehrmacht? By the SS? By Einsatzgruppen? Yes, the German occupation was without question perceived initially as liberation. Earlier, in the years of national awakening and then independence, Latvians had talked of seven hundred years of slavery under German domination. There was no trace of such talk now. After a year of Bolshevik terror, German rule appeared like the return of sweetness and light. The Germans were deemed "friends" and "saviors." People rushed to place flowers at the Liberty Monument in the center of Riga.[3]

Hope?

MORALE SEEMED TO pick up in 1948. In February, the Communist coup in Prague roused Western resolve. When on March 20 the Soviet delegation stalked out of the Control Council meeting in Berlin, the idea of four-power control of Germany wilted. In June, currency reform in the Western zones sundered the wartime alliance irrevocably. The firm line taken by the Western Allies on Berlin, after the Soviets had established a land blockade of the city, brought anxiety but also determination. The West was taking a stand on behalf of its former enemy, Germany. The city that but three years earlier had been the capital of evil was suddenly a symbol of freedom.

The pages of the *Lübecker Nachrichten* livened up considerably. Advertising increased: by October the Saturday issue of a paper that had started as a one-page Allied news sheet had four pages of ads. In November a regular column began to appear under the title "Lübeck's Spiritual Life." That was a good sign.

Negative attitudes did not disappear. The lack of a peace treaty distressed Germans and made them wonder what schemes the wartime Allies were concocting. After the village of Stolpe, on the border with the Soviet zone, was surrendered to the Russians, rumors circulated that the Red Army was about to occupy all of Schleswig-Holstein.[4] But the gradual collapse of the Grand Alliance seemed to have more positive than negative implications, for us, for most Germans, and for the world.

Ostland, 1941

WITH THE GERMAN INVASION of the Baltic in 1941, terror was unleashed once again. The endless cycle continued. Soviet activists were sought out. People were shot in the streets or taken to nearby forests to be killed. Jews were assaulted. "Death to Communists and Jews!" Jew and Communist were one and the same. On the heels of the Wehrmacht came the German security personnel, politicos, and bureaucrats. Latvian authority of any sort was not recognized.

Two months before the assault on Russia, Hitler had appointed the Baltic German Alfred Rosenberg as his deputy for Eastern European questions — his "gate-keeper of the East." Rosenberg took great pride in that designation. In his diary for July 16, 1941, he reflected on his "huge responsibility, probably the greatest that the Reich could give, the securing of Europe's independence for centuries to come."[5]

Rosenberg had been born in Reval (Tallinn). He had studied in Riga and Moscow before moving to Germany at the end of the First World War and becoming a Nazi in 1920. He had intellectual pretensions. He became the editor of the *Völkischer Beobachter*, the main Nazi newspaper, and wrote a rambling racist treatise, *The Myth of the Twentieth Century*, which catapulted him to the nominal position of party ideologue. As head of the Reich Ministry for the Occupied Eastern Territories, Rosenberg had instructions to work closely with the military, with Hermann Göring, who was in charge of economic coordination, and with Heinrich Himmler, the head of the SS and the police. But despite his sense of mission, Rosenberg could command little respect from his peers. He was saluted perfunctorily as an ideologue, but no one took him seriously as an administrator. The conflict over competence among military, civilian, economic, and police authorities led to the Ostministerium's soon being called the Chaostministerium. In the tug of war with Göring, Himmler, Bormann, and later Speer, Rosenberg repeatedly lost out: on economic matters, Göring and Speer had ultimate jurisdiction; on racial and political issues, Himmler and Bormann ruled. Even over his immediate subordinates Rosenberg exercised little control. Himmler's contact in the Ostministerium noted in the autumn of 1942 how "insecure" Rosenberg appeared, and commented that the ministry was being run like a "fire-sale enterprise."[6]

A high percentage of Rosenberg's appointments to the administration of the Ostland — which consisted of the three Baltic states and White Russia — came from northern Germany, especially Schleswig-Holstein. As Reich commissar for the occupied Ostland Rosenberg chose Hinrich Lohse, who had been Nazi gauleiter of Schleswig-Holstein. Under the Reich commissar were three general commissars and nineteen area commissars. General commissar for Latvia was Otto Drechsler, a one-legged dentist and former mayor of Lübeck. Of the nineteen area commissars, seven were from Schleswig-Holstein.

A number of the officials were Baltic Germans returning home, among them Hugo Wittrock, the new mayor of Riga. Wittrock, born in 1873 on the island of Ösel, was a friend of Rosenberg's. He had studied at the polytechnic in Riga, worked in insurance, and been active in the German community there until the repatriation of the Baltendeutsche in 1939–40. He was living in Königsberg when the call came in 1941 to return to the Baltic.

Walter-Eberhard Freiherr von Medem was appointed area commissar for Mitau and the surrounding area. His was a family name prominent in Kurland. Mitau had purportedly been founded by a Medem ancestor, the Ordensmeister Konrad Medem von Mandern, who built the first fortress there in 1265. The family had owned ten estates before Latvian independence, the grandest of which was Elley-Schloss (Lieleleja), about twenty-five kilometers south of Mitau, not far from the Lithuanian border. During the civil strife at the end of World War I, Walter-Eberhard, representing a Reich-German branch of the family, had organized the Medem Freikorps and brought it to the Baltic, where it gained a reputation as an effective strike force. However, when in 1920 the Medem lands had been sequestered by the new Latvian state, the family had, with great bitterness, rejected all offers of consolation and moved to Germany. "Il cracha. Il partit" (He spat. He left). Such, according to a French account, had been the response of the last baron of Elley-Schloss.[7]

Many of these Baltic Germans now returned to their homeland with grudges against the Latvians.

In contrast to the war in the West, which the Nazi leadership euphemistically considered a Normalkrieg, a normal war for influence rather than for tangible gain, the struggle in the East was conceived as a Vernichtungskrieg, a war of eradication. Here the Nazis envisaged radical departures. At his "generals' conference" of March 30, 1941, Hitler had denounced all international law; his impending Eastern campaign, he said, would disregard all such conventions.

The Baltic area was to become a protectorate within the greater German Reich. German authority would be supreme. According to the plans, most specifically the Generalplan Ost of 1942, the Estonian and Latvian intelligentsia would be accorded no say in administration and much of it would be resettled farther east, away from the coast and from the Baltic cities, like Riga and Reval, built and administered for so long by Germans. The only university permitted in the Ostland would be at Dorpat.

The German occupation authorities refused to acknowledge the local leadership that had tried to take the initiative in the few days between the Soviet departure and the German arrival. Instead, they appointed people they had selected to act as intermediaries and called this puppet system *landeseigene Verwaltung*, national self-administration. The first Latvian "director" appointed by the Germans was General Oskars Dankers, a military man who had fled to Germany in January 1941. Riga, moreover, was not permitted participation in even the euphemisms about "self-administration." It was given a Baltic-German mayor, Wittrock, and controlled directly. The German administration of Latvia included some twenty-five thousand German and Latvian officials.

In August, street names were changed once again. What had been Brīvības iela (Liberty Avenue) in the capital city of an independent Latvia was renamed Adolf-Hitler-Strasse, to the annoyance of all Latvians. The German argument was that they, the Germans, had liberated Riga thrice, in September 1917, May 1919, and July 1941, and thus the change in name was perfectly logical. There was also a Hermann-Göring-Strasse and an Alfred-Rosenberg-Ring, the latter replacing Raiņa bulvāris, named after Latvia's most famous playwright. All names representing Latvian national achievement, and any reference to Russian influence — streets named, for example, after Empress Elizabeth or the writer Gogol — disappeared.[8]

All signs and notices had to be in German first, and then below in Latvian. Any reference to independence or cultural distinctiveness was forbidden. The annual song festivals, dating back to 1873, and independence day celebrations on November 18 were banned. The Germans also initially refused to reverse the nationalization of property effected by the Soviets during their year of control. The economic centralization achieved by the Communist regime was, quite obviously, too useful to be disassembled.[9] Thus all significant economic enterprises were grouped into categories and put under German trusteeship.

Shortly after their arrival, the Germans began to recruit labor for the Reich — agricultural workers for East Prussia, workers for the munitions industries scattered throughout Germany, and transport workers for the Wehrmacht. At the same time, however, they rejected any military assistance, in the form of local units, in the fight against the Russians. There was to be no doubt as to who was the master and who the servant in this relationship. Of equality, for which some Balts had hoped, completely unrealistically, there was none.

The quick victory against Russia anticipated by the Germans did not materialize. On November 15 the final thrust against Moscow, a mere 125 kilometers from the German front lines, began. Three weeks later, on December 4, the Germans were but 30 kilometers from the capital. But that night the temperature plummeted. Weapons froze, tanks failed to start, soldiers got frostbite, and the German assault stopped in its tracks.

Not surprisingly, the enthusiasm that had greeted the Germans in much of Eastern Europe began soon to wane. In the Baltic, while the elimination of Soviet control was still applauded, the sense that one evil had been replaced by another grew. Farmers wanted their land back. City workers complained about food shortages. Nationalists wanted recognition. When the Dutch fascist leader Rost van Tonningen visited the Baltic in early 1942, he noted a "chauvinistic nationalism" and hostility toward the Germans in all segments of Estonian and Latvian society.[10] SS reports on the temper in Latvia expressed concern. A report on the situation in Riga in October 1942 began with the words "The mood of the population is bad."[11]

Prospects

IN 1947, as the Cold War intensified and the prospects of an early return home diminished for the DPs, the chances of escape from the camps to a new life elsewhere grew. Departures began for Sweden, England, Scotland, Canada, Australia, and Argentina. The young and the strong were taken first, to work in mines, in smelters, in forests, in kitchens, in hospitals, on farms. In England the new-comers were no longer called DPs but EVWs (European Volunteer Workers), in parlance that was meant to distance itself from the idea of servile labor. In Canada officialdom insisted on calling the DPs New Canadians.

Despite growing resolve in the standoff with the Soviet Union, the United States procrastinated on immigration issues. Its immigration policy consisted of a system, dating from the isolationist 1920s, whereby countries were allotted annual quotas. Western and Northern Europeans were favored. The annual intake from Great Britain and Ireland together was set at 84,000, from Germany at 26,000, but from Poland at 6,524, from Latvia at 236, and from Estonia at 116. As the *New York Herald Tribune* pointed out in an editorial in May 1947, "it would take 275 years to absorb all the Estonian DPs at this rate."[12] Hence it was virtually impossible for DPs to get to the United States. Both UNRRA workers and DPs were disconsolate.[13] In October 1946 the *New York Times* commented that the possibilities for emigration from the camps appeared to be "constantly dwindling."[14]

In 1948, after a bitter fight in Congress, the United States passed the Displaced Persons Act, and promised, from October of that year on, to take 10,000 refugees a month from Europe. Those promises proved difficult to keep, however. Consulates were understaffed. Security clearance for every DP took more time than expected. Harry N. Rosenfield, acting chairman of the Displaced Persons Commission, said: "We don't want any security risks — anyone who is a Commie or Nazi — coming into the United States under the DP program."[15] The security procedures prompted a *New York Times* reporter to comment in August 1948 that Germans had less difficulty in emigrating to the United States than the DPs: "As matters stand, it is easier for a former Nazi to enter the United States than for one of the Nazis' 'innocent victims.'"[16] Nevertheless, the pace picked up. Whereas by the end of June 1949 only 40,000 DPs had reached the United States, in the following six months 81,968 arrived. In the end, the United States admitted more than 400,000 refugees from the European camps.[17]

Bear Slayer

Lāčplēsis, the Bear Slayer, is the national hero of the Latvians. He is a warrior who in infancy was suckled by a bear, and as a consequence developed the ears and strength of a bear. It is Lāčplēsis who awakens his people from endless sleep, destroys the evil spirits, and restores the Castle of Light. He creates the State, protects it from its enemies, and is a model father. Even in death he continues to do battle against the Black Knight. During the years of the Latvian republic, the highest award for valor was the Lāčplēsis Medal.

When I was born, in December 1943, my parents lived once again in their seminary apartment, on Lāčplēša Street in Riga. They had returned there shortly after the German occupation when my father had resumed his duties in the seminary. Bear Slayer Street was one of a number of modern avenues that spread out in concentric circles from the old town. Actually, the Germans had renamed the street when they occupied Riga. They called it Carl-Schirren-Strasse, after a Baltic-German professor who had actively opposed the Russification measures of the tsarist regime in the previous century. "Chain up your instinct and teach it to control itself," he had admonished the Russians.

Only the Germans called Lāčplēša Street Carl-Schirren-Strasse; the Latvians continued to refer to it as Bear Slayer Street. Still, if the names differed, the sentiments they embodied did not. The bear had of course always been the Russian. Carl Schirren had been a bear slayer himself. For both Latvians and Germans the bear now was the Bolshevik Russian.

It was not in London or Washington, and certainly not in Paris, that the future of the world was decided in 1941, 1942, and 1943. It was not in North Africa or in the Pacific. It was in Europe on the Eastern Front, in its stinking pools of ethnic spite, slaughter, and revenge. It was decided in the greatest military showdown of all history, the monstrous, furious clash that had been brewing for centuries between Teuton and Slav. The war in the West for those three years was a skirmish by comparison. Before the Allied invasion of Italy in 1943, Hitler pitted only four divisions against the British and Americans — they could, as he concluded about Britain in the summer of 1941, be ignored. Against the Red Army he threw two hundred divisions. The great task was to slay the Russian bear.

Repatriation

WE WERE TERRIFIED of repatriation.

The original UNRRA plans, drawn up in 1944–45, had foreseen a relatively quick resolution of the refugee issue within six months of the surrender. At the outset, matters did in fact move apace. During May and June 1945, 5.25 million people were sent home. The Western and Northern European DPs were dealt with promptly; that operation was mostly completed by the end of June. Yugoslav and Italian DPs took a few months longer, but by the end of September they, too, had been repatriated. By then 2 million Soviet nationals had returned. In the Western zones of Germany, of 7 million DPs, fewer than 2 million remained by the end of September. But many of these proved to be difficult cases. It was the Soviet citizens and Eastern Europeans, especially the Poles, Ukrainians, and Balts, who presented the greatest problems. Many of these people did not wish to return home.

The Soviets regarded anyone who had landed in the West as guilty by association. Flight from the Soviet state, said the Soviet criminal code, was an act of treason punishable by death. Soldiers should have fought to their last breath and never been captured; those who had surrendered were traitors and defeatists. As for forced labor, no one should have worked for the enemy. On May 9, 1945, Soviet V-E Day, Beria proposed to Stalin that all these people — prisoners of war and conscripted laborers — should, on their return to the Soviet Union, be sent immediately to the gulag. As for the displaced persons who had fled their homeland, they were automatically labeled as collaborators and war criminals.

The Western Allies, too, had little patience for any non-German who had fought on the side of the Germans and thus delayed Allied victory. On June 24, 1944, Patrick Dean, then assistant legal adviser at the British Foreign Office, later a prosecuting counsel at the Nuremberg Tribunal, and from 1965 to 1969 the British ambassador to Washington, wrote: "In due course all those with whom the Soviet authorities desire to deal must . . . be handed over to them, and we are not concerned with the fact that they may be shot or otherwise more harshly dealt with than they might be under English law."[18] Repatriation of Soviet nationals, regardless of individual wishes, was the primary policy. Moreover, the Soviets were allowed to decide who was a Soviet citizen. As for the territories they occupied in 1939–40, their position was that everyone resident there in the summer of 1940 became a Soviet citizen by virtue of the various nationality decrees passed locally.

A neutral state like Sweden got into the act of bowing to Soviet pressure. On January 25, 1946, Sweden deported 146 Baltic legionnaires, 130 of them Latvian soldiers, members of the Fifteenth Division who, trapped in the Kurland pocket, had fought off the Red Army to the bitter end. While the rest of their comrades had gone into Soviet captivity and all that that entailed, these soldiers had escaped, in several different groups, from Danzig and from Ventspils and vicinity, to Sweden. Around thirty thousand Balts were already in Sweden at this point; they had come in a steady stream since the previous summer. But in June the Swedish cabinet had decided to bow to a Soviet demand, based on the armistice agreements of May, that enemy soldiers be surrendered to the nearest Allied command. For the Latvian soldiers who had fought with the Germans, regardless of whether they were volunteers or conscripts, that command was Russian. Despite intensive debate and much opposition, despite a hunger strike by the Balts in their internment camp at Eksjö, the Swedish government stuck to its decision and six months later delivered the Latvians and a few others to a Soviet ship that had arrived at Trelleborg. One young soldier, Lieutenant Pēteris Vabulis, managed to kill himself with a dagger on a bus ferrying the Latvians to quayside. A week earlier he had written to a friend: "It is not hard to die, for if such things are allowed to continue, the end of the world must be near." The Swedish foreign minister was unrepentant. "There was not the slightest reason to suspect the Soviet administration of injustice," he declared.[19] Sweden had been one of the few countries to recognize the Soviet annexation of the Baltic states in 1940.

Not the slightest reason to suspect the Soviets? Field Marshal Alexander, who had led the Baltic Landeswehr against the Bolsheviks in 1919, did have his doubts. He was troubled by the situation of the Cossacks who had surrendered in northern Italy. Some of them had in fact fought with him in 1919, and he had been decorated for his anti-Bolshevik efforts by the White Russian General Yudenich. Alexander's protestations notwithstanding, the Cossacks were returned.[20]

So were the veterans of General Vlasov's forces, mostly to applause. These were Russians who had fought against the Soviet army in the hope of overthrowing communism. In February 1946 the Americans turned some two thousand of these soldiers over to the Soviets at Plattling in Lower Bavaria. William Sloane Coffin, Jr., was there. "I saw several men commit suicide. Two rammed their heads through windows sawing their necks on the broken glass until they cut their jugular veins." The affair left him, he said, with "a burden of guilt I am sure to carry the rest of my life."[21] Vlasov and his generals were hanged by the Russians in late July 1946.

Up to 2 million people — Ukrainians, Poles, Rumanians, Yugoslavs, and Balts — were sent back forcibly by the Western Allies between 1944 and 1947. Even more, some 3.2 million, were returned from Soviet-occupied territory in Eastern Europe and Germany. Back in their native countries many of these repatriates faced a terrible fate — execution, imprisonment, or forced labor.[22]

Despite the war, despite the Holocaust, despite knowledge of the Stalinist horrors in the Soviet Union, both leaders and led in the West could simply not comprehend the brutality that was endemic in Central and Eastern Europe. The liberal mentality is basically incapable of coming to grips with human failure. "Nothing in my childhood prepared me," the American journalist Walter Lippmann once wrote in an autobiographical fragment, "for the violent and bewildering times in which I was to live and for the radical changes which have occurred in the human condition."[23] When Fiorello La Guardia, the tough former mayor of New York, was confronted by a group of Yugoslavs who said they could not return home because they rejected communism, he responded in a time-honored American manner: "That's no reason for refusing repatriation. I've disagreed with the government in my country for over twenty years now — but you don't see me running away from America on that account."[24]

British and American policy on the DPs was to soften gradually. By 1947 the position agreed upon was that no one who in 1939 had lived outside the Soviet Union's boundaries or subsequently been conscripted by the Germans to fight would be forcibly handed over to the Russians.

The Jews of Latvia

THE LATVIAN JEWS had a long history.[25] During the rule of the Teutonic Knights in the Baltic, Jews had been excluded from the territory. When, however, Kurland became a duchy of Poland in the sixteenth century, some of the Jews of Lithuanian Poland moved north. Despite frequent attempts to expel them, despite being consistently regarded as outsiders, and despite having to pay sundry special fees, taxes, and fines, the Jews flourished and grew in number. They engaged in commerce of every variety, peddling, leasing, brokering. They owned rafts that moved timber down the rivers. They controlled the rag trade. They were goldsmiths and brandy distillers, artisans and tradesmen. For a time, in the late seventeenth century, they were even hired as tax collectors in Kurland.

In the 1897 census Livland and Kurland together reported 80,753 Jews. This was 40 percent of all those Jews who lived outside "the Pale of settlement" in western Russia — the Pale consisted of those western provinces (Ukraine, White Russia, Lithuania, and Russian Poland) where Jews were officially allowed to live.[26] If one included the Jews of Latgale, in Vitebsk province, a part of the Pale, then the number of Jews in the territory of the future Latvia approached

200,000 by the eve of the Great War. By then Riga had 33,000 Jews. They were central to its economic life, particularly to the export business. Russia sent about 10 percent of its exports through Riga. Much of that business was handled by Jews. They controlled most of the export of cereals, timber, flax, and eggs. Sawmills and tanneries were often in Jewish hands, as were banks and credit societies. The clothing industry, factories and stores, owners and workers, was heavily Jewish. Many lawyers and entertainers were Jewish. Prior to 1914, almost all of Riga's dentists and many of its best-known doctors were Jewish. Mitau and Libau, too, had strong Jewish communities.

The 1914–18 war was no less disruptive to the Jews than to the other inhabitants of the Baltic provinces. The majority were uprooted and never returned. The civil strife of 1918–19 brought added suffering. The Jew was easily turned into a scapegoat for both capitalist exploitation and Communist conspiracy. When the national census was done in 1925, Latvia counted 95,675 Jews, less than half of the pre-1914 number, or 5.19 percent of the population. By 1935 those numbers had declined further, 93,479 and 4.79 percent. In independent Latvia more than 90 percent of the Jews lived in cities and towns. Almost 50 percent were involved in trade and commerce of one sort or another, compared to 1 percent of Latvians. The majority of Latvians were peasant farmers; by contrast, only 1 percent of Jews were engaged in agricultural production. Hardly any Jews were to be found in official positions — of 5,921 civil servants in 1925 only 21 were Jews — although their prominence in the professions, particularly medicine, and in the arts was still striking.[27]

The Jew spoke German and was on occasion more German than the German. The Jew spoke Russian and again could be a better spokesman for Russian culture than the Russian. The Jew was a town dweller, a cosmopolitan. The Jew was all things — but to many Latvians, caught up in a mood of growing paranoia and crude nationalism, he represented all things foreign, all things dangerous.

The invective flowed in both directions. On life in an independent Latvia, Dan Hafrey of Liepāja remarked:

Objectively speaking, the Latvians were miserable people to live with and under. Yet, in spite of the legal restrictions, which, for example, forced my family to employ a stupid and ignorant man as president of their import and export lumber business just because he was Latvian and the business could not be allowed to operate without this legal farce, we ourselves always felt very secure. Our parents succeeded very well in insulating us from the worst aspects of anti-Semitism. We felt so secure that we were in effect really quite terrific snobs. We were convinced that we were the true outpost of Western civilization.[28]

Bernhard Press, born in Riga in 1917, played as a boy the timeless children's game where you lock fingers and try to bring your opponent to his knees. "My opponent, a Latvian boy, would not, despite the pain I was obviously causing him, go down on his knees. When I insisted that he surrender, he gritted his teeth: 'I will not kneel before a Jew.'"[29]

If Jews were seen rarely in political or public office before 1940, the situation seemed suddenly to change after the Soviet occupation. Albeit even now the number of Jews in administrative offices was not large, they were more visible. A prominent Riga physician, Dr. M. Joffe, became people's commissar for health; J. Blumenthal became director of the state bank; J. Berkovits headed the propaganda section of the Central Committee of the Latvian Communist Party. Whereas previously Riga's police force of four thousand had had only one Jew, now significant numbers surfaced, particularly in the feared and hated Soviet secret police. The Jewish population of Riga increased, as young people came from the provinces and political exiles returned. "The conspicuous position of the Jews in the new regime and its political and administrative apparatus," the Israeli historian Dov Levin has concluded, "caused the Letts to identify the whole of the Jewish community with the hated Soviet regime, which had been imposed upon them by the Red Army."[30]

In Lithuania the situation was similar. An American official visiting Kaunas in March 1941 noted: "The strongest local support for the Soviet regime is found among the Jewish population. This appears to be a paradox, as the Jews were the wealthiest element in

Lithuania. Trade and industry were virtually in their hands. They lost all this, but on the other hand they have the confidence of the Reds and have been placed in key positions. All the shops in Kaunas have Jewish commissars, and by far the great majority of the employers are Jews. This has created a strong anti-Semitic feeling in the whole country, and the new regime is usually described as the 'Jewish Government.'"[31]

In the nationalist mind, disoriented and aggrieved by the upheavals and violence, by the arrests and deportations following Soviet annexation, Bolshevism and the Jew became synonymous.

Soviet Persuasion

AS ALLIED ATTITUDES became less accommodating toward the Soviets in 1947–48, they softened toward the DPs. Allied personnel were alarmed when they discovered that Soviet liaison officers had explicit instructions to subvert morale in the camps by provoking scandal, encouraging delinquency, and undermining administration. The goal, one intercepted Soviet communiqué stated, was to turn the Western occupation authorities against the DPs.[32] Soviet policy achieved the exact reverse. Instead of driving the occupation forces and the DPs apart, Soviet tactics brought them together.

The treatment of Soviet repatriation teams by the Western Allies was indicative of the shifts in policy. These teams, consisting of NKVD (secret police) officers, were initially given free range of the DP camps. They brought magazines, pictures, and films from home, on occasion mail for camp residents, and sought to persuade people to return. The Western Allies did much at the beginning to facilitate the Soviet effort. Fliers encouraging repatriation were distributed throughout the camps. Fourteen issues of an UNRRA news sheet called *Repatriation News* were published, the last in June 1947. That final issue devoted several pages to an appeal to Latvian DPs to return to their homeland. "Every honest Latvian has to return home . . . Think of your children who want to grow up in their homeland and be taught in their home language. The

Soviet Government guarantees you freedom and invites you home."[33]

The DPs were not convinced. Rumors spread about informers in their midst and kidnappings. Stories circulated that when Soviet agents had names of DPs they would threaten to harm relatives back home unless the DPs "volunteered" to return. DPs hesitated even to write home. Consequently, they greeted the Soviet repatriation teams with a blend of fear and outrage. Soviet officials often encountered violence. One was stabbed. Stone throwing and physical assaults were common.

In January 1947 instructions went out to military supervisors in the British zone to take more care over the Soviet visits to the camps of Balts and Ukrainians.[34] Finally, in February 1949, during the Soviet blockade of Berlin, General Lucius Clay ordered the departure of the last Soviet repatriation officials from the Western zones. By then, my family, though still frightened, had left.

The Soviet success rate had been paltry. Around Christmas every year the numbers had picked up slightly. A friend of my father's who had left his family behind found Christmas alone most painful. He gave up the struggle at the end of 1947. On December 29 he shuffled off to the repatriation center, the Brandenbaum transit camp at Lübeck. His prize possession, several albums of postage stamps, he left with my father. We never saw or heard from him again.

Holocaust

IN LATGALE, the eastern province of Latvia, revenge massacres of Jews began immediately after the cessation of Soviet counterattacks, on June 29, 1941, days before the German Einsatzkommando units, police, and security officials arrived. In Daugavpils on that second to last day of June, all male Jews between the ages of sixteen and sixty were ordered to assemble in the market square. Some of these were summarily shot in the train station garden behind the prison, the rest incarcerated. More than a thousand Jews would be murdered

here before the German killing squads arrived. Some Latvians probably aimed to please their "liberators"; most, however, aimed to
satisfy their own impulses. Moral feeling had been blunted again
and again in this part of the world. Bolshevik and Jew were the same.
As in 1918–19, extermination was the only answer.[35]

In Rēzekne the victims of the NKVD had barely been buried
when the next round of murders started. When he arrived on July 6,
a German army chaplain, Walter S., assisted in a ceremony for the
victims of the Soviet slaughter for which most of the town's survivors turned out. The German pastor read several passages from the
New Testament. From Revelation 21:4, where the vision of a new
heaven and a new earth is summoned, he cited the voice from on
high: "God . . . will wipe away every tear from their eyes, and death
shall be no more, neither shall there be mourning nor crying nor
pain any more, for the former things have passed away." No sooner
had the interdenominational service ended than the killing began.

"The squaring of accounts didn't take long," Walter S. wrote to
his wife later that day. "The Jews, who have been the wire pullers
behind the whole thing, were destroyed wherever they were found.
The worst of them naturally got away again to safety in Russia.
Those who remained were simply struck down, if necessary with
only a spade." Among the perpetrators were Latvians but also German members of Organisation Todt, who were working on road
repair. That kind of spontaneous violence and indiscipline annoyed
the military, Walter S. commented to his wife. "Put them against a
wall and shoot them. To that everybody was agreeable. But not this
random killing."[36]

It was the "gangster types" that annoyed Rudolf Höss, too, commandant of Auschwitz and veteran of the Baltic wars of 1918–19.
The task of extermination was a serious one; it had to be done
properly, with appropriate order and commitment. The elimination
of the Jews and other objectionable elements in society was not to be
regarded as murder. Murder is a negative act; what the new German
order was involved in was positive: it was a cleansing, an improvement, a morally purposive policy. It was like clearing weeds from a
garden. Höss's superior, Heinrich Himmler, told his SS officers in

October 1943: "Most of you will know what it means to deal with a hundred, or five hundred, or even a thousand corpses. To have endured this and — a few exceptions of human weakness aside — to have remained decent, that has made us tough. This is an unwritten and never to be written page of glory in our history."[37] To exterminate human beings and at the same time to remain decent — that was the essence of Nazism. Such behavior had a long history in the borderlands.

Incidents similar to those in Daugavpils and Rēzekne took place elsewhere in the country. In Riga mass arrests, pillage, and random killing of Jews occurred during the night of July 1–2, prompted as much, it appears, by the enthusiasm of Latvian right-wing elements as by German orders. On July 4 the synagogues of Riga burned, including the large choral synagogue on Gogol Street. Nearly a week later, on July 8, a German decree finally made all Latvian police and security initiatives subordinate to German authority.[38]

During the summer and fall of 1941 at least fifteen thousand, and perhaps as many as thirty thousand, Jews were killed.[39] A German official noted in mid-August that the hatred, particularly among the Latvian peasantry, for Bolsheviks and Jews was "monstrous." The locals, he pointed out, had already done much of the dirty work before the Germans could intervene.[40]

Much of the killing was done by Kommando Arājs, a security unit of the Latvian auxiliary police created shortly after July 8. Its leader was Viktors Arājs, who came from a Latvian peasant family that had been ruined by the Great War. Born in 1910, the same year as Artūrs Vajeiks, Arājs had lived for a time near Code (Zohden); his mother was the daughter of a prosperous farmer of the district who may have been a neighbor of Grieta Pluta's. Arājs attended secondary school in Jelgava. After graduation in 1930, he completed his army service and then joined the police, working his way up to the rank of lieutenant. Still, he obviously harbored all kinds of resentments. Evidence that he was hoping to make a career under Soviet occupation, along with his subsequent behavior under Nazi rule, point to a personality craving extreme solutions.[41]

Herberts Cukurs, another activist, was a spiritual confrère of

Arājs. He had been a Bolshevik sympathizer in 1919, and in the 1930s had become the Charles Lindbergh of Latvia, flying from Riga to Gambia, and later Riga to Tokyo. He was involved in mass shootings of Jews in 1941. He came to be known as "the butcher of Riga."

When Arājs began, in July, to look for volunteers for his unit of auxiliary police, his first recruits were university students and members of Thunder Cross. While the unit would grow to number 1,176 members in March 1943, early on it consisted of probably no more than several hundred men. Photographs of the unit suggest youth, vitality, and intelligence. Many of the men are distinctly handsome. They are clean-shaven, lean, and alert. The color of the buses that ferried Kommando Arājs from one murder site to the next denoted cleanliness and purpose. Like the sea that figured prominently in the country's sense of self, and like the eyes of its prized maidenhood, that color was blue. All told, Kommando Arājs murdered at least 26,000 Latvian Jews.

Just a few days after the German army had entered Jelgava, a yellow banner appeared on the railway overpass with a fierce announcement in black letters: MITAU JUDENFREI (Mitau is free of Jews). Einsatzgruppe A reported from Jelgava in mid-October 1941 that of the 1,550 Jews who had lived in the city before the war, none remained — "all had been removed, without exception, by the local population."[42]

In two major "actions," on November 30 and December 8, 1941, organized by the newly arrived SS General Friedrich Jeckeln, fresh from murderous successes in the Ukraine, most of Riga's Jews were slaughtered, in the quiet pine forest with its not so quiet name of Rumbula, on the outskirts of the city.[43] Women, children, and old folk were taken to the forest, in some cases forced to dig their own graves, and shot. Some twenty-five thousand Jews were killed in the two days of slaughter. The Jewish historian Simon Dubnow, who had fled Berlin in 1933 to find shelter in Riga, was executed, according to one account,[44] by a German who had been a former student. General Jeckeln had his headquarters in the feudal Ritterhaus in Old Riga.

By the end of 1941 the German onslaught on Eastern Europe and

Soviet Russia had killed half a million Jews. A period of administrative consolidation followed, which included the ghettoization of the remaining Jews.

When was the decision to proceed with "the final solution," the complete elimination of the Jews of Europe, taken? Was it the upshot of apparent military victory — in the summer of 1941 — as German might smashed its way toward Moscow? Did the exuberant participation of some Latvians, Ukrainians, and other "liberated" peoples in dealing drastically with the Jews encourage that decision? Or was the step in fact taken later in the year, when the German onslaught had slowed and doubts first arose about victory? The Jew-Bolshevik was resisting yet again, preparing to fight another day. He had to be eradicated completely if Germany was ever to be great, ever to be stable, prosperous, and safe.

The Wannsee Conference, convened in January 1942 in a glorious lakeside setting on the outskirts of Berlin, was long considered to have been the venue at which the decision to proceed with extermination was taken. It is now regarded as the point at which the policy was confirmed rather than initiated. It remains an important juncture, however, the moment when barbarism and technology joined together in the most demonic alliance ever. If Hitler found "willing executioners" among his own people, he also found them among his conquered subjects. The Holocaust was far from being merely a German-Jewish phenomenon. The Holocaust was enacted in the fevered dreamscapes of Eastern Europe where right and wrong were seldom on opposite sides and where fear and hatred were a way of life. This was a frontierland where borders and peoples had fluctuated throughout history and where the Jew and the Gypsy were symbols of transience and instability. Holocaust was a state of mind here before it was Nazi policy.

The new dimension that the Germans introduced in 1941–42 was the idea of planning. Generalplan Ost and the murder of the Jews were part of the same effort: the application of bureaucracy and technology to issues of complex historicity.[45] The Nazis were not the first to apply such methods, or the last. Lenin, Trotsky, Stalin, and the Bolsheviks were prepared to use a similar approach to national-

152 Walking Since Daybreak

ity questions. And of course they did apply these methods to the collectivization of agriculture and the general issue of class. After the war, with the knowledge and agreement of the Western Allies, some twelve to fifteen million Germans would be expelled from territories in Eastern Europe that they had settled centuries earlier. "A clean sweep will be made," Winston Churchill told the House of Commons. He said he was "not alarmed by the prospect of the disentanglement of populations."[46]

The final solution of the Jewish question was to be merely a prelude to the wholesale reorganization of Central and Eastern Europe and Russia.

"The Years Disappear"

THE MOOD IN THE CAMPS, as in Germany as a whole, slumped badly in 1946 and 1947. Despite the efforts of UNRRA and its successor, after July 1947, the IRO, the international community was not keen on helping to resolve the refugee problem in the first years after the war. "None is too many" was a Canadian bureaucrat's comment about the Jews of Europe who were seeking refuge, but it was a sentiment applicable to the postwar DPs as a whole.[47]

General Eisenhower had addressed the issue of DP morale in a letter to President Truman on September 18, 1945: "The hopelessness of the ordinary displaced person comes about from fear of the future, which involves questions, always of international politics, and from the practical impossibility of participating, at this time, in any useful occupation."[48] "Profound dejection" is what the medical officer at the Funk Kaserne in Munich observed among the DPs of his camp in June 1946. "Among people who have already for years suffered deep psychological wounds, such a factor cannot be taken lightly."[49]

The lowest point of morale in those years came at the time when good cheer and hope normally prevail, at Christmas and the New Year. "The entire last year we can write off as a loss," wrote my father on January 1, 1947. He resented that the year had been spent thinking almost exclusively about food and clothing. The main motif in his diary as a whole is the desperate wish to get out of the camps and away to some kind of predictable existence. "Otherwise the years disappear, and life with them, without any gain." In a front-page editorial comment on Christmas Eve 1947, the *Lübecker Nachrichten* decried the fact that another year had passed without begetting the slightest trace of hope.

Ghetto

AT THE END of Bear Slayer Street was the Riga ghetto. It was in what was called the Moscow suburb. In fact two ghettos existed, the "small" one where Latvian Jews were quartered and the "big" one containing Jews deported from Germany and Central Europe.

The Latvian Jews in the Riga ghetto, some forty-five hundred of them, were the survivors of the massacres of women, children, and old people on November 30 and December 8, 1941. They were mostly young men. They had been spared because their labor was required by the new German order.

They worked unloading supply ships in the harbor; they worked in factories, sawmills, and army installations; they worked in peat bogs. Their property had been seized. They were not paid. When the Latvian Jews did not suffice for this work, Jews from Central Europe were brought in to meet the need. Twenty thousand arrived between November 1941 and February 1942. Most came from Germany, some from Austria and Czechoslovakia. These German-speaking Jews were housed in the big ghetto next to the Latvian one. The relationship between the two ghettos was as strained as the relationship between Eastern and Western Europe. The Ostjuden were considered by the Westerners as uncultured and unreliable. The Western Jews in turn were regarded as materialistic and soulless interlopers whose behavior had brought on the crisis. The small ghetto had a modicum of food, the large ghetto less.[50]

The Riga ghetto was dissolved in November 1943. The survivors were sent to Kaiserwald concentration camp, near the exclusive residences of the Riga rich; a few went to other work camps. As the Russian armies approached in the summer of 1944, the Germans evacuated several thousand remaining Jewish workers to Stutthof concentration camp, thirty-five kilometers from Danzig. The "Moscow suburb" of Riga that had housed the ghetto now became, true to its name, the home of Russian refugees fleeing the advancing Red Army.

Of the Latvian Jews who went to Russia in 1941, perhaps four thousand — one in three — survived; of the roughly eighty-three thousand who fell into German hands in Latvia, not more than nine hundred survived; and of the more than twenty thousand Western Jews sent to Latvia, only some eight hundred lived through the deportation until liberation. This was the highest percentage of eradication in all of Europe. Such thoroughness was not merely imported or imposed by the German conqueror; it had to be an expression of the local situation.

The Holocaust was enacted in borderlands, ethnic and psychological, where victory and defeat were up in the air, where your brother could be your foe, where anxiety and hysteria had become the norm. Throughout history these borderlands had provided fertile soil for extremes; in the twentieth century they became a hothouse for madness.

Camping

CAMPING, the irreverent might say, was the most popular activity in the age of the dictators and its immediate aftermath. There were camps galore. Camps for this and camps for that. An UNRRA assessment of personnel assigned to Camp 553 in Pasing, a district of Munich, contained the comment: "Mr. Spencer (American) has had considerable camp experience. He ran 112 camps for Japanese in the U.S."[51] A Canadian official, A. H. Brown, suggested in December 1946 that the camps used to intern Japanese Canadians during the war could now be used to house arriving DPs.[52] The implication was that the DPs, coming from the camps of Europe, would feel right at home in the camps in Canada.

Eventually more than nine hundred camps were set up for displaced persons, in Germany, Austria, Italy, France, and North Africa. The vast majority of these were in Germany, in the three Western occupation zones.

In postwar Germany, finding space for this camping frenzy presented a problem. Right after the war, in the spring and summer of 1945, vanquished German soldiers, too numerous to process quickly, were simply put in fields like farm animals, without shelter, without sanitation. Wilderness camping, one might call it — at Sinzig, Remagen, Kripp. The Swiss consul general in Cologne heard that sixty to one hundred people were dying in these open-air prison camps every day.[53]

Later, all sorts of facilities were employed: warehouses, schools, movie theaters, barracks, ships in harbor, guest houses, barns, and stables. In Lübeck more than a hundred different locations were eventually used as camping facilities. Appropriately, the Nazi Party's rally field in Nuremberg, the site of Hitler's greatest glory, became in 1948 a huge DP camp, the Valkalager, which in time housed 4,400 people of twenty-one nationalities.[54]

Because of the bad reputation the dictators had given camping, the Western Allies preferred not to use the word "camps." They coined expressions like "assembly centers." But these wouldn't take.

The postwar camps were set up to try and bring some order to the chaotic condition of a wretched humanity: to house people, to clothe and feed them, to tend to them medically. Yet despite the good intentions, at first everything was in short supply: food, clothing, shoes, cutlery, bedding, blankets, even straw. Bugs, lice, and rats were, however, plentiful. In June 1945, for the 572 people housed in the Timm Kröger School in Flensburg only two washbasins were available. Because of shortages of coal and electricity, what bedding there was could be washed only once every three or four months. In the Funk Kaserne in Munich, in the spring of 1946, three toilets had to suffice for almost two thousand people.[55]

But still, the irreverent would continue, what a life! Fresh air and exercise. Free food. No overeating. No responsibilities. What could be finer? Trouble was, the weather was mean. The first winters after the war were wretchedly cold, the summers dismally hot. The winter temperatures stood at minus 15 to minus 20 degrees Celsius for days at a time. In January 1947 thirty people were found frozen to death in Hamburg. Sixty kilometers of the Rhine froze. In a country where fuel was in short supply and the railway system in chaos — in the British zone, fewer than half of the sixty-five hundred locomotives were usable — the frozen river, the main north-south artery, compounded problems of transport and communication. The cold of winter brought despair to the camps. The heat of summer brought lethargy.

Some camps had central kitchens and mess halls. In others individuals or families cooked for themselves. The low ration level and the limited ingredients at hand meant that prepared food was bland and monotonous. We cooked for ourselves. In his diary my father celebrated on one occasion the acquisition by my mother of a little fat — that would make food taste immeasurably better!

Illness was rampant. If the dreaded epidemics of deadly disease did not strike, less dangerous maladies like whooping cough, bronchitis, and tonsilitis ravaged malnourished populations. Rates of diphtheria, scarlet fever, tuberculosis, and rickets far exceeded the norm. I was afflicted by rickets and still bear minor osteal malformations as mementos.

Clothing was scarce. The refugees had left with what they could carry. To make haste, many had jettisoned belongings en route. Consequently, as one UNRRA report from the American zone put it, "the DP looks like a bum." The report went on to point out that U.S. military personnel were influenced by appearances: "The German civilian is still unusually well dressed and presents a neat respectable appearance . . . The German looks like a gentleman (or a lady) and the US soldier accepts him as such; the DP man or woman looks like . . . a tramp and that is the way they are regarded." Self-respect among the DPs was, not surprisingly, low.[56]

Total Mobilization

IF DISSATISFACTION with the German occupation was widespread by 1942, confidence in German victory against Russia was still strong through much of that year. Despite shortages, living conditions in the Baltic were seen as superior to those in other parts of warring Europe. In a conference on food supplies organized by Göring in August 1942, attended by the Reich commissars for the Baltic, complaints surfaced that life in Latvia was perhaps a little too good — since, among other items, baby prams were still being manufactured there![57]

When it became clear in late 1942, and especially in 1943, that the German offensive against Russia had stalled, the war moved into a new phase. For Germany it necessitated the mobilization of all available resources, both material and human — total mobilization, as it was called. Policy in the occupied areas now changed significantly. Cooperation, compromise, and assistance, both military and economic, were sought. Instead of being an exclusively German concern, the East — the war against Bolshevism and the settlement of conquered territory — became, in Nazi parlance, a European issue.

In the military effort, national units — ethnic SS legions — were set up; in the economy, reprivatization and improvement of the rationing system were begun; and politically, more substance was to be given to the idea of "national self-administration." In return for cooperation in the war effort, Latvian nationalists wanted promises of Latvian independence after the war. Although the German authorities were unwilling to go quite that far, some concessions were granted.

The national song festivals, banned in 1941, were permitted again in 1943. On July 11 two thousand voices sang for an audience of forty thousand in Riga. The program had a marked nationalist flavor: it included not only a large number of emotion-laden folksongs but also a cantata by Andrejs Jurjāns entitled *Tēvijai* (For the Fatherland). A fortnight later, on a beautiful summer's day, forty-five choirs and sixteen hundred singers participated in a regional festival in Jelgava.[58] The Latvian national anthem was permitted again, as was the national flag. Implicit in all the new measures was a recognition of ethnic individuality, even if Nazi officials refused to acknowledge this distinctiveness openly. Thus, while any mention of independence was still forbidden, Latvians were permitted, by early 1944, to speak publicly of their struggle for survival as a people.[59]

The decree for reprivatization was issued on February 18, 1943. Its sole purpose was to encourage productivity for the war effort, and since all applications were screened with this in mind, in practical terms only small commercial enterprises, farms, and houses were affected. The reprivatization bureaucracy worked sluggishly: the paperwork and investigations were extensive and the decisions slow in coming. All large industrial and commercial ventures were kept under German control. Anyone receiving property back had to sign an affidavit agreeing to work in the interest of the Führer and the German people. Many peasants found the reprivatization ceremonies a source of amusement.[60]

My grandfather Jānis Vajeiks received his farm back in the summer of 1943.[61] His land was part of an early group of properties to be returned to their owners. Why he was among the first to have his property restored is not clear. Some of his neighbors had to wait until the end of the year, others until January 1944.

Reprivatization was the carrot. Four days later came the stick: conscription. On February 24, 1943, the Reich commissar for the Ostland decreed that all men born between 1919 and 1924 had to report for military duty. "With Adolf Hitler to victory, to arms, to work!" read the proclamation. All Estonians, Latvians, and Lithuanians between the ages of nineteen and twenty-four would either serve in the ethnic SS legions or do other war-related work.

The draft was gradually widened to include both older and younger men. By the late summer of 1944 the range in Latvia had been extended to include all those born between 1906 and 1928 — in other words, between the ages of sixteen and thirty-eight. By July 1, 1944, Latvia had 31,446 legionnaires under arms in three units, and a total of 146,510 men serving in various military roles.[62] For nationalists the dream now was to keep the Red Army at bay until the Germans had been defeated in the West. Renewed independence for the Baltic states would then, they thought, be a possibility.

In the immediate postwar world, the West would regard these legionnaires with suspicion. Proto-fascist collaborators, they were often called, supposedly more interested in killing Jews and Slavs than in national independence. The quick judgments came from Western commentators for whom Stalin was, for the time being, a comrade-in-arms rather than a threat. What determined behavior during the war was above all the issue of survival, personal and national. When they donned German uniforms, most Latvians did so to fight against Bolshevik Russia rather than for Nazi Germany. Postwar judgments about collaboration in Eastern Europe often came from people who knew little about the region and the moral ambiguities endemic to life in the borderlands.

If German occupation policy could be harsh within Latvia, in the frontier areas bordering Russia it was oftentimes cruel beyond comprehension. In early 1943 SS General Friedrich Jeckeln decided to create a forty-kilometer-wide no man's land along the border between Latvia and Russia, the purpose of which was to protect Latvia from infiltration by partisans. Four thousand troops, mostly Latvians, and seven hundred vehicles were involved. Jeckeln led the campaign personally. A confidential report describing the action surfaced in July 1943.

When the troops entered a town or village, all men between the ages of sixteen and fifty were immediately shot. When the Wehrmacht had moved through this area in 1941 all able-bodied men had been encouraged to leave. Those who were now found were assumed to be partisans. The old and the disabled were shot, too, because they would not be able to keep pace in an evacuation. Women and children, all that remained, were then marched off to camps in the Latvian interior, Salaspils near Riga being the largest. Here the women were separated from their children and sent off to Germany to work. The children were housed among the local population. The evacuated villages were razed.

As the campaign proceeded through the spring of 1943, partisan resistance grew. In many cases Jeckeln's forces entered empty villages that the Russians had already evacuated and destroyed. Some terrible mistakes were made: the pleas of families who could prove that they were hostile to the Bolsheviks were ignored. The wife of a village priest who had been sent to Siberia was shot. An elderly couple, whose son had been deported to the snow and ice of Archan-

gel and whose daughter was working in Emmendingen in Baden,
were shot. In the village of Muschino, everyone, men, women, and
children, was herded into a barn and shot. The confidential German
report deemed the Jeckeln campaign a huge failure.[63]

As the fortunes of war turned, the German leadership in the
Baltic, never of one mind to begin with, began to quarrel openly. The
military and civilian authorities blamed each other for setbacks.
Reich commissar Lohse — "puffing, exploding, neckless"[64] — was
at the center of the turbulence.

In contrast with some of his underlings, Lohse had always been a
hard-liner, intent on centralizing the entire administration of the
Ostland and unwilling to bow to any local aspirations. Others, like
the general commissar for Reval, Karl Litzmann, had been trying for
some time to introduce more flexibility into occupation rule.[65] But
Lohse, determined to preserve his fiefdom and powers, was even
working on a scheme to remove the Ostland from the jurisdiction of
Rosenberg's ministry. His cabal brought out the knives.

On April 20, 1944, the Führer's birthday, after an official celebration in the Riga Opera House followed by a reception at the Guild
Hall, Lohse was involved in a skirmish over protocol with General
Friedrich Braemer, the Wehrmacht representative for the Ostland. It
was all a question of whose car should leave first, that of the leading
civilian or of the military authority in Riga. The general insisted he
be allowed to depart first. When Lohse protested, Braemer called
him a "stupid asshole" *(dummes Luder)*. The civilian then punched
the general in the nose, knocking him to the ground. Lohse's victory
at fisticuffs was to be a Pyrrhic one, however. Rosenberg, his patron,
turned on him, and Martin Bormann, Hitler's adjutant, told Lohse
to take a holiday.

That summer Lohse's world crumbled. SS General Jeckeln declared that he could no longer work with him. Jeckeln and others
were now insisting that a measure of compromise was essential if
the local populace was to be kept in check. Jeckeln's position was
simple. Promise the Balts their independent states, he said. When
the time came to set up these states, the Germans would have the
last say anyway. But Lohse would not agree.

In August General Schoerner, who had been given command of Army Group North on July 23, with the express purpose of stopping the rot in the northern army, had a member of the civilian administration arrested in Riga because the latter had not saluted him as he drove by. When proof was presented that the civilian could not have seen the general, Lohse intervened and released the man. Schoerner was incensed. His response was to call for the immediate execution of five members, chosen at random, of the civilian staff of the Reichskommissariat Ostland. That, he claimed, would quickly put an end to the insubordination and restore order.[66] The command was not carried out, but the administration was clearly unraveling.

Camp Activities

IN THE DP CAMPS activities were certainly not lacking. With the assistance of UNRRA, schools were set up, as were sundry recreational groups. Orchestras, choirs, dance and theater companies flourished, despite a shortage of instruments, scores, and equipment. Most of the Latvian ballet company escaped and reconstituted itself in Lübeck; a Latvian opera company started up in Oldenburg. Between 1945 and 1950, 1,179 books were published by Latvians in exile in Sweden, Denmark, and Germany[67] — more than one thousand titles produced by just over one hundred thousand people, perhaps the most intensive rate of per capita publishing ever. Any sort of creative activity was permitted and encouraged as long as it had no direct political implications. The vibrancy of DP cultural life was such that one American official could hardly keep up: "There was an invitation on my desk every week to a play, a ballet, a show, even banquets."[68]

In Hamburg in December 1945, a "Baltic University" was established. It opened its doors and held its first lectures in March 1946. Robert C. Riggle, an UNRRA staffer on leave from Ohio State University, was the chief sponsor of the project. The Latvian Fricis Gulbis was the first president. The British authorities who supervised the operation were not always supportive. Given the impromptu nature of the "university," its unpredictable future, and the shortage of space and study materials, the military government refused to recognize it officially as a university, insisting that it be called the Baltic Study Centre.

The organizers were not discouraged. If British officials preferred to call the institution a "study centre," so be it. Among DPs and in the broader world, the name Baltic University stuck. By the end of 1947 three hundred courses had been offered. At the peak of its activity in 1947, it had some twelve hundred students and two hundred faculty. By October 1948 the library had grown to ten thousand volumes. The enterprise was so successful that in 1946 it was moved, in order to gain more space, to former Luftwaffe barracks in Pinneberg, a suburb of Hamburg. "I cannot speak too highly of this great creative effort," wrote one visitor from Geneva. "I urge most strongly the strengthening of this project as a morale builder and creative undertaking for these peoples."[69]

Such opinions had echoes. In 1948 a group of fifty U.S. and Canadian educators, led by the dean emeritus of Princeton, Christian Gauss, and including the distinguished political philosopher Sidney Hook, of New York University, and the principal of McGill, Cyril James, backed an attempt to move the Baltic University, faculty, students, and all, to North America. In May 1948 the Gauss committee issued this statement:

> Mass executions and mass deportations have so decimated the ranks of the Baltic intelligentsia that the mere survival of the Baltic cultures has come to depend more than anything else on the several thousand Baltic scholars who succeeded in escaping abroad. It would be a terrible tragedy if this unique institution were to go out of existence. It is imperative that the cultures of the Baltic peoples which are today being destroyed by a genocidal foreign regime should be kept alive and that there should be at least a small body of Baltic intellectuals prepared and able to assist in their countries' recovery . . . when they regain their freedom.[70]

American officials pointed out, however, that they would accept only individuals, never an institution. Negotiations shifted to Canada. Cyril James of McGill expressed an interest in attaching the

Baltic operation to his university as a "centre." Late in 1948 only the matter of funds — it was estimated that $1 million to $1.5 million was needed — seemed to stand in the way of a transfer. But in the end, the monies did not surface; the discussions dragged on too long; the Baltic University shrank in size as people emigrated; and nothing came of the plans for a block transfer.

Sports — soccer, volleyball, basketball, and track and field — were popular in the camps. Although they required little equipment, even that little was hard to find. My father managed to attend the Baptist World Congress in Copenhagen in 1947, and he brought back a soccer ball for his young son. In the Artillerie Kaserne, ownership of a football brought extraordinary prestige and power to a four-year-old — but also, as I recall, a rock thrown at my head.

It was not any lack of activities but the sense of limbo that took its toll, the uncertainty about the future, the marginalization. Few DPs were employed. Some worked part-time for the military. The American authorities preferred to hire DPs rather than Germans, but still, the numbers involved were small. If a DP was found to be working for remuneration for the Germans, he could lose his ration privileges. Anything to get away from the camps — that was the attitude.

My father worked as an interpreter for the British and as a teacher of English at the Baltic University. He had numerous contacts abroad. The principal of his Bristol college, the Reverend J. B. Dakin, was in the Refugee Division of the World Council of Churches. Drs. Lewis and Rushbrooke of the Baptist World Alliance took up his cause. However, none of these associates could short-circuit the laborious immigration policies of their respective countries. My father wanted to believe that his friends were not to blame, but as the days and years passed he felt abandoned and even betrayed.

Frederick Morgan sensed the depression of the DPs but felt helpless to relieve it: "What could be done? . . . What was wanted was some means of spiritual uplift, some way of persuading them that, in spite of appearances, not every man's hand was against them."[71] Kathryn Hulme, who worked for UNRRA and later went on to fame as the author of The Nun's Story, spoke of "the strange half-world of the DP camps." Much of her work she found enormously frustrating: "I despised the insanity of international relief that imagined something could be done with this ruin in the human soul, so much more fearful than all the mountains of rubble strewn over the face of Europe." After screaming at the DPs on one occasion, she noted: "The DPs' prompt obedience to anger and threats seemed almost the worst discovery I had yet made about them."[72]

Some of the DPs risked life, limb, and whatever money they had to get away. In Schleswig-Holstein, a local fisherman, desperate for some earnings and hence willing to smuggle refugees to Sweden, could always be found. The going rate was about 2,000 marks per person. The newspapers reported the failed runs, not the successful ones. Similar schemes, with different destinations, were afoot throughout occupied Germany.[73]

Of the children in the camps Dorothy Macardle suggested that they had suffered "immeasurable harm." You could quantify the orphans and the diseases, "but there are other injuries," she said, "which are imponderable. The hurt to the children's mental growth and nervous balance, to their faith in life and their natural feelings, cannot be estimated." It was impossible to say what would happen to these children in the future, but she was not hopeful.[74]

Foreign Relations

ANGLO-AMERICAN POLICY on the Baltic, as on most of Eastern Europe, diverged. President Franklin Roosevelt, confident that he could handle Stalin, was much less willing to give in to his territorial demands; the U.S. position was that territorial issues should be discussed in the wake of victory, not in the midst of battle. Prime Minister Churchill had a more practical bent. Aware that British fortunes were linked to the resistance of the Soviet army, Churchill, who had been so keen on guaranteeing Baltic independence in 1919, was willing by early 1942 to offer Stalin the Baltic. In March he told Roosevelt "that the principles of the Atlantic Charter ought not to be construed so as to deny Russia the frontiers she occupied when Germany attacked her." Churchill's position was transmitted to Molotov when he was in London in May.[75]

By the beginning of 1944 the changed military situation had reinforced Churchill's views. "The Russians may very soon be in physical possession of these territories," he wrote in a personal minute to his foreign secretary on January 16, 1944, "and it is absolutely certain that we should never attempt to turn them out." Churchill sympathized with Roosevelt's propensity to shelve territorial issues until a postwar peace treaty could resolve them, but he doubted that this would be possible in the matter of the Baltic states.[76] His foreign secretary, Anthony Eden, saw no reason why the Soviets should even bring up the issue of the Baltic states, since they presumably assumed that the matter had been resolved, even if informally, in the discussions of 1942.[77]

In the United States, despite Roosevelt's procrastination, policy was evolving in a similar direction. A reorganization in the State Department in January 1944 put Charles Bohlen in charge of relations with the USSR, Poland, and "other areas of Eastern Europe." These "other areas" were left undefined in Bohlen's job description, even though countries far smaller than the Baltic states, like Andorra, Liechtenstein, San Marino, and Monaco, were mentioned in other descriptions. The Baltic states were becoming unmentionables.

In April 1944, in the wake of the Moscow and Teheran conferences, the Latvian Social Democrats voiced their foreboding: "What is the meaning of the silence regarding the problems pertaining to the western frontiers of the Soviet Union?" And they concluded: "With much horror we are bound to state that in the case of a return of the Soviet occupation everything that does not agree with the Communist imperialism and their dictatorship will be exterminated by sword and fire; fear and bondage will be again the lot of the Baltic peoples who already have so much suffered from this war, dictatorships and occupations." The head of the Latvian legation in London, Kārlis Zariņš, or Charles Zarine as he was known in English circles, forwarded this statement to Christopher Warner at the Foreign Office. He asked that Warner pass it on to the leaders of the Labour Party, mentioning Clement Attlee and Herbert Morrison as apt recipients of this plea from fellow Social Democrats. Warner, however, did not oblige. It had become Foreign Office policy not to acknowledge official notes from Zarine or any of his Baltic colleagues — in other words, not to acknowledge the existence of the Baltic states. Within the cold formality of protocol, administered with such aplomb by the British, all traces of emotion were eliminated. When, at the end of August 1944, Zarine warned of "the utter destruction of the Latvian nation," Warner simply commented: "I am afraid this report is very likely to be true."[78]

Hour of Women, Hour of Mothers

IN HIS FAMOUS commemorative address to the German parliament forty years after the Second World War, Richard von Weizsäcker, then president of the Federal Republic of Germany, praised the women of all nations. They, he suggested, had borne the greatest burden in the war. "Their pain, renunciation, and silent strength are all too easily forgotten by history. Filled with fear, they worked, bore human life, and protected it . . . In the years of darkness, they ensured that the light of humanity was not extinguished . . . It was thanks first of all to women that nations did not disintegrate spiritually in the wake of the destruction, devastation, cruelties, and inhumanity, and that they were able slowly to pull themselves together after the war." Nineteen forty-five was, he said, the Hour of the Woman.[79]

The male population of Europe had been decimated. In Germany adult males were now only one third of the total population while adult women constituted roughly half. Women took the initiative. They nursed, they fed, they bartered, they begged. And they cleared the bombed cities. They moved rubble by hand; they cleaned bricks for reuse. The *Trümmerfrau*, the woman of the rubble, who in many cases was a rape victim as well, became a symbol of the German experience. She became a saint.[80]

Often, however, sin was just around the corner. The occupation soldiers, especially the Americans, were a great attraction. They had food, cigarettes, nylon stockings, and more. They offered a dream of plenty. American boys had no trouble finding German female companionship. An army investigation concluded that well over half of American occupation troops "fraternized" with German women in 1946.[81] The *Ami-Liebchen*, the Yank sweetheart, was despised by her fellow Germans. She was a symbol of the Fall, of moral collapse and degradation. The journalist and polemicist Curzio Malaparte had scorn for the base manner of surrender to the Americans. Freedom was paid for "not in the most noble sacrifice but in cowardice, in prostitution, in treachery, in everything that is rotten in the human soul."[82] Because of the humiliations of defeat and occupation, many Germans were to regard the occupation years as more traumatic than the preceding years of dictatorship and war.

Saint and sinner. Such was the image of the German woman.

As Weizsäcker pointed out, women elsewhere played an equally significant role. My impression is that my mother was the key to our survival as a family in these years of flight and fear. She was the one who foraged. She found food, a few sticks of firewood, and the odd luxury like a spoon of bacon drippings. To her, appearances mattered less than reality. She had been raised on the land, mostly at Nightingales, so she was less citified than my father. In the camps she became a YWCA Girl Guide leader, less because of the Baden-Powell ideals spouted by the British occupation authority than because of the practical results of leadership: a better ration card. My father filled out applications; he worried about his image as man and intellectual. He was profoundly depressed by the humiliations of refugee life. My mother went out and did what she considered necessary. She sustained us and brought us through this purgatory. In 1945 she was twenty-seven but already had a lifetime of experience.

Shortly after their marriage in 1937, my father had decided that his young wife should improve her foreign-language skills if she was to keep pace with his ambitions. She had only recently completed secondary school in Jelgava. With the help of his contacts in Britain, he found her a domestic position with a family in London. She would live in, help look after two young children, do some housework, and, most important, learn English. The household chores included, as it turned out, emptying and washing sundry chamberpots every morning. When, in a spot of homesickness, she reported this to her husband by letter, he became incensed. This was an indignity to his wife, he wrote the host family. Grieta would have been proud of him. He pulled my mother out almost immediately and sent her instead to an interdenominational school for church teachers in Birmingham. There, at West Hill College, she spent the better part of a year, learning the important language of English and, perhaps more significantly, making friends with whom she corresponds to this day. She returned to Latvia in the summer of 1939.

Black Market

FOOD. FOOD. FOOD. In 1945–46 people thought about food all the time. Food was interchangeably the object of passion, the means of bribery, and the goal of criminal activity. Of 816 cases of burglary in Hamburg in October 1945, 540 involved food stores. No one bothered counterfeiting money: it was ration coupons and cards that one tried to replicate. In the spring of 1946 food riots broke out in occupied Germany. The elected official responsible for economic and food matters in the Lübeck senate was called, appropriately, Emil Knapp. *Knapp* means tight.

A black market in Germany had existed throughout the war, but in the postwar emergency illegal trading exploded. In the summer of 1946, when the average factory worker earned 50 marks a week, one Chesterfield cigarette was worth 6 marks, a pound of butter 200 to 250 marks, a jar of Nescafé instant coffee 130, and a pound of coffee beans 400. Cigarettes had in fact become the accepted currency in trading. No one trusted the mark. Otherwise, barter was the norm.

If you were willing to pay, you could get anything, even that rarest commodity, fresh fruit and vegetables. Cigarettes could buy you food, but also jewelery, antiques, Meissen porcelain, a bicycle, or, if you fervently wanted one and had enough cartons of Chesterfields or Lucky Strikes, even an army jeep. A grand piano could be had for just fifty cartons of American cigarettes. And the U.S. Army shipped everything home free for its boys.

Of the nine thousand cases awaiting trial by the German courts in Hamburg in October 1945, nearly three thousand were for black-market offenses. Sentences that month for black-market activity ranged from fines of 50 to 100 marks to nine months in prison. In November, inflation took hold in sentencing as well as in the economy: as the mark lost value, the maximum fine jumped to 10,000 marks and the prison term to eighteen months.[83]

The black market was everywhere, on the street, in the countryside, at the workplace. But the DP camps were often centers of illegal enterprise. The directors of UNRRA were sensitive to this complaint. In November 1946 a warning was issued: "Any person trafficking in goods or currency in the black market — seller as well as buyer — shall immediately lose his status as a displaced person and be instantly expelled from our camps."[84] Such caveats had little effect, however, particularly since the occupying forces who were supposed to reeducate Europeans in democracy and decency were as deeply involved in the black-market economy as anybody else. One might argue that this illicit activity, not the official Allied efforts, was the crucial experience in the reeducation of Germans. "Anyone who did not freeze to death in a destroyed city could only have stolen his wood or his coal," wrote the novelist Heinrich Böll, "and anyone who did not starve to death must have acquired his food, or had someone else acquire it in some illegal fashion."[85]

The German criminal and railway police conducted surprise checks on waiting rooms in stations, on cyclists, motorists, carters, and farms to try to deter the activity, but with small results. In Schleswig-Holstein in the month of March 1946, the British supervised 2,041 spot checks. These led to 153 arrests but only 57 convictions. Of 143 farms checked in the British zone in May 1946, only 34 were found to be abiding by the law. Farm produce was being hoarded; most of the farms had more pigs, cattle, and horses than they reported. Police raids achieved little other than to make black marketeering a slightly less open, less public activity. British authorities complained about the apathy of German officials; the latter, said one report, merely shrugged their shoulders and mumbled something about "normal human nature."[86]

My mother traveled to the countryside often with the cigarettes that were part of the special rations she received for her work as a Girl Guide leader. These she traded to farmers in exchange for potatoes, vegetables, perhaps a little butter, or bacon.

At midnight on Sunday, June 20, 1948, a new currency called the deutsche mark was introduced, replacing the reichsmark. Every inhabitant of the three Western zones could get sixty new marks in return for sixty old ones, forty immediately and twenty the next month. Overnight, shop windows filled up as if by magic. Products that had not been seen for years suddenly reappeared.

Palazzo

THE RASTRELLI PALACE in Jelgava, built for the dukes of Kurland, had been rebuilt after its destruction by the Bermondt forces in 1919 and turned into an agricultural academy. The transformation of this ostentatious symbol of the *ancien régime* into an educational institution highlighting the economic and cultural essence of an independent Latvia was a move full of symbolic intent. Not surprisingly, when the Germans returned to Jelgava in 1941, the area commissar, Walter-Eberhard Freiherr von Medem, installed his offices in the palace alongside the agricultural school. When the conquest of the East was complete, the Germans presumably meant to reoccupy the whole of the Rastrelli palace, as in days of old.

But the victory in the East did not come. The attack stalled. The following spring, in May 1942, air-raid drills began in the Jelgava palace. The alarm signal was a huge gong in the courtyard. When it sounded all work was to cease, all fires were to be doused, and water and gas turned off. Everyone was to descend rapidly to the basement of the palace until the next gong gave the all-clear signal.[87]

When German military fortunes began to turn in 1943, part of the palace was turned into a military hospital. By December 1943 it was treating 250 wounded soldiers. The plan was to expand to a one-thousand-bed facility.

6

Odyssey

Then thus I turn me from my country's light.
To dwell in solemn shades of endless night.
WILLIAM SHAKESPEARE

Up the Reds! Aren't they heaven, quite my favourite allies.
NANCY MITFORD

Ubi solitudinem faciunt, pacem appellant
(They make a wilderness and call it peace).
TACITUS

April Calm

IT WAS THE SPRING OF 1944. My three-year-old sister was not
well. My mother decided to take her and me, her newborn, from
Riga, where food shortages were common, to my grandfather's farm
near the village of Tetele, a few kilometers from Jelgava. Here there
would at least be berries, eggs, milk, and the beauty of the Lielupe
River. The parish of Tetele had, according to a head count two
months earlier, a total of 1,126 inhabitants. We arrived on my sister's fourth birthday, April 19, and increased that number temporarily by three. My father's responsibilities kept him in Riga.

By now the German campaign in Russia was not going well.
Setbacks were accumulating. The capitulation of the Sixth Army at
Stalingrad at the end of January 1943 was an enormous blow to
morale. Ninety thousand Germans had been killed there, another

110,000 taken prisoner. The defeat denied Hitler the oil-rich Caucasus. That summer the German attack on Kursk failed, with a
terrible cost in manpower and armor. In January 1944 the Russians
liberated Leningrad after a thousand-day siege during which a million citizens had died of starvation.

Goebbels urged Hitler to find some way of ending the war with
Stalin. If a good part of the Baltic and some of Eastern and South-
ern Europe had to be surrendered to the Soviets, so be it, he said.
But Hitler would not listen: a few setbacks did not mean the war.[1]
By early 1944 the Red Army was on Napoleon's route of 1812,
but heading in the opposite direction. That meant that Jelgava, the
Rastrelli palace, Stalgene, Mežotne, and Tetele would again see
war.

By early 1944 the office of the area commissar in Jelgava was
seriously concerned about air raids. Blackouts had been in effect
since the Stalingrad disaster, but now any sign of laxness by inhabitants in following blackout orders was punished. However, from my
parents' point of view, the front was still distant, the other side
of Pskov, Vitebsk, Bobruisk. And the defenders were Germans after
all. The countryside would be healthier and safer than Riga. And so
off went my mother, my sister, and I to Tetele, leaving my father
behind.

Operation Bagration

MAY AND JUNE 1944 were lovely. The fruit trees, glorious in their
blossom, promised a rich harvest. Strawberries appeared. My sister
had the first three. The fourth she saved for me. Bronzed by the
sunshine, her body revived. We swam in the river.

Then suddenly, in late June and in July, the Red Army burst
forward, smashing through German defenses. Their great summer
offensive of 1944, Operation Bagration, the Russians started on
June 22, three years to the day since Germany's attack on the Soviet
Union. The name Bagration was Stalin's idea, to honor the Russian
commander who had been mortally wounded opposing Napoleon at

Borodino in 1812. Bagration would be revenge, and then some, for Barbarossa; it would outdo Barbarossa in ferocity and match it in terror. It would be revenge for Brest-Litovsk and for Tannenberg too.

The assault came less than three weeks after the Allies had landed at Normandy. The Germans had expected the next major Russian thrust somewhere in the south, perhaps between the Pripet Marshes and the Black Sea, with Bucharest and the Ploesti oil fields as targets. The location of the Soviet attack, its spectacular size and energy, came as a total surprise. Like Stalin in June 1941, Hitler refused to believe the early military reports.

The Russians had focused on Belorussia. They had built up, in secrecy, an assault force of 166 divisions, supported by some 30,000 guns, mortars, and rocket launchers, around 4,000 tanks and self-propelled guns, some 6,000 planes, and 43,500 machine guns. They stockpiled tons of ammunition, fuel, and food. In the attack they were to outnumber the Germans 2 to 1 in manpower, 2.9 to 1 in guns and mortars, 4.3 to 1 in tanks, and 4.5 to 1 in planes.[2] The Russian "steamroller" that rival military planners had conjured up for decades as a monstrous threat — much like the giant ogre in a fairy tale — finally became reality. However, before the onslaught of the steamroller came the hammer blow.

The campaign began on four fronts, three Belorussian fronts driving westward toward East Prussia, Poland, Lithuania, and southern Latvia, and one Baltic front thrusting across and down into Estonia and Latvia. The German Army Group Center, commanded by Field Marshal Ernst von Busch, was devastated within days. Russian armor made a breach forty-five kilometers wide at Vitebsk, poured through the gap, and raced forward in both emulation and escalation of the blitzkrieg tactics the Germans thought they had perfected.

Vilnius was captured on July 13. By then Chernyakhovsky's Third Belorussian Front was ready to strike into Poland as well as northwest toward the Baltic Sea. General Bagramian's First Baltic Front kept up its pressure against the German Army Group North, which was forced to surrender three divisions to assist the beleaguered Army Group Center to the south.

Within three weeks the Germans lost some 350,000 troops, or twenty-eight of their forty divisions. On July 17, 57,000 German soldiers were paraded through Moscow on their way to prison camps. Crowds lined the streets. They were oddly silent.

Hitler's world was collapsing. On July 20 an attempt was made on his life at his briefing headquarters at Rastenburg in East Prussia. He barely survived the bomb attack. But the word "retreat" was still not in his vocabulary. On July 23 Russian troops entered the concentration camp of Maidanek, near Lublin in Poland. Here was the first tangible evidence of the attempt to exterminate European Jewry. The discovery of Treblinka and Auschwitz-Birkenau would follow.

In the Baltic the offensive had begun on July 5. On July 15 evacuation of the area around Daugavpils in Latgale started. Two days later Russian forces crossed the Latvian border, even as SS General Jeckeln was issuing a Führer Order for the creation of a fortress wall along the Latvian frontier. Driving toward the Gulf of Riga from the south, to try and cut off the entire North Group of the German army in Latvia and Estonia, the Soviet Fifty-first Army arrived virtually without warning directly across the Lielupe River from my grandfather's farm.

We could see them. The Germans were right behind us. We were trapped once again between the age-old enemies.

In the autumn of 1943 Himmler had issued orders for the eventuality of German withdrawal: "Not a human being, not a single head of cattle, not a hundredweight of crops and not a railway line is to remain behind. Not a house is to remain standing, not a mine is to be available which is not destroyed for years to come and not a well which is not poisoned."[3] But the Soviet advance had been so stunningly rapid that in most areas that fell to the Russians, no evacuation orders, let alone the scorched-earth policy that Himmler had called for, could be implemented. In a huge swath, people, livestock, and crops fell into Russian hands. In the first month of the Soviet attack the Germans lost thirty-three divisions, with, according to one estimate, 381,000 men killed and 158,000 captured. In materiel, two thousand armored vehicles, ten thousand guns, and roughly sixty thousand other vehicles were lost.

Šiauliai (Schaulen) fell on the twenty-sixth, as the Red Army pushed northward toward Jelgava. What was the Soviet objective? Were they driving toward Riga or would they suddenly wheel left toward the coast in an attempt to cut off all land routes to Germany? The Germans were puzzled and increasingly distraught. Resources were insufficient to cover both possibilities.

As July drew to a close, the German military viewed Jelgava as an essential outpost of the larger Riga salient and the Lielupe River as a boundary that the Soviets were under no circumstances to cross. But panic was spreading in the German high command. The leadership of Army Group North had changed hands four times since the beginning of the year. The commanders of this group wanted to withdraw their forces to the Daugava and make a stand there, but Hitler would not hear of it. General Ferdinand Schoerner, ideologically the most committed of Hitler's military staff, was put in charge on July 23 with orders to eliminate all talk of retreat.[4]

Schoerner, who had recently commanded the South Ukraine Army Group, was a Bavarian and an officer of the Gebirgstruppen, the alpine troops. The son of a policeman and a professional soldier himself, he was, ironically, one of the officers who had helped put down Hitler's Beer Hall Putsch in 1923. Bespectacled and gentle in appearance, he was gruff and crude in behavior. "His manner of speaking," stated a colleague, "can only be described as coarse."[5] His ideological outlook was in keeping with his alpine military association. He believed in the supremacy of ideas over all physical and material constraints. His favorite adjective was "fanatical." "Mountain movies" were Hitler's favorite genre of film; the "mountain general" became a favorite too, part of Hitler's "fire brigade," to be used in emergencies. He came to be known as the "strength through fear" general and may have been the most disliked officer in the entire German high command.[6] Hitler was to appoint Schoerner a field marshal on April 5, 1945, and to designate him in his last will and testament as his commander in chief.

In peppering his language with the word "fanatical," Schoerner was taking his cue from the regime's propaganda chief. In February 1943 Goebbels had held a huge rally in the Sport Palace in Berlin. Its purpose was a "proclamation of fanatical will" — "for the salvation of Germany and civilization."

Upon appointment, just days after the attempt on Hitler's life, Schoerner displayed his colors: "Every meter of ground, every position must now be defended with glowing fanaticism . . . Our homeland is looking to you, men of the Army Group North, with passionate concern. They know that you hold the fate of the war in your hands. Our unflinching faith in our Führer, whom providence has so clearly preserved for us, gives everyone strength and resolve for a fanatical defense in these difficult hours . . . Long live the Führer!"[7]

Four days after Stauffenberg's bomb exploded beside Hitler, not all that far away in East Prussia, Schoerner's appeal was bound to evoke extreme reactions, either the fanatical support he called for or disdain. The Soviets, on learning of the assassination attempt, immediately dropped propaganda leaflets behind German lines pointing out to soldiers and civilians alike that the German leadership was collapsing and that if the struggle continued, lives would be lost for naught.

South of the Lielupe, the much decorated General Philipp Kleffel commanded his own army group, the Generalkommando Kleffel. A fifty-six-year-old professional soldier, he had in 1940 commanded the First Infantry Division through the Netherlands, Belgium, and France, and then after 1941 on the eastern front. For his efforts, some of them spectacularly successful, he was rewarded with the command of an army corps named in his honor. He now had orders to reopen the Šiauliai–Jelgava road along which the Russians were pushing north.

But the task both Schoerner and Kleffel faced was enormous. Shortages of munitions, antitank weaponry, and radio equipment plagued the German effort. Gasoline was in such short supply that the Germans would soon begin scuttling some of their vehicles, including tanks, so as to have fuel for the rest. The Allied bombing campaign against Germany was responsible for many of these shortages. Between March and September 1944 oil production in the Reich had fallen drastically, from 316,000 to 17,000 tons. In August Rumania with its productive oil fields fell to the Russians. By March

1945 Goebbels could remark with sarcasm: "We are now hardly able to fill our cigarette lighters."[8]

Manpower, too, was dwindling fast. German losses during the summer of 1944, on all fronts, were appalling: nearly two million dead and wounded, almost as many as had been lost in the entire war to that point. Morale was sinking at a comparable pace; the desertion rate was climbing, among soldiers but also among civilian personnel employed by the occupation authorities. Every unit, military and administrative, was short-staffed. Everyone was overworked and tired. Commanders complained about the lack of troops and the poor quality of the troops they had. Dissension grew. Schoerner tried tough measures — the summary execution of deserters, the flogging of shirkers, along with orders to take the initiative in battle — all to little avail. As his personal frustration mounted, he became increasingly scornful of his own army, and especially of the local Baltic component in it. The Latvians, he said repeatedly, were cowards, drunkards, and ne'er-do-wells.

The Soviets, paradoxically, did not have such a negative view of their enemy in the Baltic. Before Operation Bagration was launched, the Soviet general staff worried that an attack might come from Army Group North against the Soviet northern flank and that the defenses there might not hold.[9]

But here my family was caught between the two.

Lübeck

LÜBECK. The name reverberated in Baltic history. Many of the German settlers to the eastern Baltic had set sail from Lübeck, and over the centuries Lübeck and Riga developed a flourishing commercial and cultural relationship. Cities both of many spires, Lübeck and Riga were soul mates. The main crossing over the Daugava in Riga was called the Lübeck Bridge. Many Baltic Germans might have said that the next-best place to Riga was Lübeck, and not surprisingly a good number of them, when forced on Hitler's orders to leave the Baltic in 1939–40, resettled in Lübeck, Thomas Mann's home, the

gateway to the Baltic, a city of solidity and integrity.[10] In contour
and scent, too, Schleswig-Holstein was similar to the eastern Baltic,
a flat land of pasture and marsh, farmers and fisherfolk.

During the war the air-raid alarms of Lübeck howled 1,353 times.
Of those alarms, 51 involved actual attacks on the city, and 10 of
those were designated as *Tiefangriffe*. The most devastating of these
"deep raids" occurred on the night of March 28–29, 1942, when the
Royal Air Force used Lübeck as an early test site for its incendiary
bombs. Much of the old town with its gabled merchant houses and
towering church spires was wiped out.[11]

At the time, Tita Jahnke was finishing her schooling at the Er-
nestinenschule, a school founded in 1804. Five days before the RAF
raid she read to her classmates, in a graduation ceremony next to the
cathedral church, an essay entitled "Under the Magic Spell of an Old
City." Clearly inspired by Thomas Mann's much acclaimed speech
in 1926 on the occasion of the seven hundredth anniversary of the
founding of Lübeck, these youthful reflections on nature and life
celebrated the potential for vital experience in a city full of beauty
and history.

Later that year she penned her impressions about the night of the
raid. In the midst of the inferno, as her city surrendered to insatiable
flames, she was struck above all, she said, by the "great silence." No
one screamed, no one shouted, no one whined. As people went about
trying to contain the fires, they talked in whispers.[12] Art and history,
beauty and mystery, had been reduced to silence.

By the end of the war five of Lübeck's seven famous spires had
crumbled.[13] When in April 1945 Sigrun Becker arrived in Lübeck
from Neustettin in Pomerania, grass was growing on the walls of
the bombed-out buildings. Spring flowers were blooming. The mag-
nolias were magnificent.[14]

In the wake of the Potsdam accords on zones of occupation,
Lübeck became a border city, only a few kilometers from the Rus-
sian zone. As the "iron curtain" descended in the following months,
Lübeck found itself on the front line in the Cold War.

As a port and border city in a divided Germany and a divided
Europe, Lübeck became a way station for thousands of refugees who

Flensburg, like Riga and Lübeck a city of spires, was the
last capital of the Third Reich.

Dug into a hill is the bunker, on Flensburg's Südergraben,
where we used to take cover during air raids.

Barrack 12, Artillerie Kaserne, Lübeck — our "home" for four years.

The author in the family's room in Artillerie Kaserne. We covered the wall
with magazine pictures to hide its decrepit condition.

Rūdolfs Ekšteins, at right, in conversation with an UNRRA official.

Biruta Ekšteins (second row, center) as a DP camp Girl Guide leader.

Rūdolfs Ekšteins at a distribution point for CARE parcels.
His pleasure can hardly be contained.

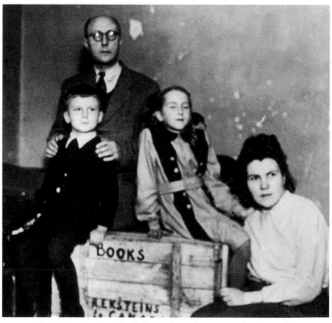

The Ekšteins family before their departure for Canada.

Our first home in Canada, 1019 Selkirk Avenue, in Winnipeg's North End.

King Edward Public School in Winnipeg. Is this Byron's notion
of "a palace and a prison on each hand"?

Field Marshal Montgomery inspecting the author
(front row, second from right), 1960.

The author as a British bobby (rear, third from right) in a school
production of *The Pirates of Penzance*. (*Herb Nott & Co., Ltd.*)

The author with Sir Edward Peacock at the official opening of the new library at Upper Canada College, September 1960. (Jack Mitchell, *Globe and Mail*)

The author with Richard von Weizsäcker, former president of the
Federal Republic of Germany, June 1996. (Frost Photographic)

came by sea and by land. They began arriving in 1944, from East Prussia and Silesia. The DP wave came at the end of the war. The German expellees from the East came in droves after that. In a marshaling operation the Allies called Swallow, 195,600 refugees passed through the Pöppendorf transit camp, with its eighty huts, between February 1946 and January 1947.[15]

Schleswig-Holstein had the highest concentration of refugees and DPs in Germany. *Flüchtlingsland Deutschlands,* it was called, Germany's refugee state. By October 1945 the newcomers had reduced the average living space per person to 3.5 square meters. And still they kept coming. All community facilities were crawling with them. Some schools were closed so as to house them. In late July 1946 the state assembly of Schleswig-Holstein, sitting in Kiel, adopted unanimously a resolution calling for a complete stop to the refugee influx. There was simply no room, or tolerance, left.[16]

The theaters in Lübeck were always sold out, no matter what movie was playing.

"Serene Warm Weather"

THE HEAD OF the German Sixteenth Army's economic staff always concluded his weekly assessment of events with a weather summary. *"Schönes warmes Sommerwetter"* was the last of his report for the week ending July 29, 1944. His summary for the next week was one degree better: *"Heiteres warmes Sommerwetter."* Not just "beautiful warm weather" but "serene warm weather."[17] The weather for the Russian advance that June and July was perfect.

It was perfect for their artillery, of which the Russians seemed to have endless supplies. "Artillery," Stalin had said, "is the god of war." The shelling was now constant. As the Germans were pounded, they could only quiver with fear and envy. The weather was also perfect for air raids. On the afternoon of July 27, shortly after four o'clock, Jelgava was subjected to three preliminary attacks from the air, aiming at the railway station, which was crowded with refugees and with several troop and munitions trains. The first and last attacks were relatively harmless; the middle one, around five o'clock, was disastrous. The station took a direct hit, as did a munitions train loaded with artillery shells and bombs. The huge explosion detonated gas tanks nearby.

The attack was plainly visible from Nightingales. One Soviet plane was shot down. As it spiraled to the ground in flames, four parachutes appeared. My sister, four years old, watched the drama with intense interest and mounting anxiety. Afterward she wouldn't leave my mother's lap.

"A plane shot down before our eyes just before tea: . . . a scuffle; a swerve; then a plunge; and a burst of thick black smoke." That was Virginia Woolf describing an incident in the Battle of Britain.[18] The words might have been apt for the Battle of Jelgava too. The mood, however, was completely different.

Early on the twenty-eighth, Jelgava came under Russian artillery fire. By midmorning tanks were approaching the city. In the next days this impressive city, capital of Kurland, would be reduced to rubble. The last rail link to East Prussia, the line from Jelgava to Ventspils, was cut. The Soviet advance had been so swift that Area Commissar Medem learned of the imminent danger only when armored columns began entering his city. He fled immediately to Liepāja, along with most of the German civilian authorities. When General Commissar Drechsler saw him a short time later, Medem, he said, appeared a broken man.[19]

Along with the artillery, the tanks seemed to be everywhere. By July 30, tanks of the Soviet Eighth Guards Mechanized Brigade had penetrated as far as Tukums, mere kilometers from the coast. The forward units of the brigade rushed for the Gulf of Riga. The German Army Group North was about to be cut off. As serious a threat as this was, and as much as it upset the military, it did not disturb Hitler greatly. The key, in his view, was to hold the ports, especially Riga, so that supplies could get in. Fortress ports — Cherbourg, La Rochelle, Calais, Dunkirk, Odessa, Memel, and Riga — they had to be defended to the bitter end. Some of them were.

Kleffel's corps was now responsible for the territory that remained between Riga and the front line, including the north shore of the Lielupe River where my grandfather's farm stood. Kleffel's orders were to keep the Russians from crossing the river.[20] An army in retreat is always torn between, on the one hand, timely evacuation of civilians and movable stock, to prevent these from falling to the enemy, and on the other hand, maintaining the pretense that all is under control, so as to buttress morale and avoid panic. In the Baltic in the summer of 1944, the speed of the Russian advance removed the first option and left the Germans with only the pretense.

The Lielupe had once again become a historic battlefield. Upriver at Bauska, where the Teutonic Knights had built their fortress, plans went ahead for a German counterassault westward on Elēja, on the Šiauliai–Jelgava road, where the Medems had had their family seat. At Staļǵene, a few kilometers upstream, where Napoleon's Tenth Army had set up headquarters in 1812, the Germans blew up the bridge on the twenty-eighth. On the twenty-ninth they destroyed the bridges at Jelgava. On the morning of the thirtieth the Russians launched a major assault at various points on the river. They tried to cross at Staļǵene and at Mežotne, the former Lieven estate, but were thrown back at both points.

At Valaki, a mere two kilometers downriver from Tetele and my grandfather's farm, a contingent of 150 men, of the Ninety-first Guards Division, did make it across in the morning without being noticed. Once the Russians were across, the fields of mature grain and the frequent wooded thickets provided cover. They had instructions to lie low for forty-eight hours and then to spread out through the sparsely defended area. The aim was to filter through the German defenses, then to strike from the rear and capture two important links to Jelgava.

At Valaki, the river curves; the Jelgava–Bauska road and the Jelgava–Krustpils railway line come within half a kilometer of the river, run parallel to each other for a while, until the rail line dips and crosses the road. By striking here at Valaki the Russians could disrupt both road and rail communication with Jelgava and gradually isolate the city. These strategic points had been fought over in the Great War and again during the civil war. In 1919 the Bermondt

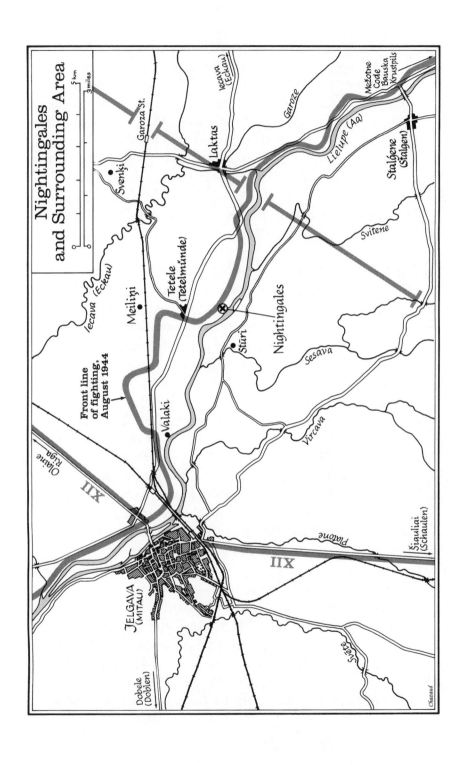

Nightingales
and Surrounding Area

5 km
3 miles

Iecava (Eckau)

Garoza

Mežotne
Code
Bauska
Krustpils

Garoza St.

Laktas

Lielupe (Aa)

Svenķi

Staļģene
(Stalgen)

Iecava (Eckau)

Tetele
(Tetelmünde)

Meiliņi

Svitene

Nightingales

Sturi

Sesava

Front line
of fighting,
August 1944

Valaki

Vircava

Olaine
Rīga

XII

IIX

Platone

Šiauliai
(Schaulen)

JELGAVA
(MITAU)

IIX

XII

Dobele
(Doblen)

Šete

Chazaud

rebels, consisting then of Russians and Germans who insisted that only in Russian-German friendship could either people prosper, had run their armored train along the line, destroying everything in their path.

Now, on July 30 and 31, 1944, the Russians managed to cross the road and the railway line. A group then moved eastward through the fields, following the road, which now forked away from the train tracks, to Tetele, past the ruin of the Behr manor house, past the village cemetery, where Rūdolfs Vajeiks and a number of fallen German soldiers from the Great War were buried. History seemed unwilling to leave the area in peace. In late July 1944 this history engulfed us.

A Dream Ends

ON OCTOBER 4, 1945, an UNRRA official came to see us in Flensburg, a city on the border with Denmark, where we were living in the basement of the Baptist church on the Südergraben. He told us that we had been granted visas for Sweden. Our joy was indescribable. On October 16 an UNRRA vehicle picked us up and took us to Lübeck, to an UNRRA transit camp. Four days later we were loaded onto a British truck and taken — glory be — across the Danish border to a quarantine station at Krusá. We were out of Germany at last! A new life, a better life, was about to begin.

Several days later, however, we heard words of absolute dread. "Your papers are not in order — *Ihre Papiere sind nicht in Ordnung.*" The words rang out like a death sentence. What was not in order? Our papers? Who says? Why were we brought this far for nothing?

On the dismal drive back to Lübeck, on October 25, in darkness and rain, we were, my father noted in his diary, "utterly disconsolate." Three months later, in January 1946, the Swedish decision was confirmed in writing. No reasons were given. "The Swedish dream is over," wrote my father. The Swedish dream, which had begun the day we left Riga in August 1944, was a dream of neutrality and order. The alternative was confusion and insecurity.

Josef Katz, a Lübeck Jew, had a similar experience with modern bureaucracy. He had spent the war years in ghettos, camps, and slave labor units in Riga, Liepāja, and Danzig. He survived and returned to Lübeck after the war. "I go to the police department to register, and find the same clerk who took my keys from me so long ago sitting at the desk. 'But Mr. Katz,' he says, 'where have you been all this time? You never notified us of your departure.'"[21]

We were now put in a camp for "displaced persons," the Meesen Barracks, a brick-and-stucco military compound not far from the center of Lübeck that had been built at the turn of the century and had once housed the locally beloved 162nd Lübeck Infantry Regiment. We were placed first in a small room with another family, whose raucous behavior my parents found unbearable, and then in a larger room with ten other people.

After many entreaties we were moved again, on January 24, 1946, this time to a new camp, occupied until recently by Hitler's Wehrmacht, the Artillerie Kaserne, a large complex of wooden barracks in a suburb of Lübeck. Here we finally got our own quarters, Room 7 in Barrack 12. The room had two beds, a stove, and a window. This camp, with a capacity of 2,200 inhabitants, was reserved exclusively for Balts. It was one of many such camps. By September 1946 Lübeck, whose indigenous population of 136,000 had swollen to 236,000, had twenty-eight DP camps within its urban borders.

Crossᵃre

FIRST SURPRISE CONTACT with the Russians was made at around five o'clock in the morning on that August 1, 1944, by two separate German units, a group of grenadiers from the 639th Regiment and a company of engineers from Battalion 660.

Both contingents were being brought into position from different directions, one moving east from the vicinity of Jelgava and the other west from the nearby hamlet of Svenķi. Both consisted of motley crews, mostly elderly engineers and cyclists. The troops averaged about forty-five years of age, were poorly armed and few in number. The 639th Regiment was led by a forty-nine-year-old, Colonel Armand du Plessis, the 660th Battalion by a forty-five-year-old, Lieutenant Colonel Eugen Ruf. While the officers were experienced, the soldiers under their command were not combat troops. Of the engineers in Battalion 660 their commanding officer said: "The troops were exhausted from the preceding week-long marches, poor food and lack of sleep. Their weapons and organization were inadequate: they were not fit for front-line duty."[22] The few Latvians in the group were not trusted. Latvian soldiers as a whole had a good reputation as attacking troops but were considered unreliable in defensive positions.

Battalion 660 had in fact been due in the day before, but owing to a great deal of troop movement on July 29–30, as the Germans shortened their front-line defenses, and owing also to critical fuel shortages — tankers had not reached the port at Riga on time — their transport trucks had arrived a day late. The unit had been trucked from Krustpils only the previous evening and had been unloaded at Svenķi shortly after midnight. The transportation foul-up was an indication of how badly things were going for the hard-pressed Wehrmacht.

From Svenķi the 660th had then trudged, exhausted and disoriented, through the darkness toward their positions along the river. Companies 2 and 3 were heading along the road toward Valaki; they had to cover more than fifteen kilometers on a road that had been turned to dust by the exceptional heat of July. Company 4 had a slightly shorter march; after ten kilometers en route it was deployed around Tetele and my grandfather's farm, arriving about three-thirty in the morning.

As dawn was breaking on August 1 and as the weary troops destined for Valaki were moving into position, they were suddenly enveloped by machine-gun, mortar, and antitank fire. The Russians had even managed by then to get two tanks and several light vehicles across the river. The two German units that were supposed to meet up, Company 2 of the 660th Battalion coming from Svenķi and a contingent of the 639th Regiment coming from the west, were unable to establish contact, compounding the sense of confusion.

Moreover, no one let the commander in Jelgava, General Pflugbeil, know what was happening. How many Russians were there and how far had they penetrated? No one could tell. German losses in this first encounter were heavy.

As the day advanced and as the strength of the Russian infiltration gradually came to light, Company 4 of the 660th was withdrawn from the riverside at Tetele in the direction of the main road and railway line. The resulting vacuum around my grandfather's farm was promptly filled by the Russians. After the Soviet advance party had settled in, five hundred men were quickly ferried across the river from Stūri, a hamlet directly opposite Tetele, to consolidate the bridgehead. Some of this group dug in right at Nightingales. They cut down trees — my mother especially regretted losing the fruit trees, bursting by midsummer with promise — and built trenches in the farmyard.

As they discovered the extent of the Russian intrusion, the Germans scrambled to plug the hole and to keep the railway line free. The command of Army Group North was incensed that the Russians should have been able to slip across the Lielupe without being seen and demanded an investigation. General Schoerner ordered an immediate counterattack: "Our traditional understanding of defense, holding a position to the last man, must be revived with determination. Our front soldier must be convinced that everything depends on him and him alone and that we shall win the war if he holds his position, if necessary by sacrificing his life."[23]

That afternoon a company of the 281st Infantry Division was quickly sent in to Laktas, a nearby crossroads, to support the 660th and to engage the enemy. Artillery and air support was called up. Two tank units, one from Iecava, another from Olaine, were dispatched to the Lielupe front. Shortly after 8 P.M. the German counterattack, commanded from Jelgava by General Pflugbeil and led on the spot by General Windisch, began. It was launched from Meiliņi, from the very point, just across the railway tracks, where my grandfather's house had stood in 1919.

By midnight one German section had pushed as far as the center of the village of Tetele, a kilometer north of the river and our farm.

Here, however, they ran into tough resistance. Shortly before midnight General Pflugbeil reported on the telephone to General Kleffel that though the attack had been costly, it would nevertheless be resumed the next morning with fresh troops from the Ninety-third Infantry Division.

At dawn the German assault recommenced, now with artillery support. German shells rained down on Nightingales. Every shell that exploded among us carried the weight of centuries.

We took cover in the large cold-cellar of the former manor house, where since the civil war of 1919 only ruins remained. It was dank and dark. The firing seemed to go on without respite. The German attack on August 2, by the Ninety-third Infantry Division, met with fierce Soviet resistance, including air support, and stalled just at the edge of our farm. Finally there was a lull. My mother decided to take me, her eight-month-old, out from the fetid dark into the fresh summer air. All of a sudden, a shell came whistling toward us and exploded but meters away.

I, needless to say, have no memory of that moment, but there is a mother's diary. Its commentary is straightforward. It states that I was grazed in the temple by a fragment from that shell and expresses relief that my sister, who was in the cellar asleep at the time, was not with us. A German medical orderly patched my head.

Nearby a soldier was killed by enemy fire. A German officer, my mother recounts, removed the dead man's wallet. It contained, among other things, three photographs: one of his wife, one of his child, and one of his girlfriend. The officer took the picture of the girlfriend, pocketed it, and returned the wallet.

Russian prisoners captured and interrogated that night declared that their comrades in the Ninety-first Infantry Division had no intention of relinquishing the bridgehead. And at two o'clock in the morning Russian counterattacks began at Roņi, just over the main road about a kilometer away.

On August 3 the German assault resumed. General Kleffel ordered that first of all the front line be straightened and reconnected. "It is also a matter of narrowing the bridgehead bit by bit with well-prepared individual attacks against enemy strongholds and especially dangerous nests of Russians."[24] The shelling continued. This time, the Russians were beaten back across the river with heavy losses. As they left, they burned down my grandfather's barn and stables, taking his horses with them. Most of the other animals had been killed in the crossfire. Dead chickens littered the farmyard.

The goose, however, had survived. After the Germans had reappeared, at the next pause in the firing, we ran. The goose led the way, head held high. We moved, heads down, through fields, along ditches, across roads and railway tracks. We spent a night and a day at a neighboring farm. Alerted about our predicament, my father came, by bicycle and on foot, from Riga in search of us. He found us at the neighbor's. Together we set out for the return to Riga. After two days and nights — one night spent in Olaine, the German staging center for the battle for Jelgava — we reached Riga.

My grandparents, who had escaped to the neighboring farm with us, decided to stay there, to be close to their home. The goose stayed with them. We never saw any of them again.

In the meantime, the battle for Jelgava raged. As the Lielupe front line seesawed back and forth, the city was pulverized by artillery, air raids, and tank shells. The Rastrelli palace, so often the object of attack in the past, became yet again a prime target. All the training drills and precautions of the past year, introduced by Area Commissar Medem and designed for an occasion such as this, came to naught. The palace was leveled. Much of the city was razed in ferocious street fighting. Gone were the churches and schools, as well as the splendid villas on the Palaisstrasse and the Bachstrasse, the former city residences of the von der Pahlens, Lievens, and Medems.

Some in the German high command had written off Jelgava by July 30, insisting that forces be withdrawn toward Riga and the coast to try and keep a corridor open to East Prussia. Still, a skeleton force of defenders under General Pflugbeil managed to hold off the Russians for a good part of August, allowing much of the civilian population to escape. General Kleffel's overtaxed forces put up a commendable resistance along the river. After the successes on August 3 and 4, at Jelgava, Stalģene, and Mežotne, visions appeared of

German bridgeheads across the river and counterattacks in the direction of Elēja. On August 4 Army Group North issued figures claiming that in the previous six weeks its soldiers had destroyed 1,197 Soviet tanks and taken 2,509 prisoners. Some grounds for optimism did exist.

But the optimism was brief. Kleffel's troops were outmanned and outgunned and despite brave resistance stood little chance of winning back territory. The emphasis now was on defense. On August 6 General Schoerner decreed: "Every village, every town will become a fortress! Riga too!"[25] A day later: "We must accept the idea of keeping the Ostland in its present shape for some time. We must stop the enemy attacks now. If we achieve this, quieter times will come."[26] But even this was wishful thinking.

Weapons were being lost at a disturbing rate. "Hang on to your weapons as if they were your honor!" read the order of the day on August 7. Artūrs Vajeiks could have written that order. The Sixteenth Army's quartermaster reported that, aside from weapon shortages, ammunition would not suffice to repel a prolonged enemy onslaught. Supplies, for instance, of two-centimeter flak and twelve-centimeter mortar shells were completely exhausted. In the event of a heavy attack, artillery munitions might last three to four days, he pointed out, infantry munitions perhaps five to six.[27] And on August 13 orders went out for a general evacuation of the area between Riga and the front. Animals and foodstuffs were to be moved first, between the fourteenth and eighteenth, and the civilian population in the next two days.[28]

Panic

IN JULY 1944 the Archbishop of Canterbury had asked Foreign Secretary Anthony Eden if press correspondents might accompany the Russian armies when they occupied the Baltic states. He was concerned, he said, that the brutality displayed by the Russians in 1940–41 might be repeated, especially against churchmen. Eden's reply came on July 20:

I sympathize with what you say in your letter, but I am afraid that this is not a matter which it would be either wise or profitable for me to take up with the Soviet Government. They have always shown themselves very sensitive as regards foreign criticism of their activities in the Baltic States, and from all our information, I feel quite certain that the Russians would not give facilities in that area for press-correspondents or other observers which they have not given in other parts of the front. They would merely be resentful; nor are we in a position to make and persist in a demand.[29]

In Riga panic was mounting. The city was flooded with refugees from the countryside. My father preached his last sermon in the Baptist seminary church on August 13, using as text the words of Jesus in John 13:7: "What I am doing you do not know now, but afterward you will understand." One or two of you, my father told his congregation, expect the imminent arrival of the Lord. "Excuse me," he hastened to add, "if I tell you that the Bolsheviks are much more likely to come than the Lord." The notes he had before him at the pulpit had been, in contrast with his usual neat hand, scrawled in great haste. In his peroration he repeated the text: "What I am doing you do not know now, but afterward you will understand."[30] It is unlikely that either he or his parishioners ever did understand.

A week later my parents locked the door to their apartment, leaving everything in place, beds made, table set, on the assumption they would be back shortly. They never returned. To the end of his life, my father was obsessed with what might have happened to his library, much of which he had acquired in his years of study abroad.

We were not the only ones leaving. We joined a growing flood of frightened, fleeing people.

While the Wehrmacht staff opposed evacuation of civilians at this stage, because it suggested defeatism and because the inevitable traffic congestion hampered the movement of troops and supplies, the civilian occupation authorities encouraged it. There was not enough food to feed the local population beyond the end of the year; labor, moreover, was needed in the Reich. The officials in the Reich Commissariat for the Ostland expressed great resentment toward the army when it was discovered that roughly four hundred thousand head of cattle had fallen into Soviet hands during the recent retreat.

The exodus from Latvia would eventually number three hundred thousand. Much of that exodus was by ship. The German army was now being supplied exclusively by sea, for on August 17 the Russians reached the East Prussian border and were threatening to cut off all land traffic around the Baltic coast. German supply ships, after unloading their cargo at the ports of Riga, Ventspils, and Liepāja, took on refugees whom they ferried back to Germany. Many of these were engaged as laborers.

The land route west was still an alternative, but an extremely risky one because of the Soviet advance. In addition, General Schoerner became preoccupied with the idea that his own soldiers were deserting in droves — the morale of the troops at Stalingrad was better than the mood here, he ranted in mid-August — and he called for "brutal measures" against the rats trying to jump ship. The incidence of desertion in the Sixteenth Army did go up after the middle of July. Offenses involving officers increased 60 percent between mid-July and mid-October.[31]

Flight

WE CAUGHT A TRAIN NORTH. A member of my father's congregation was a high railway official; he supplied tickets and travel papers. The direction chose itself. If one was to escape the German and Soviet yokes, one had to get to Sweden. From the port of Riga the only destination was Germany. The overland route south through Lithuania was very long and treacherous, especially with children, and that way, too, should one escape the furious Russian advance, would lead only to Germany. So we headed north.

Tallinn, the Estonian capital, was the first destination. The stretch, less than three hundred kilometers, took two days owing to delays caused by military priorities. The Russian push had created havoc in the area's rail system, a complex network of narrow- and wide-gauge track.[32] We were fortunate just to get away by train. Passenger traffic would cease within days of our departure. We arrived in Tallinn on August 22.[33]

The city's port was besieged by refugees. We spent three days looking for an avenue of escape. None appeared, so we headed for the Baltic coast, to the port of Haapsalu, and from there on a ferry to the Estonian island of Hiiumaa, or Dagö as the Germans called it. The aim was to find a fisherman with a boat who would take us to Sweden, to neutral, safe Sweden — or, for that matter, anywhere beyond the guns. Paris, which had just been liberated on August 24, would have been nice, thank you. But on Dagö the fisherfolk were gone, or else they were unwilling to take risks for small compensation. Both the Russian and German navies, as it turned out, had orders in place to sink all unauthorized ships and boats.

We spent a balmy, unreal September on Dagö, indeed for the moment beyond the guns. We slept on straw on the floor of a doctor's house. The doctor had long since departed. My father, the clergyman, toured the island on a bicycle, looking for the fisherman-savior. He never found him. We had little news of developments on the mainland — of the German decisions on September 17, for instance, to evacuate Tallinn and, five days later, to destroy the port facilities at Haapsalu; or of the Soviet vise that was tightening around Riga. We knew nothing of the reports in the Swedish press that thirty-six thousand refugees had arrived in Sweden in the last two weeks of September — some thirty thousand of these from Finland, the rest from the Baltic states — and that the Swedes were not particularly welcoming toward the arrivals because they feared that their cherished neutrality might be compromised.[34] A Foreign Office official in London noted: "These Balts and Finns will give the Swedes a good deal of trouble with the Soviet authorities. Anybody who makes a getaway from Soviet occupied territory will automatically be dubbed a Fascist. So will those who try to help them or even express any sympathy with them."[35]

Some daring escapes were made by sea from Latvia even after the fall of Riga on October 13 and right up until the end of the war when the Kurland pocket finally surrendered. A young girl, Helen Peterson, wrote to a friend in Dublin at the end of October, telling him of her harrowing trip in a fishing boat that sailed from Ventspils and reached Farosund at the northern tip of Gotland eighteen hours later, its forty passengers cold, wet, and sick. Her letter ended with an appeal: "Pray that the Bolsheviks will be destroyed and that we will be able to go back to our home."[36] Among those who fled in precarious vessels was our former neighbor the poet and nationalist Kārlis Skalbe. His exile was to be brief: he would die in Stockholm a few months later. In May 1945, when the last hopes had been extinguished, people took to sea en masse from the burning harbors of Ventspils and Liepāja. Mostly women and children, they fled in sailboats, dinghies, tugboats, and even rowboats. Some of these craft made it to Gotland. Many were sunk by Russian patrol boats, their passengers left to perish.[37]

Of the broader war, too, we knew nothing — that, for example, the first V-2 rocket had smashed into England on September 8 and that American troops had crossed the German border near Aachen four days later. However, when at the end of the month Soviet planes began to appear overhead, we knew it was time to move on.

The only possible direction was south, to the island of Saaremaa, or Ösel. From there, as the islands were coming under Soviet attack, we were evacuated to the German mainland. As we were assembling on the pier at Arensburg (Kuresaare),[38] another Baltic town with connections to the Teutonic Knights, a squadron of Russian planes zoomed in to bomb and strafe the exposed harbor. We dove for cover. The boats stayed afloat. On a packed troopship crawling with lice, through a terrible storm, we reached, on October 3, Danzig, the city that had served as pretext for Hitler's attack on Poland. Perhaps the storm had been a godsend. Russian submarine activity in the Baltic was increasing. Just a few days earlier the *Moero* had been torpedoed, with a loss of twenty-two hundred lives. The sinkings multiplied. In January the liner *Wilhelm Gustloff*, overloaded with perhaps as many as eight thousand desperate passengers who had been waiting in snowstorms on the quays of Gotenhafen, would be sunk in the worst maritime disaster in history.

We left in time. On October 2 the Russians landed on Dagö. On October 7 they took Arensburg.[39]

West, ever westward, that was now the goal, away, as far as possible, from the advancing Russians. First a train to Berlin. There my father contacted a friend in Prague who said the trains to Switzerland were still running. Neutral Switzerland with its mountains and chocolate — what a vision! We must get to Prague, and then to Switzerland. Off we went. The trains were packed, people fleeing in every direction. The bulging, bursting coaches reminded two passengers, Ruth Andreas-Friedrich and Magda Denes, of bunches of grapes.[40] The rising in Warsaw, which had begun on August 1 when we had been trapped on the Lielupe River, ended on October 5; two hundred thousand Poles had died in less than six weeks.

When we got to Prague the trains had stopped running. The vision of Switzerland proved a mirage. Because I was ill, we were permitted to stay for one month, in a room ominously facing the city crematorium. But at the end of the month the German security police insisted that we return to Berlin. And so back we went, to the capital city of hell, a city now being pounded by Allied bombs. We were to be stuck there for three months.

Riga fell on October 13 to Bagramian's First Baltic Front. During the previous fortnight the Germans had set about destroying as much as they could: factories, power stations, railway lines, bridges. The huge power plant at Ķegums, for example, which supplied 40 percent of the country's electricity and which had been put into service only in December 1939, was blown up section by section over three days with 17,220 kilograms of munitions.

When Riga fell, Army Group North withdrew into the Kurland peninsula. To the south, the land route west had been cut off by the Soviet advance. The Kurland army, a full thirty divisions, was encircled — almost. It could still escape, or be supplied, by sea. General Guderian, chief of staff, insisted to Hitler that the army be pulled out and used to defend the Reich. Hitler refused. The Kurland army, he said, would be the basis for his next spring offensive against Russia.[41] On March 1, 1945, twenty-two divisions were still there.

The Kurland pocket would hold out until May 9, 1945, and give rise to all kinds of illusions among the locals as well as the German soldiers. One of these visions focused on the arrival by sea of the

Western Allies as the occupation army of the Baltic. The British, Americans, and French would repeat their heroics of 1919 and help drive out the Bolsheviks. Field Marshal Alexander would return. In the end, in May, about 190,000 troops, including 14,000 Latvian soldiers, were abandoned to the Russians. Field Marshal Alexander went to Canada instead, as governor general.

Yalta

WHILE THE CENTER OF EUROPE was exploding in a finale of cacophonous fury, the "Big Three," Roosevelt, Churchill, and Stalin, were meeting in the Crimean resort of Yalta to decide on the frontiers and administration of postwar Europe. At their summit in Teheran in November 1943, the three leaders had agreed to "work together in war and in the peace that would follow," and furthermore to "seek the cooperation and active participation of all nations, large and small, whose peoples in heart and mind are dedicated, as are our own peoples, to the elimination of tyranny and slavery, oppression and intolerance."[42]

Mindful of such rhetoric, Latvian officials abroad pleaded with the Western Allies to parlay these words into action. In the days before Yalta, the Latvian ministers to Switzerland, Belgium, and Estonia cabled the British prime minister, from Geneva, urging him in his upcoming meeting with Stalin and Roosevelt to uphold the spirit of the Atlantic Charter. In forwarding the message to the Foreign Office, John Colville, private secretary to Churchill, noted: "I do not consider that any reply to the enclosed telegram is necessary, greatly though I sympathise with the Latvians."[43] The world situation had relegated the Baltic states to their familiar position of margin and silence.

When the fate of the Baltic was raised in the House of Commons on December 21, 1944, the official response was similar. Sir Herbert Williams asked if the British government still recognized the governments of the three Baltic republics. No, not since the changes in June 1940, replied George Hall on behalf of the foreign minister. Sir

Herbert pressed his point: "As these changes are in conflict with the principles of the Atlantic Charter . . . , why have we left these people in the lurch?" Hall's response was again evasive: No government in the area had sought or been granted recognition since 1940. Sir Herbert: "Is not our treatment of these countries identical with the treatment of Czechoslovakia by Germany? What is the moral difference?"

At Yalta, February 4–10, 1945, Roosevelt, who had not wished to go to the Crimea, accorded Eastern and much of Central Europe, including a large part of Germany, to Stalin and the Soviet Union. These territories were grouped in Stalin's sphere of influence. Roosevelt's purpose was to placate "Uncle Joe," whose armies in the East were now rolling inexorably forward, and to persuade him to assist in the forthcoming assault on Japan. As one of his State Department officers put it, in an attempt to explain what he called "our obscure foreign policy," "President Roosevelt was thinking of winning the war; the others were thinking of their relative positions when the war was won."[44]

Poland, whose integrity was the *casus belli* to begin with, was surrendered to Stalin, its borders rearranged in keeping, roughly, with the agreements Stalin had made with Hitler. Implicit in the rearrangement of borders was a massive transfer of peoples. The repatriation of nationals was part of the agreement.

The fate of the Baltic states was never debated at Yalta. Silence prevailed. The British and American position was to admit de facto Soviet administration of the states but not to admit their incorporation into the Soviet Union. Had the Cold War not hotted up shortly after the conclusion of hostilities and precluded a peace settlement, it is more than likely that the Soviet absorption of the Baltic statelets into its Union would have been formalized by international accord. It was the breakdown of East-West relations after 1945 that consigned the Baltic states to a kind of unwilling common-law relationship with the Soviet Union, which everyone accepted but no one outside the USSR openly recognized.

According to the former U.S. ambassador in Moscow William C. Bullitt, Roosevelt's attitude toward Stalin was: "If I give him everything I possibly can and ask nothing from him in return, *noblesse oblige*, he won't try to annex anything and will work with me for a world of democracy and peace."[45] Roosevelt died, on April 12, 1945, before he could witness the results of his policies.

If Churchill regretted developments, his Foreign Office staff did not. Nor did the newly reconstituted Quai d'Orsay or the American State Department. Baltic independence had originally been accepted with reluctance. In the twenties and thirties no Western statesman seriously considered it an issue worth taking a stand on. After 1945 the stubborn refusal by the Western Allies to formalize the de facto situation in the Baltic states was provoked by Soviet aggression and intransigence in Central and Eastern Europe, not by any particular sympathy for the peoples of the Baltic.

Those peoples have always regarded Yalta as the great betrayal.

Land of Culture

WHEN THE LITERARY-CRITIC-TO-BE Marcel Reich-Ranicki was leaving Poland for Berlin in 1929, his teacher said to him: "You are going, my son, to the land of culture."[46] By 1944 the land of culture was a moonscape of ruin. Leonardo da Vinci had imagined the airplane as a kindly bird that would carry snow from cool mountaintops and sprinkle it over hot cities in summer. These few centuries later, kindness could find no room in the cargo holds of bomb-laden planes.

My father was a man of education and reflection, although his diary for those winter months of 1944–45, when we were in Berlin, indicates little of that. The entries revolve around food, lodging, illness, and fear. The acquisition of an apple was celebrated; the theft — from baggage we left in storage at Anhalter train station — of a bit of bacon saved from Dagö was lamented at great length. An October 1944 report of the state attorney's office on legal matters in the Reich capital pointed out that railway station theft had increased markedly. So had death from methyl alcohol poisoning.[47]

Then there was the cold, the terrible cold. One slept fully clothed

owing to the lack of heat but also because the air-raid alarm would
leave no time to dress. We found quarters in central Berlin, near the
Anhalter station. Its lower reaches served as a bomb shelter. Some
days we ran to it in panic three or four times. "If only people
wouldn't crowd around the entrance so," noted my father in frustration.

For Christabel Bielenberg the station had become

> a symbol of disintegration; its huge domed roof, once glassed in, stood
> out like a skeleton greenhouse against the sky. Along the platforms
> the propaganda posters hung unnoticed in red and black tatters from
> the shrapnel-pitted walls. "*Führer* we thank you." "To Victory with
> our Leader," "National Socialist Order or Bolshevik Chaos."

She went on to describe some of the patrons of the famous station:

> The tall Mongol in the fur hat and his little wife in her black shawl —
> perhaps some Russian collaborator, with revenge hard on his heels; a
> bustling Party official, still in his brown uniform, who tried to keep
> order when pushing started from behind, and whose commands pe-
> tered out to futile mutterings when confronted by the silent, hostile
> gaze of his neighbours; the straggling group of silent children, with
> labels round their necks, shepherded by a thin anxious woman in Red
> Cross uniform; the soldiers in their shapeless uniforms, some of them
> mere boys; the rather helpless woman, wearing her Mother's Cross in
> silver, who had asked me if I knew whether trains were still going to
> Leipzig — two of her children had been evacuated there with their
> school and she was hoping to find them before the Russian wave went
> over them.[48]

The German war effort was full of paradoxes. One was the lack
of air-raid shelters in Berlin. Only three deep bunkers in the entire
city offered genuine security from the bombs, providing space for
around sixty thousand people — out of a population that had at first
declined from, but then, owing to the influx of refugees, swelled
back to about four million. The other shelters used — including the
subway and train stations — were not deep enough to assure safety.
Nevertheless, transients like us clung to the train stations, those
symbols of escape, hope, and home. Hans-Georg von Studnitz, com-

ing from Hanover in late October 1944, arrived at the Zoo station in the middle of the night to find it "crammed with refugees and homeless who spend the night there whether there is a raid or not. There are clear signs that the nerves of the people are cracking; inexpressible anxiety, horror, bitterness and fatalism are stamped on all their faces."[49]

By March 1945 Goebbels shared these sentiments. Berliners, he noted, had become "nervous and hysterical" from the nightly attacks. To spend every evening in the air-raid shelter "is a torture which overstrains the nerves in the long run, particularly when people are firmly convinced that for the present no end to these nightly raids is in sight."[50]

In Canada the Holt Renfrew department store suspended Wednesday deliveries to its customers to save on fuel. "Will it not THRILL you," it asked in an advertisement, "to think that non-delivery of your dress on Wednesday will aid in the delivery of a 'block-buster' over the Ruhr . . . Naples . . . Berlin . . . ?"[51] It certainly THRILLed the inhabitants of Berlin.

Germans now called the British and American fliers *Luftgangster* and *Mordpirate*, air gangsters and killer pirates. Accuracy was not the hallmark of Bomber Command. Assessing one raid on Berlin, the record book of the RAF's Eighty-third Squadron commented: "The success of the attack was not due to our accurate bombing but to the Germans for building such a large city!"[52] One German citizen wrote to the Propaganda Ministry in early January 1945 to suggest that British and American prisoners of war should be distributed throughout the German cities.[53] Goebbels called the air war a "great tale of woe": "The situation becomes more intolerable daily and we have no means of defending ourselves against this catastrophe."[54]

On January 14, 1945, my father, the clergyman, damned the British and American airmen for not observing Sunday as a day of rest. My sister had a high fever. We had to run for cover three times that day, the first time around noon, the second in the early evening, and a third time toward midnight. After the second raid, as we returned from the Anhalter station shelter, the stones and debris kept getting larger and larger as we neared our building. On the Möckernstrasse, a block from our temporary quarters at the Hotel Quandt, we found a huge crater that augured ill for our few possessions. Amazingly, however, our hotel, on the Hallesche Strasse, was untouched. But not for long.

Just before midnight the sirens blasted us from our beds again. Once more we ran, over rubble and sand, in utter darkness, to the shelter. As we sat in one of the train cars, below ground level, the world around us trembled mightily. This time, my father noted, it was not a joke. The all-clear signal came near one o'clock in the morning. Back we trudged, to the sound of broken glass underfoot. Third time unlucky. The Quandt was still recognizable, but only just. A large incendiary bomb had landed one street over, on the Kleinbeerenstrasse. Our building, while still standing, had been badly damaged. The windows were all gone, the walls unstable. The jar of honey my mother had battled to acquire the day before for her sick daughter lay shattered on the floor. A flower she had found, in the midst of winter, and put in a vase on the windowsill lay crushed among the ruins. "I often ask myself," wrote Mathilde Wolff-Mönckeberg, "what this period of time will look like in our memory. Which particular picture will demand precedence over the others, and will there ever be a time without screeching sirens, without above us the deafening crashes of explosions and within us fear and worry? . . . Whenever I listen to Beethoven, I cry."[55]

We were now *Bombenbeschädigte*, bomb victims — oddly enough, a privileged caste in the Hades that was Berlin in 1945. We found what might be termed heaven-sent quarters in Dahlem, the arbored residential district in the southwest of the city. We were given a room in the Diakonissenhaus Bethel, a Baptist social mission founded in 1887 and located on the Kronprinzenallee (Crown Prince Avenue). The basic premise of the mission's founder was that body and soul were equally important; neglect of one was bound to harm the other.

The minutes of the meeting of the mission's board of directors on January 28, 1945, record the recent arrival, along with us, of thirty-seven female missionaries and various other church personnel from

branch offices in the East, most on this occasion from Litzmannstadt
(Łódź) in Poland and Insterburg in East Prussia, the latter a town
razed by the advancing Russians.[56] My mother's excitement could
hardly be contained: the room accorded us was warm! There was
even an air-raid shelter in the basement. No more frantic running
to train stations in the middle of the night. No longer were we in
Bezirk Mitte, the central district. In Dahlem the chances of survival, physical and spiritual, were far better. My father, too, was
delighted. Next to a bright fresh flower in our room was a note
with greetings and two passages from the Bible, one from Psalms 42
and a second from John 13:7: "What I am doing you do not know
now, but afterward you will understand." This had been the text of
my father's last sermon in Riga. He thought the coincidence an excellent omen.

Capital of the Future

THE 1939 GRIEBEN TRAVEL GUIDE to Berlin called it "the world
city of the future." Rome, Paris, London, and Vienna revel in their
beautiful past; New York, with its skyscrapers, is the expression of
technology and capitalism; but Berlin heralds the future.[57] By 1945
that assessment had assumed a frantic irony.

Göring's famous statement that if Allied bombers ever reached
Berlin he would change his name to Meier had been swallowed long
ago by the swirling eddies of sarcasm that the issue of bombing
provoked among Berliners. The first Royal Air Force attack on the
German capital took place in August 1940 during the Battle of Britain. But though Berliners were dumbfounded, those early raids were
little more than pinpricks. When during the night of November 7–8,
1941, the RAF lost 12 percent of its attacking force over Berlin,
Churchill suspended long-distance bombing raids in order to prepare the carpet-bombing runs, of more than a thousand planes, that
would, from 1943 on, reduce German cities to ash and rubble. As
early as July 8, 1941, he had stated: "There is one thing that will
bring [Hitler] down, and that is an absolutely devastating extermi-

nating attack by very heavy bombers from this country upon the Nazi homeland."[58]

Air Chief Marshal Arthur Harris shared those sentiments. In February 1942 he said: "There are a lot of people who say that bombing cannot win the war. My reply is that it has never been tried yet. We shall see."[59] In November 1942, Air Chief Marshal Sir Charles Portal, head of Bomber Command, sent a memorandum to the chiefs of staff committee stating that in the next two years his force would be able to drop approximately one and a quarter million tons of bombs on Germany, which could destroy six million houses and a proportional number of industrial and public installations. Close to a million Germans would be killed and another million seriously injured; twenty-five million would be rendered homeless. John Terraine, the British military historian, would subsequently ask: "What is one to think of the calm proposal, set down in a quiet office, to kill 900,000 civilians and seriously injure a million more? One thing emerges, with absolute clarity: this was a prescription for massacre, nothing more nor less."[60]

Between 1941 and 1945 the Allied technology for strategic area bombing improved exponentially with the development of new planes, bombs, and optical and navigational instruments. In this new war the Baltic coastline proved an important testing ground. The timbered medieval ports of northern Germany would reveal what incendiaries could achieve. The first practice run by the RAF was against Lübeck in late March 1942. The old town was, Harris sneered, "built more like a fire-lighter than a human habitation."[61] The incendiary bombs left the city a charred hulk. In April it was Rostock's turn. The result was the same. The two runs delighted Butch — for "Butcher" — Harris; he felt they squared the account with Germany. But squaring the account was not good enough. The attacks on Hansa cities were followed by the raid on Cologne, on May 31, 1942, and would culminate in Operation Gomorrah, the firebombing of Hamburg in July 1943, when in one week almost as many people were killed in that city as would die in Britain from bombing during the entire war. The center of the Hamburg fire-storm reached 1,400 degrees. People melted. Brains tumbled from burst temples. Intestines erupted. Small dead children on the pavement reminded one survivor of fried eels.[62]

Margot Schulz lived in Bergedorf, the first town outside Hamburg on the road to Berlin. She remembered the Hamburg survivors trudging past: "It was the most pathetic sight I had ever seen. If I think back on it now, I don't think it can have been true. They were in their nightdresses — half burned sometimes — and pyjamas, sometimes a coat thrown over their shoulders." One woman gave birth on the pavement. Another sat nearby breast-feeding. "She was dressed only in a nightdress," recalled Schulz, "and all her hair was burnt away. And, all the time, the exodus went on."[63]

And this was in preparation for the "Battle of Berlin." The air assault on the German capital began in earnest in November 1943. Between November and the end of March 1944, Berlin was subjected to sixteen heavy raids, almost half the major bomber sorties to Germany during that period. One and a half million of its residents were made homeless, and two thousand acres of the city were destroyed. All told, forty-five thousand tons of bombs would be dropped on Berlin during the war.

In the aftermath of a raid in November 1943, Ursula Gebel wrote:

A terrible smell lingered above the total destruction of my beloved Zoo. There were blasted and dead animals everywhere. The only living thing, in his big pond, was a big bull hippopotamus called Knautschke, still swimming while above him his shelter burned down . . . All the brown bears, the polar bears, the camels, the zebras, the antelopes, the ostriches and all the beasts of prey — lions, tigers, panthers, leopards, hyenas — were dead; the keepers had been forced to shoot many of the burning and crazed animals. All the wild birds were gone. Of the apes, only one orang-utan — a female called Cleo — managed to escape into the nearby park. She had been found sitting in a big tree with her baby but she had died from a heart attack and her body was hanging in the tree.[64]

The raids dominated life in Berlin. "Alarm, alarm, and again alarm," wrote Ruth Andreas-Friedrich on February 4, 1944. "You hear nothing else, see nothing else, think nothing else. In the S-

Bahn, on the street, in shops and on buses — everywhere the same
bits of conversation buzz about: totally bombed out . . . roof blown
away . . . wall collapsed . . . windows out . . . doors out . . . certificate
of damage . . . everything lost."[65]

But the Royal Air Force was hurt too: 2,690 bomber crew members died in the Berlin raids, and another thousand men became
prisoners of the Germans. "The results," said one pilot, "didn't
appear to come anywhere near justifying the losses and the hardship."[66]

The British sought assistance. In 1944 the U.S. Eighth Air Force
joined in the attacks. The British preferred night raids, the Americans daylight bombing. For Germans that combination, the inces-
sant alarms, was utterly nerve-racking. During the rest of 1944
Berlin would face constant harassment. Then in February 1945 the
last and darkest phase of the battle would begin. By then the Luftwaffe had lost more than fifty thousand aircraft, and in the air
Germany was virtually defenseless.

The Russians Are Coming

THE RED ARMY KEPT COMING. The refugees kept streaming into
Berlin. At the Silesia train station in the east of the city, an open
wagon car had arrived full of frozen children. They had been
crammed like herrings into this car and subjected to the winter cold,
without relief, for ninety-six hours. The wind howled, the snow
covered them. They cried. They died.[67]

Zhukov's First White Russian and Konev's First Ukrainian fronts
were poised on the river Oder, ready to launch the final assault.
Artillery and armor were the essence of the Russian advance. For
tactical sophistication there was no need. In Berlin, trenches were
dug, barricades built. Berlin would be the downfall of Bolshevism,
said Hitler: "The Bolshevik will once again experience the old fate of
Asia, that is, he will and he must bleed to death before the capital of
the German Reich." Hitler hoped that what Moscow had been to
him in 1941, Berlin would be to Stalin in 1945.

Many Berliners, however, had had enough of the rhetoric. How long would it take the Russians to conquer Berlin? they asked. Two hours and five minutes, a wag replied. For two hours they'd stand in front of the barricades and laugh, and then in five minutes they'd climb over. Still, the situation could not be regarded as truly critical, said another jester, until you could get to the eastern front on the subway.

The air raids, too, were multiplying. Operation Thunderclap — massive Allied air attacks against four cities, Berlin, Leipzig, Chemnitz, and Dresden — was designed to support the Soviet advance. Berlin suffered a heavy raid on February 3; some estimates, probably bloated, put the death toll from that attack at twenty to twenty-five thousand. From mid-February on, the city would be hit on thirty-six successive nights. Built largely in the nineteenth and twentieth centuries, of stone, brick, and concrete, with many broad boulevards, Berlin refused to burn in the manner of Lübeck, Rostock, and Hamburg, with their timbered gables and winding streets. It never experienced a firestorm. Dresden, old and beautiful, did. Full not only of museums and churches but of refugees from the East, many of them Balts, this fairy-tale city of cobblestones and spires was firebombed on February 13–14. It exploded into flame. Perhaps one hundred thousand civilians died. The National Committee for Latvia was in session in Dresden that very night when the planes arrived.

Gerhart Hauptmann, the great German playwright from Silesia, was in a sanatorium not far from Dresden. He could see the city burning. "Whoever has forgotten how to cry," he wrote, "will learn again from the destruction of Dresden. I stand at the end of my life and envy all my dead spiritual friends who have been spared this experience."[68]

At the end of January forty to fifty thousand people a day were flooding into Berlin. Only three or four thousand of those moved on daily. Hans-Georg von Studnitz noted that a set of false identity papers cost 80,000 reichsmarks. "Large sums are also being offered for Jewish Yellow Stars!"[69]

With the bombing of Dresden and then the final battle for Berlin, which began on April 21, the symphony of war reached its climax, a mighty crescendo of percussive destruction. Elena Rzhevskaya was an interpreter in the Soviet army. She arrived in Berlin that spring. On May 4 she noted in her diary: "We went over the Spree by bridge. On the bridge sat a woman, her face held toward the sky, her legs outstretched before her, and she was laughing loudly. I called her over. She stared at me with absent, transparent eyes, politely nodded her head, then, exactly realizing who I was, in a wild, guttural voice, screamed: 'All is lost!'"[70]

Older Generation

MY GRANDPARENTS, we found out years later, had survived but had not been permitted to return to their farm for several months. The crops, plentiful because of the splendid weather, were not harvested that summer of 1944. The remaining animals had died or disappeared.

"The potato harvest will be a good one," the Sixteenth Army's office of the intendant had reported earlier.[71]

Jānis Vajeiks died at the end of the war. One report said that he was removing a bomb from the attic of his house at Nightingales when it suddenly exploded. Another suggested that he, like his son Artūrs, had been shot. He is buried beside his first son, Rūdolfs, in the cemetery at Tetele. He rests among Baltic-German barons, German soldiers of the Great War, and ordinary Latvians like himself.

Paulīne Vajeiks lived until 1959. She stayed at Nightingales for a few years after the war. Though the land was taken from her, she was allowed to remain in her house as long as she shared it. Three women, two sisters and a daughter, were lodged with her. They were assigned the living room. Somehow Paulīne had acquired two cows. She wrote about them with affection. One was called Spīdola. Increasingly incapacitated by age, she decided in the mid-1950s to sell the house her husband had built. In the care of a distant relative in her last years, she died in Riga. Her last letter to us was in February 1947. It was addressed to her daughter, Biruta, at "1221/G Camp,

1221/DP Assembly Centre, BAOR, via Great Britain." "When you are all well again," wrote Paulīne, "come home. I miss you very much."

My father died in 1977. He never went home. To the end, he was frightened. In the 1950s we started receiving Soviet publications from Riga urging us to return to our homeland. Who gave them our address? What other lists were we on? For my father the KGB was everywhere. He refused to open, let alone read, the journals from Riga.

Late in 1976 he was boarding a Toronto subway train, heading for the printer's with materials for the next edition of a small religious journal that he edited. His briefcase was weighted down with electrotype plates. The train started abruptly and the bulky briefcase caused him to lose his balance. He fell awkwardly and shattered his leg. He never recovered and died two months later.

"When you are all well again, come home . . ."

Horsemen of Apocalypse

WHERE TO RUN, where to hide? For every ton of bombs the Germans dumped on England, the British and Americans eventually dropped 315 on Germany. But while those bombs from the West caused fear and occasionally outrage, the approach of the Russians provoked absolute dread. "There'll be nothing left but to take poison," said one north German matron.[72] Those in the path of the Russian advance did not, however, take poison; they took to the roads.

In the Soviet advance the horsemen of the apocalypse had been unleashed, to rape, pillage, murder, burn, and rape again. "Follow the words of Comrade Stalin," Soviet propagandists urged, "and crush forever the Fascist beast in its den. Break the racial pride of the German woman. Take her as your legitimate booty. Kill, you brave soldiers of the Victorious Soviet Army."[73] Perhaps as many as two million German along with thousands of refugee women were raped by Russian soldiers, many of them repeatedly.[74] The young were raped, and the old, the lame, and the pregnant. "Why Germanski make my three brother kaputt?" roared the drunken Russian officer.[75]

Aleksandr Solzhenitsyn took part in the Russian invasion of East Prussia in January 1945. The gruesome rampage, gang rape, and death he described in *Prussian Nights*. At Höringstrasse 22, the protagonists include a mother, a daughter, and an entire platoon. The daughter died. The only civility belonged to a clock, which continued to measure time "honorably," though its hands did tremble ever so slightly.[76]

In Silesia a group of Russian officers came across a herd of cattle. "A lieutenant unsheathed a knife, walked up to a cow, and struck her a death-blow at the base of the skull. The cow's legs folded under, and she fell, while the rest of the herd, bellowing madly, stampeded and ran away. The officer wiped the sharp edge on his boots and said: 'My father wrote to me that the Germans had taken a cow from us. Now we are even.'"[77]

As he watched the town of Insterburg in East Prussia burn in January, a Soviet reporter wrote: "There is rarely more uplifting theater than the sight of a burning enemy town. You search your soul for some feeling that might be comparable to pity, but you can't find it . . . Burn, Germany, you've earned nothing less. I cannot and will not forgive you . . . Burn, damned Germany, burn."[78]

When questioned about the rape and looting by Milovan Djilas, Stalin said with irritation: "Can't he understand it if a soldier who has crossed thousands of kilometers through blood and fire and death has fun with a woman or takes some trifle?"[79]

"Enjoy the war," Berliners had remarked wryly in the summer of 1944, "the peace will be awful."

The columns of refugees were endless, most on foot, a lucky few in horse-drawn carts. Women, old folk, and children. Young men were rare. The refugees had come in waves, from Russia, from Lithuania. From January on, East Prussia emptied, then Silesia, Pomerania, and Brandenburg. Freezing, starving people scurried as best they could to escape the scourge from the East, until they could scurry no longer. "They spoke not a word. You heard only the scraping rattling sound of the boxes and cases. And round about endless snow-loneliness, as in the retreat of the Grande Armée 130 years ago."[80] Cold and hunger destroyed many; Soviet T34 tanks crushed others, like papier-mâché dolls, in brazen victory.

Many who reached Berlin, too tired to go on, stayed. For its final battle the capital city was bloated with a forsaken humanity.[81]

Detritus

AMIDST THE DETRITUS OF WAR the homeless refugee was the symbolic centerpiece.[82] In 1945 no one knew for certain how many refugees there were in Europe. A State Department report in June estimated the total number at thirty-three to forty-three million.

The roads of Europe were clogged. *Life* magazine calculated that in the week following V-E Day nine and a half million people were on the move. "Trudging on foot, hitching rides on bicycles, motorcycles, looted German cars, trucks and hay wagons, this stumbling mass of humanity moves steadily on, urged by one fixed idea: to get home."[83] In some cases this desire to get home was a little more complicated than the picture magazine suggested. It certainly was in the case of our family. Writing under her pseudonym Genêt, Janet Flanner would point out in *The New Yorker* some months later that "the displaced persons are willing to go anywhere on earth except home."[84]

The numbers of displaced persons turned out to be far greater than the Allies had anticipated. In fact, the mounting size of the problem in early 1945, as hundreds of thousands of people fled westward, terrified them. In May 1945 the military blew up bridges leading west in order to stanch the tidal wave of fleeing humanity.[85]

If you had to be in Europe in May 1945, Germany was probably the safest place to be. Elsewhere a terrible vengeance was exacted. Partisans dealt with collaborators, Communists rooted out fascists, and the Soviet liberators sought out enemies of the people. The French minister of justice would report in April 1952 that 10,519

Frenchmen had been executed since the liberation, only 846 after legal procedures.[86]

Escape

ON GROUNDS that the northern coastal areas of Germany, the provinces of Mecklenburg and Schleswig-Holstein, were full of refugees needing not merely physical but also spiritual sustenance, my father won permission to leave Berlin. What a victory that was! "Away, away from this Babel in ruins!" he wrote in his diary.

We found our way, again on crowded trains, to Flensburg, in the northernmost part of Schleswig, on the border with Denmark. Everyone seemed to want to get to Schleswig-Holstein, that flat peninsular land that divided the North Sea from the Baltic Sea, whose very protrusive shape suggested escape from the turmoil of the mainland. The German soldier Dieter Wellershof was part of a ragtag group that was supposed to defend the eastern approaches to Berlin against the Russians but decided, as order and purpose broke down, to try and make it through to the Americans or the British. "The general direction is Lübeck, still so far away."[87] The key was to get away from the Russians. As the war ground down in chaos and confusion, rumors circulated that the Americans and the British had joined with the remnants of the German army in the West . . . to fight the Russians. In Lübeck, in the basement of a villa on the Eschenburgstrasse, Heinrich Himmler was discussing with the vice president of the Swedish Red Cross, Count Folke Bernadotte, the favorite idea of the Balts, of the Baltic Germans of yore, of the Freikorps and others: the idea of a separate peace with the West. Neither Himmler nor the ghosts of sundry Balts hovering in that basement room got very far in these negotiations.

On May 1, at 9:30 in the evening, after some solemn excerpts from Wagner and the slow movement of Bruckner's Seventh Symphony, Hitler's death was announced on Radio Hamburg. "Our Führer, Adolf Hitler, has fallen this afternoon at his command post in the Reich Chancellery fighting to the last breath against Bolshevism and for Germany." He had in fact shot himself. His successor,

Admiral Dönitz, then came on the air. "He recognized beforehand," he said of Hitler, "the terrible danger of Bolshevism and devoted his life to fighting it . . . His battle against the Bolshevik flood benefited not only Europe but the whole world." Turning to his own role, Dönitz said: "It is my first task to save the German people from destruction by the Bolsheviks and it is only to achieve this that the fight continues. As long as the British and Americans hamper us from reaching this end we shall fight and defend ourselves against them as well. The British and Americans do not fight for the interests of their own people, but for the spread of Bolshevism." Dönitz's speech was followed by the German national anthem and the "Horst Wessel Lied," and then three minutes of silence.[88] Hitler had of course committed suicide not that afternoon but a day earlier.

In Flensburg the air-raid alarms sounded even more frequently than in Berlin because the city was on the flight path of so many of the Allied bombing raids. But actual attacks on the city had been relatively few, and these had been directed at the docks and at industry. Only twenty-six houses in Flensburg had been destroyed. The population of the city had risen from 68,000 in May 1939 to more than a hundred thousand by the spring of 1945. We were among 34,678 outsiders who had found refuge there. Most of the others were Germans from the East, but 3,800 were Poles and 1,250 were Latvians.[89] We were four of those Latvians.

By the end of April the British had crossed the Elbe. Their approach, while eagerly awaited, was not without danger. The local fanatics erected tank defenses and barbed-wire barricades. On May 2 we spent four hours in a bunker dug into a hillside as the earth shook around us. The next day, however, the Oberkommando of the Wehrmacht declared Flensburg and Kiel to be "open cities" and hence not to be defended.

That declaration may have had something to do with the company we were keeping. We were unaware at the time that we were amidst a raft of nefarious characters and that Flensburg had in effect become the new capital of the German Reich. We were trying to get away from this whole crowd; they insisted on following us everywhere.

Much of the Nazi hierarchy had fled to Schleswig-Holstein at the end of April because it was the last pocket of Germany to remain unoccupied by Allied troops. Admiral Dönitz had been based in Plön but moved on May 3, as the British drew closer, to the naval school at Flensburg-Mürvik, where he had been a student in 1911. Most of his ministers and military commanders followed: Himmler, Speer, Schwerin-Krosigk, Rosenberg, Keitel, Jodl, Schellenberg. We were refugees all, some more desperate than others to get away.

Erich Koch, gauleiter of East Prussia and at one time Reich commissar for the Ukraine and then, after Lohse's dismissal, for the Ostland, had also arrived. He had forbidden residents of East Prussia, upon pain of death, to flee the Russians. He, brave fellow, now wanted to catch a submarine to South America. Lohse, his predecessor in the Ostland, was also in Flensburg with the same demand. Alfred Rosenberg was at the naval school in Mürwik. One day he was found barely conscious. The immediate assumption was that he had tried to commit suicide. It turned out that he was merely drunk.

Himmler went into hiding without his mustache, wearing, like Captain Hook, a black patch over one eye and calling himself Hitzinger. He survived for three weeks, until the British Second Army found him in Bremervörde, a town between Hamburg and Bremerhaven, and told him to stop being so silly. During interrogation he bit on a cyanide capsule and in fifteen minutes was dead. Himmler's intimate, SS Gruppenführer Karl Gebhardt, exchanged his SS uniform for a Red Cross outfit in his attempt to get away. The fury ended, as always, in farce.

On May 5 the British arrived in Flensburg. On the seventh the Germans capitulated. On the ninth all firing ceased. What days those were! Flensburg was the last provisional capital of the Reich but also the city from which the German surrender was announced. In his brief diary entry for May 9, my father, obviously overcome by fatigue and emotion, was reduced to an inarticulate exclamatory recitation. He wrote the word "Peace!" over and over again.[90]

In his radio broadcast, at 3 P.M. on May 8, Winston Churchill said: "We may allow ourselves a brief period of rejoicing; but let us not forget for a moment the toil and efforts that lie ahead. Japan, with all her treachery and greed, remains unsubdued. The injury she has inflicted on Great Britain, the United States, and other countries, and her detestable cruelties, call for justice and retribution. We must now devote all our strength and resources to the completion of our task, both at home and abroad. Advance, Britannia! Long live the cause of freedom! God save the King."[91]

Édouard Herriot, the veteran French politician, had been interned by the Germans since 1942 and liberated by the Soviets a few days before V-E Day. He heard Churchill's speech in Moscow. "You will understand if I weep today," he said to Churchill's wife, Clementine, who was also in the Soviet capital, "I do not feel unmanned."[92]

On May 1, Mathilde Wolff-Mönckeberg had written in her diary: "When one recalls Hitler's flaming victory speeches, his prophecies and inflated promises that all would be well in the end, one can only regard our present situation as the quintessence of irony in the whole history of the world . . . We will never get over this bloody calvary. We have grown old and weary to death. One sits and searches one's brain for an explanation . . . What was the point of it all, what rhyme or reason was there for this desperate, ruinous destruction? Was it just a satanic game?"[93]

Hour Zero

IN 1933–34, after Hitler's advent to power, the artist Werner Heldt had done a charcoal drawing of a huge crowd in Berlin. The sea of heads in the drawing consisted of thousands of small, painstakingly drawn zeros. In 1945 the hour of those zeros, their summation, had arrived. Kazimir Malevich's *Black Square* had also come into its heritage. The Russian artist had first hung his canvas, consisting of a black square centered orthogonally on a white square, thirty years earlier in Petrograd, in the middle of the Great War. He had called his work *Zero*.

"Surviving, finding something to eat and drink, was less difficult for me," said a former Nazi, Anna Hummel, "than the psychological emptiness. It was incomprehensible that all this was supposed to be over, and that it had all been for nothing."[94] Nothing. The defeat in the form of an unconditional surrender, the occupation and partition of the country by the former enemy — against a backdrop of utter devastation — came to be called *Stunde Null*.

Hour zero? The end? At the time, life of course went on despite the horrors and privation. No one had a proper overview of the disaster that had befallen Europe, not the statesmen, let alone the dazed survivors wandering the byways of the continent. Despite briefings and mental preparation, everyone who visited Europe from outside in 1945 was astounded. No one was prepared for the magnitude of destruction.

Germans reached into their cultural knapsacks and drew out whatever they could use to sustain themselves. Certain values were so deeply ingrained that even the agonies of war could not extirpate them. One soldiered on, in a manner of speaking, regardless. Historians would, as a result, subsequently question the notion of a *Stunde Null* and prefer to emphasize the idea of continuity rather than disruption.

Economic recovery and the emergence of political stability in postwar Europe would erode the concept of *Stunde Null* as a time beyond convention, beyond understanding, indeed beyond the realm of history and enlightenment. Intellectual bridges would be built over the chasm and connections reestablished. But despite the bridges, the chasm remains. "Even if surrounded with explanations," Günter Grass has written, "Auschwitz can never be grasped."[95] The same is true of the murderous military strategies of the two world wars, of Stalin's homicidal policies, and of the firebombing of civilians in undefended cities. Nineteen forty-five marked the nadir of Western civilization.

The Allies tried to make the atrocities against the Jews known to Germans. They forced locals to visit the death camps; they distributed the documentary film *Die Todesmühlen* (The Death Mills) widely. But even then, proportionately few Germans were forced to confront, through personal experience or Allied reeducation efforts, the reality of the Third Reich's vicious onslaught on civilization. The extermination camps had been located for the most part outside Germany; the horrors of the Einsatzgruppen took place beyond

Germany's borders; of the Jews murdered by the Nazis only a small
percentage were German, the vast majority Polish and Russian. Jews
had never constituted more than 1 percent of Germany's population;
they were concentrated in the big cities, Berlin, Frankfurt, and Hamburg. To most Germans the Jew was a myth, not a reality.

By contrast, most Germans did encounter Allied atrocity, in the
form of impersonal bombs raining down from the sky. German
cities were flattened. Millions of Germans encountered Soviet brutality during the advance of the Red Army. Some twelve to fifteen
million Germans were expelled from Central and Eastern Europe;
perhaps two million of them did not survive.[96] This for Germans was
tangible, palpable horror.

When the war was over, the mood in Germany was an indefinable
mixture of confusion, fear, and anger, but not guilt, certainly not
collective guilt. The attempt by the Western Allies to force repen-
tance on the Germans evoked much cynicism and mockery. The
Allies had no moral authority to "reeducate" others. Lübeck's most
famous son, Thomas Mann, who had gone into exile in 1933, said
that the Germans even felt a kind of pride that the greatest tragedy
in world history was their tragedy.[97] A British intelligence report
remarked that the Germans "tend to glory in the distinction of
being misunderstood, and maintain that it is not the Germans who
are to blame but the rest of the world for driving Germany towards
nationalist feelings."[98] Of her husband, Emil Wolff, a professor of
English and now the newly elected pro-rector of the University of
Hamburg, Mathilde Wolff-Mönckeberg wrote in mid-May 1945:
"W. is deeply depressed . . . He was so passionately devoted to Great
Britain and all it stood for. Now he is disillusioned by the limitless
arrogance and the dishonesty with which they treat us, proclaiming
to the whole world that only Germany could have sunk so low in
such abysmal cruelty and bestiality, that they themselves are pure
and beyond reproach." She shared his anger. "And *who* destroyed
our beautiful cities, regardless of human life, of women, children,
and old people?" she asked in rhetorical rage. "*Who* poured down
poisonous phosphorus during the terror raids on unfortunate fugi-
tives, driving them like living torches into the rivers? *Who* dive-

bombed harmless peasants, women and children, in low-level attacks, and machine-gunned the defenceless population? *Who* was it, I ask you? We are all the same, all equally guilty."[99]

The very house in Potsdam, at Kaiserstrasse 2, in which Truman and Churchill made the decision, on July 24, to drop an atomic bomb on Japan had witnessed only weeks earlier the gang rape by Soviet soldiers of the daughters of the German publisher Gustav Müller-Grote.[100]

Moreover, as awful as the war had been, it could have been worse. The weapons of war in Europe had been gruesome, especially the impersonal bombs and rockets from the air. Those weapons could, however, have been even more deadly. During the summer of 1944, when it seemed for a time that the Normandy invasion had stalled, and when London was being subjected to a steady dose of V-1 rocket attacks, Churchill and his advisers did give thought to gas and bacteriological warfare. But they backed off for the moment.[101] A year later, after the fighting had stopped in Europe, the Americans, who in relative terms had had a light war, did not twitch as they dropped their new atomic bombs on Japan. Had these been available earlier, would they not have been used on Germany? Many Germans were convinced they would have. Guilt? Morality? In a Central and Eastern European context these were far more complex issues than the victorious Anglo-American Allies seemed able in the spring of 1945 to imagine.

A creed of destruction — a normalization of horror — had evolved, especially among soldiers but within the political leadership as well. You destroyed so as not to be hurt yourself. The church steeple had to be shattered; it might house a sniper. The haystack deserved a tracer; it might be hiding a treacherous enemy. Shoot first so as not to be sorry afterward. Bomb first before the kids grow up to bomb you.[102] The Cold War began in earnest at this point too.[103] Once the Americans had the Bomb, they could disregard their Soviet ally — in contrast with Roosevelt's wooing of Stalin as long as an invasion of Japan was thought necessary. Now the natural distrust and rivalry that were inherent in any relationship between capitalism and communism could blossom. In this moral swamp the

Allied decisions to try the German leaders for crimes against humanity and to reeducate and hence supposedly to civilize the Germans elicited scorn in many quarters.

In the aftermath of the First World War the Germans could not stop talking, complaining, and denying defeat. After the Second World War they did not talk, least of all about the defeat. After a visit to Germany in early 1947 a British Conservative member of parliament remarked on the spiritual vacuum in the land.[104]

Solly Zuckerman, Churchill's scientific adviser, was humbled by his experience of the destruction. After a visit to Aachen in early 1945 he dined with Cyril Connolly in London and promised to write an essay entitled "The Natural History of Destruction" for Connolly's journal *Horizon*. "It was never finished," Zuckerman commented later. "My first view of Cologne, and particularly of the cathedral, cried out for a more eloquent piece than I could ever have written."[105]

Of course life went on in 1945; of course there were elements of continuity and of new beginnings. But none of this could overcome the fissure that had been the great civil war of Western civilization.

Liberations

LIBERATION BY THE ALLIED ARMIES was full of ironies, a few of them sweet, most of them bitter. As an adolescent of fifteen, the Czech Ota Filip was liberated thrice in Prague in May 1945. The first liberation came at the hands of the *Hausmeister* of his apartment building, who, on the morning of May 5, as the Czech uprising against the withdrawing Germans was beginning, decided he would free his building of Germans.

A German woman doctor lived on the third floor. Her husband had been killed on the western front in March; in April she had given birth to a baby boy. Dressed in an Afrika Korps uniform looted from the Germans, weapon in hand, the crazed caretaker stormed up the stairs to the third floor. A brief altercation followed; then a small bundle, the baby, went flying past Filip down the stairwell. The soft thud in the darkness below was followed by one shot. The building had been liberated.

The second liberation came three days later, in the dawn hours of May 8, when Prague was occupied by the Vlasov army, an army led by a general who had been Stalin's favorite in 1941 but who had surrendered to the Germans at Leningrad; then, aware of his fate should the Russians win the war, he had turned against his comrades and fought alongside the Wehrmacht, until the approach of the Americans, when once again Vlasov changed sides. It was this army of traitors that liberated Filip early on May 8.

Finally, on May 9 Filip was liberated a third time in the space of four days, this time by tank divisions of the Red Army, who would occupy Czechoslovakia for the next forty-four years. "If therefore I think back on May 8th, 1945, I feel cheated by history. I was denied the genuine liberation to which a fifteen-year-old, on the threshold of life and peace in May 1945, had a right."[106]

Waste Land

ON VISITING COLOGNE after the devastating air raid of May 31, 1942, the former mayor of the city, Konrad Adenauer, remarked: "Just think, I did not even recognize it, and I had trouble finding my way about — and Cologne was my life's work."[107]

All German cities were similar. James Stern had been in Frankfurt before the war. He returned to that city at the junction of the Rhine and Main rivers when the war was over but, seeing nothing as it had once been, could not convince himself that he had actually ever been there before.[108] Munich in turn evoked for Stern only visions of refuse: "Munich's ruins in pouring rain looked like a million overturned garbage carts multiplied in size many times. The creatures crawling over the acres of filth were the shining rats emerging to gorge themselves on the decomposing graveyard when the last man on earth had been buried alive."[109] Graves, decomposition, rats, garbage.

General Lucius Clay, Eisenhower's deputy in Germany, called

Berlin "a city of the dead."[110] William S. Rogers, a young Canadian UNRRA supply officer, evoked a similar image: the German cities were "lifeless, as lacking in individuality and as devoid of their former beauty as a row of skulls."[111] "My exultation in victory was diminished as I witnessed this degradation of man," wrote Clay.

Between 1943 and 1945 the Allies had stepped up the air war with relentless determination. Their air forces dropped about 1.25 million tons of bombs on German soil. All told, about 600,000 civilians were killed and 780,000 injured. Some 3.6 million houses were damaged or destroyed, leaving 7.5 million people homeless. In Berlin alone, about 50,000 people were killed, and by the end of the war some 612,000 houses in the German capital had been destroyed. The worst damage was in the center of the city. *Bezirk Mitte* came to be known as "the Waste Land."[112]

Destruction was so pervasive that the normal seemed perverse. When Heinrich Böll saw his first undestroyed city, Heidelberg, he broke into a cold sweat. "In a dual sense, esthetically and morally, it seemed to me improper, a particularly deplorable form of disaster for the city to have escaped disaster in this way."[113]

Numbers

SOME 140,000 LATVIANS had fought with the Germans, some 65,000 with the Russians.

Among the last defenders of Hitler's Reich Chancellery and Himmler's State Security Headquarters in Berlin were eighty Latvian soldiers, from the Fifteenth Battalion of the Fifteenth Waffen-SS Division. The last commander of this battalion, Lieutenant Neilands, would act as interpreter for the talks on German surrender between the commander of Berlin, General Krebs, and the Soviets. Yet another Latvian, the Soviet Colonel Nikolajs Bērzzariņš, would become the first commander of Russian-occupied Berlin.

Russian deaths in the Great Patriotic War are now thought to have exceeded 27 million.

The Germans lost 3.8 million soldiers killed, most on the eastern front. Probably an equal number of civilians died. Another 3 million soldiers were captured by the Russians, and of these about 1 million did not survive.

British losses on all fronts amounted to 388,000. American to 295,000. Canadian to 41,700.

The number of human beings who died in this conflict was staggering enough, but something else was gravely wounded: the entire Enlightenment tradition. It could not, contrary to some assertions, emerge from the war strengthened. As T. S. Eliot put it, Germany and Japan, "these two aggressive nations, . . . did but bring to a head a malady with which the world was already infected; and their collapse only leaves the world with the disease in every part of its body."[114]

Babel

COLLABORATORS, resistance fighters, SS soldiers, Jews, peasants, professors, prostitutes, children, paupers, bankers, criminals, clergymen. Every nationality, age, social class, type. They were all present amidst the devastation.

They headed in every direction. Frightened, dirty, bewildered. Carrying, pushing, stumbling, hobbling, pleading. Air Marshal Tedder had always insisted that disrupting transportation and communications would be the key to the Allied bombing offensive.[115] That spring, in 1945, he could say that his success was there for all to see.

As a boy, I once poured kerosene on an anthill and lit a match. That, too, disrupted traffic.

For regret and tears there was no time, no point.

Someone once said that war poetry is the love poetry of our age. The girl with the flaxen hair would surely agree.

Acknowledgments

While writing this book I have benefited from much kindness. First and foremost I must thank the Social Sciences and Humanities Research Council of Canada for its generous assistance, without which the archival research essential to this project could not have been accomplished. The Connaught Fund of the University of Toronto also awarded me a fellowship at a crucial stage when I needed time to think things through. The direction of the project changed dramatically as a result.

My family's story is based in large part on interviews with relatives and friends of the family, on the war diaries of my father and mother, and on my own memory. Some of my sources have requested anonymity. My cousin Juris Ukstiņš helped in genealogical matters. My mother, Biruta Ekšteins, née Vajeiks, I have showered with questions over the years; she has tried gallantly to answer them all. My sister, Mudīte, joined me in a memorable exploration of Latvia in 1993 and has consistently provided sustenance of every sort.

In Latvia, Ralfs and Rute Tannenbergs, Hardijs Rozenbergs, Pāvils and Ineta Pallo, and Jānis Tervīts gave guidance. Among my fellow historians, I have derived much from the eminently sensible work and patient advice of Andrejs Plakans, who suggested some of my Latvian research and then read the manuscript, and from the extraordinary compilatory diligence of the late Edgars Andersons. William Dick saved me, yet again, from a number of pratfalls; Piotr Wróbel gave me some tips; and the work and suggestions of Dominic Lieven, whose family figures prominently in this story, were most helpful.

Wilhelm Lenz guided me through appropriate materials in the Bundesarchiv in Koblenz, and Hans-Heinrich Fleischer pointed me in the right direction in the military archives in Freiburg. Anne Summers did the same in the Department of Manuscripts of the British Library. The directors and staff of the Public Record Office in London, the Archives de l'Occupation Française en Allemagne et en Autriche in Colmar, the Landesarchiv Schleswig-Holstein in Schleswig, the Stadtbibliothek in Lübeck, the archive of the Nordelbische Evangelisch-Lutherische Kirche in Lübeck, the Archiv des Diakonischen Werkes der Evangelischen Kirche Deutschlands in Berlin, and the Diakonissenhaus Bethel in Berlin were gracious and forthcoming in response to my requests, as were Hans-Friedrich Schütt, of the Flensburg city archive, and Valda Pētersone and Valda Kvaskova at the Latvian State Historical Archive in Riga.

William S. Rogers shared with me his experience as a displaced persons officer in UNRRA. Vid Ingelevics lent me documentary materials about the DP camps. His own attempt, as photographer and artist, to grapple with the problems of history, art, and memory stimulated me greatly. Douglas LePan evoked unusual ideas and connections in the course of several delightful conversations. Gaston Lacombe did some digging for me in Riga. Barbara Moon, Peter Fritzsche, Barbara Gover, Tom Mohr, and, as always, John and Valerie Bynner helped in important ways.

Paul Thompson and John Warden, my colleagues at the University of Toronto at Scarborough, gave administrative and moral support. Ken Jones helped with the photographs. Countless students, both undergraduate and graduate, have stimulated me with ideas and provocation.

Portions of this book have appeared in different guise in *Saturday Night, Maclean's, Queen's Quarterly, Border Crossings,* and *The Globe and Mail.* My hosts for a variety of lectures in recent years will also recognize some of the ideas herein. For their invitations and repartee I thank the Liberal Arts College of Concordia University, the Faculty of Humanities at Brock University, the Institute for the Humanities and the Koerner Foundation at Simon Fraser University, Green College at the University of British Columbia, the Legacies Project in Vancouver, the Vancouver Public Library, both the University and the Stichting Literaire Activiteiten of Amsterdam, the Durham Region Secondary School History Teachers, the Universidade Federal de Minas Gerais in Belo Horizonte, and the Fundação Casa de Rui Barbosa in Rio de Janeiro.

Most of the photographs come from the family album. In a few cases, where provenance is external to the family, I have been unable either to derive the original source or to establish ownership of rights.

Jayne, companion, wife, and mother, has contributed to this book more than she might modestly accept; she has often, as if by magic, conjured up calm where before there was only storm. Beverley Slopen, critic and friend, has been all one could want of an agent. At Houghton Mifflin, Peter Davison has, once again, provided inspiration and wisdom, and John Radziewicz good counsel. Before Larry Cooper, my manuscript editor, I can only grovel.

Despite all my doubts about causality and continuity in history, I know that I am my father's son. My children, whether they like it or not, are my offspring. To them this book, about great travail and equally great hope, is dedicated. With love.

Toronto, January 1999

Concordance of Place Names

Aa	Lielupe	Lieliecava	Gross-Eckau
Arensburg	Kuresaare	Lielupe	Aa
Bauska	Bauske	Liepāja	Libau
Bauske	Bauska	Memel	Klaipeda
Cēsis	Wenden	Mesothen	Mežotne
Code	Zohden	Mežotne	Mesothen
Dagö	Hiiumaa	Mitau	Jelgava
Danzig	Gdansk	Ösel	Saaremaa
Daugava	Düna, Dvina	Reval	Tallinn
Daugavgrīva	Dünamünde	Rēzekne	Rositten
Daugavpils	Dünaburg	Rositten	Rēzekne
Dobele	Doblen	Saaremaa	Ösel
Doblen	Dobele	Schaulen	Šiauliai
Dorpat	Tartu	Šiauliai	Schaulen
Düna	Daugava, Dvina	Stalgen	Stalģene
Dünaburg	Daugavpils	Stalģene	Stalgen
Dünamünde	Daugavgrīva	Stettin	Szczecin
Dvina	Daugava, Düna	Szczecin	Stettin
Eckau	Iecava	Tallinn	Reval
Elley	Lielelēja	Tartu	Dorpat
Garossen	Garoze	Tetele	Tetelmünde
Garoze	Garossen	Tetelmünde	Tetele
Gdansk	Danzig	Treiden	Turaida
Gross-Eckau	Lieliecava	Tuckum	Tukums
Haapsalu	Hapsal	Tukums	Tuckum
Hapsal	Haapsalu	Turaida	Treiden
Hiiumaa	Dagö	Üxküll	Ikšķile
Iecava	Eckau	Valka	Walk
Ikšķile	Üxküll	Valmiera	Wolmar
Jelgava	Mitau	Ventspils	Windau
Klaipeda	Memel	Walk	Valka
Kreuzburg	Krustpils	Wenden	Cēsis
Krustpils	Kreuzburg	Windau	Ventspils
Kuresaare	Arensburg	Wolmar	Valmiera
Libau	Liepāja	Zohden	Code
Lielelēja	Elley		

Notes

ABBREVIATIONS

ADW   Archiv des Diakonischen Werkes, Berlin
AOF   Archives de l'Occupation Française en Allemagne et en
         Autriche, Colmar
AOK   Armee Oberkommando
BAK   Bundesarchiv Koblenz
BAM   Bundesarchiv-Militärarchiv, Freiburg im Breisgau
FO   Foreign Office
IRO   International Refugee Organization
LE   *Latvju Enciklopēdija*
LFP   *Lübecker Freie Presse*
LN   *Lübecker Nachrichten*
LVVA   Latvijas Valsts Vēstures Arhīvs, Riga
OMGUS   Office of Military Government, United States
PRO   Public Record Office, London
RKO   Reichskommissariat Ostland
UNRRA   United Nations Relief and Rehabilitation Administration

PROLOGUE

1. In Ron Rosenbaum, "Explaining Hitler," *The New Yorker*, May 1, 1995, 66.
2. From Ruth Evans's epilogue to her mother's diary, Mathilde Wolff-Mönckeberg, *On the Other Side. To My Children: From Germany, 1940–1945*, trans. and ed. Ruth Evans (New York: Mayflower Books, 1979), 161, 163.
3. Diary letter, April 26, 1945, Wolff-Mönckeberg, *On the Other Side*, 116.
4. Charlotte Delbo, *Auschwitz and After*, trans. Rosette C. Lamont (New Haven: Yale University Press, 1995), 239.
5. Theodor Adorno, *Minima Moralia: Reflections from Damaged Life*, trans. E. F. N. Jephcott (London: Verso, 1978), 143.
6. Richard Rodriguez, *Days of Obligation: An Argument with My Mexican Father* (New York: Viking, 1992), 2.

1. THE GIRL WITH THE FLAXEN HAIR

1. Marijas Gimbutas, *The Balts* (London: Thames and Hudson, 1963); and Andrejs Plakans, *The Latvians: A Short History* (Stanford: Hoover Institution Press, 1995).

2. Arnolds Spekke, *The Ancient Amber Routes and the Geographical Discovery of the Eastern Baltic* (Stockholm: M. Goppers, 1957), 3–5, 40.

3. William Urban, *The Baltic Crusade* (DeKalb, Ill.: Northern Illinois University Press, 1975).

4. Wolfgang Wippermann, *Der "Deutsche Drang nach Osten": Ideologie und Wirklichkeit eines politischen Schlagwortes* (Darmstadt: Wissenschaftliche Buchgesellschaft, 1981).

5. Heinrich von Treitschke, quoted by Hermann Schreiber, *Teuton and Slav: The Struggle for Central Europe,* trans. James Cleugh (New York: Alfred A. Knopf, 1965), 86.

6. [Elizabeth Rigby], *Letters from the Shores of the Baltic,* 2nd ed. (London: John Murray, 1842), I, 199–200. Elizabeth Rigby (1809–1893) became Lady Eastlake when in 1849 she married Sir Charles Eastlake, the painter and president of the Royal Academy.

7. *The Chronicle of Henry of Livonia,* trans. and ed. James A. Brundage (Madison: University of Wisconsin Press, 1961), 241. To translate Heinrich von Lettland as Henry of Livonia only leads to confusion. Heinrich, born around 1188, probably came from Lower Germany. See Norbert Angermann, "Die mittelalterliche Chronistik," in Georg von Rauch, ed., *Geschichte der deutsch-baltischen Geschichtsschreibung* (Cologne: Böhlau Verlag, 1986), 6.

8. J. G. Herder, "Ideen zur Philosophie der Geschichte der Menschheit," in *Herders Werke in fünf Bänden,* ed. Regine Otto, vol. IV (Berlin: Aufbau-Verlag, 1978), 394–95.

9. In Bernd Nielsen-Stokkeby, *Baltische Erinnerungen* (Bergisch Gladbach: Lübbe, 1990), 47.

10. In G. P. Gooch, *History and Historians in the Nineteenth Century* (London: Longmans, 1913), 302.

11. Michel Serres, "L'univers et le lieu," in *L'Arc* 72 (Aix-en-Provence, n.d.), 65.

12. Peter Novick, *That Noble Dream: The "Objectivity Question" and the American Historical Profession* (Cambridge: Cambridge University Press, 1988); Jacques Revel and Lynn Hunt, eds., *Histories: French Reconstructions of the Past,* trans. Arthur Goldhammer and others (New York: New Press, 1995).

13. Pierre Nora et al., *Les lieux de mémoire,* vol. I (Paris: Gallimard, 1984), xix.

14. Ernst Troeltsch, "Über die Massstäbe zur Beurteilung historischer Dinge," *Historische Zeitschrift* 116 (1916), 1–47, esp. 46. In the few years remaining to him, Troeltsch went on to develop his ideas on historical relativism. See, above all, *Der Historismus und seine Probleme* (Tübingen: Mohr, 1922).

15. Martin Heidegger, "The Word of Nietzsche," in *The Question Concerning Technology and Other Essays* (New York: Garland, 1977), 62–3.

16. Jacob Burckhardt, *Historische Fragmente,* in *Gesamtausgabe,* ed. Albert Oeri and Emil Dürr (Stuttgart: Deutsche Verlags-Anstalt, 1929), VII, 227.

17. [Rigby], *Letters,* II, 140–41; also Hubertus Neuschäffer, *Katharina II. und*

die baltischen Provinzen (Hannover-Döhren: Verlag Harro v. Hirschheydt, n.d.).

18. Gustav Keuchel, in Anders Henriksson, *The Tsar's Loyal Germans. The Riga German Community: Social Change and the Nationality Question, 1855–1905* (Boulder, Colo.: East European Monographs, 1983), 16; also Margarethe Lindemuth, "Krišjānis Valdemārs und Atis Kronvalds, zwei lettische Volkstumskämpfer," *Baltische Hefte* 13 (1967), 89.

19. [Rigby], *Letters*, II, 181–82.

20. Dominic C. B. Lieven, *The Aristocracy in Europe, 1815–1914* (London: Macmillan, 1992), 49–50.

21. "On Being Canadian, Forever," *The Globe and Mail*, July 1, 1997, A10.

22. In Priestley's introduction to *The Bodley Head Leacock* (London: Bodley Head, 1957), 10.

23. Richard Gwyn, *Nationalism Without Walls: The Unbearable Lightness of Being Canadian* (Toronto: McClelland and Stewart, 1995), 243–48.

24. In ibid., 248.

25. Dieter Hassenplug, "A Little House in a Theme Park," *Shift*, September 1997, 24.

26. Lewis Namier, "Princess Lieven," *Vanished Supremacies* (London: Hamish Hamilton, 1958), 17–20.

27. In Harold W. V. Temperley, ed., *The Unpublished Diary and Political Sketches of Princess Lieven Together with Some of Her Letters* (London: Jonathan Cape, 1925), 40–41.

28. In H. Montgomery Hyde, *Princess Lieven* (London: Harrap, 1938), 275.

29. Letter, May 8, 1839, Dorothea Princess von Lieven, *The Lieven–Palmerston Correspondence, 1828–1856*, trans. and ed. Lord Sudley (London: John Murray, 1943), 188.

30. *The Private Letters of Princess Lieven to Prince Metternich, 1820–1826*, ed. Peter Quennell (London: John Murray, 1937), 344.

31. See the father's letter to Constantine, May 3/15, 1829, in which he denounces his son's "dépravation" and "conduite désordonée." Lieven Papers, vol. 47408, British Library. The father sought assistance from many friends, the Pahlens and the Benckendorffs among them, to get Constantine back on course. See the correspondence in vol. 47411.

32. R. Staël von Holstein, *Fürst Paul Lieven als Landmarschall von Livland* (Riga: Häcker, 1906), 2.

33. Ibid., 247–49.

34. In ibid., 266–67.

35. In Temperley, ed., *Lieven*, 197.

36. Letter, March 19/31, 1835, Princess Lieven, *Lieven–Palmerston Correspondence*, 80.

37. Edward C. Thaden, "The Russian Government," in Edward C. Thaden, ed., *Russification in the Baltic Provinces and Finland, 1855–1914* (Princeton: Princeton University Press, 1981), 43–44.

38. See Robert Sloan Latimer, *Dr. Baedeker and His Apostolic Work in Russia* (London: Morgan & Scott, 1908), 77–80. Princess Lieven contributed an introduction to this volume.

39. In Edmund Heier, *Religious Schism in the Russian Aristocracy, 1860–1900: Radstockism and Pashkovism* (The Hague: Martinus Nijhoff, 1970), 52. The more recent work by David Fountain, *Lord Radstock and the Russian Awakening* (Southampton: Mayflower Christian Books, 1988), adds a few details to the English background of the story.

40. Lieven, *Aristocracy*, 150. On the conversion of some of the Lievens to a Radstockist evangelicalism, see Dominic C. B. Lieven, *Russia's Rulers under the Old Regime* (New Haven: Yale University Press, 1989), 145.

41. LVVA 630 f., 1 apr., 808 i., 478 lp., Latvian National Archive, Riga.

42. In Madeleine Bingham, *Princess Lieven: Russian Intriguer* (London: Hamish Hamilton, 1982), 2.

43. Peggie Benton, *Baltic Countdown* (London: Centaur, 1984), 33.

44. [Rigby], *Letters*, I, 142.

45. In Gerhard Bauer, "Gesellschaft und Weltbild im baltischen Traditionsmilieu. Eine soziologisch-volkskundliche Untersuchung über die Gesellschaft und Mythologie bei den baltischen Völkern, dargestellt anhand historischer und volkskundlicher Quellen," doctoral diss., Heidelberg, 1972.

46. Andrievs Niedra, cited in Stanley W. Page, *The Formation of the Baltic States* (Cambridge, Mass.: Harvard University Press, 1959), 19.

47. In Astrida B. Stahnke, *Aspazija: Her Life and Her Drama* (New York: University Press of America, 1984), 90.

48. G. Reinbeck, *Travels from St. Petersburg*, trans. (London, 1807), in Bingham, *Princess Lieven*, 7.

49. *Memoirs of Catherine the Great*, trans. Katharine Anthony (New York: Tudor, 1935), 41.

50. For a lady of the nobility to indulge in such antics was unacceptable, unless she was the empress of Russia. Fräulein von Tiesenhausen was drowned, along with her lover, because he was middle-class scum! Hermann Schreiber, *Teuton and Slav: The Struggle for Central Europe*, trans. James Cleugh (New York: Alfred A. Knopf, 1965), 113.

51. Robert Cullen, *Twilight of Empire: Inside the Crumbling Soviet Bloc* (New York: Atlantic Monthly Press, 1991), 132. See also the important account by Anatol Lieven, *The Baltic Revolution: Estonia, Latvia, Lithuania and the Path to Independence* (New Haven: Yale University Press, 1993).

52. Juris Dreifelds, *Latvia in Transition* (Cambridge: Cambridge University Press, 1996), 2.

53. Eduard von Keyserling, *Bunte Herzen* (1909; Berlin: S. Fischer, 1937), 133.

54. Constantin Mettig, *Baltische Städte* (Riga: Jonck, 1905), 250.

2. A MAN, A CART, A COUNTRY

1. *Latvju Enciklopēdija* (hereafter *LE*), ed. Arveds Švābe, 3 vols. (Stockholm: Apgāds Trīs Zvaigznes, 1950–51), I, 826, grudgingly acknowledges the positive German role in education.

2. In Hermann Schreiber, *Teuton and Slav: The Struggle for Central Europe*, trans. James Cleugh (New York: Alfred A. Knopf, 1965), 92.

3. Arveds Švābe, *Latvijas vēsture, 1800–1914* (Uppsala: Daugava, 1958), 16.

4. *Time,* February 1, 1993, 32.

5. Edgar Anderson, "Die ersten kurländischen Expeditionen nach Westindien im 17. Jahrhundert," and the two-part "Die kurländische Kolonie Tobago," all in *Baltische Hefte* 8 (1961), 13–35, 129–55, 216–32; also "Tobāgo," *LE,* III, 2499–2501.

6. Ernest Daudet, "Les Bourbons et la Russie pendant l'émigration," *Revue des Deux Mondes* t.71 (October 1 and 15, 1885), 526–60, 790–823; Josi von Koskull, "Der König von Mitau," *Baltische Hefte* 17 (1971), 7–132.

7. Constantín Mettig, *Baltische Städte* (Riga: Jonck, 1905), 323; Kārlis Kangeris, "Napoleona kaŗaspēks Latvijā," *Archivs* 25 (1985), 67–88.

8. Wilhelm Schlau, "Die Kurländische Gesellschaft für Literatur und Kunst und das Kurländische Provinzialmuseum zu Mitau," *Baltische Hefte* 14 (1968), 5–107.

9. Edgars Andersons, ed., *Cross Road Country Latvia* (Waverly, Iowa: Latvju Grāmata, 1953), 130.

10. Andrejs Plakans, "Peasants, Intellectuals, and Nationalism in the Russian Baltic Provinces, 1820–1890," *Journal of Modern History* 46 (1974), 466.

11. Konrad Adenauer, *Erinnerungen, 1945–1953* (Frankfurt: Fischer, 1967), 9.

12. Astrida B. Stahnke, *Aspazija: Her Life and Her Drama* (New York: University Press of America, 1984), 90.

13. Henry W. Nevinson, *More Changes, More Chances* (London: Nisbet, 1925), 154. The parson was August Bielenstein, who, ironically, a year earlier had published a memoir entitled *Ein glückliches Leben* (A Happy Life).

14. Arnolds Spekke, *History of Latvia: An Outline* (Stockholm: M. Goppers, 1957), 313–14; Ernst Benz, "Die Revolution von 1905 in Estland, Livland und Kurland (1)," *Acta Baltica* 28 (1991), 19–167. A hardline Baltic-German view of the events of 1905 can be found in the memoirs of Baron Adolf Pilar von Pilchau, "Die Memoiren des livländischen Landmarschalls Baron Adolf Pilar v. Pilchau: Bilder aus meinem Leben als Landwirt, Verwaltungsbeamter und Politiker von 1875 bis 1920," *Baltische Hefte* 15 (1969), 5–60.

15. Nevinson, *More Changes,* 152.

16. Walter Duranty, *'I Write as I Please'* (London: Hamish Hamilton, 1935), 64–65.

17. The German viewpoint on these relations is given in an interesting discussion by Hamilkar von Foelkersahm, "Baltischer Adel und lettische und estnische Landbevölkerung in ihren gegenseitigen Beziehungen," *Baltische Hefte* 11 (1965), 3–35.

18. Lewis Namier, *Germany and Eastern Europe* (London: Duckworth, 1915), 13.

19. Edgars Dunsdorfs, *Mūžīgais latviešu kaŗavīrs* (Melbourne, Australia: Goppera Fonds, 1966), 193–208.

20. Edgars Andersons, *Latvijas vēsture, 1914–1920* (Stockholm: Daugava, 1967). See chapter 3 for an extensive treatment of the evacuation and refugee issue.

21. A colorful memoir describing the plight of the Kurland refugees from the area of Mitau and Bauska is Kristaps Bachmanis, *Latvju tauta bēgļu gaitās* (Riga: Saule, 1925).

22. Jānis Freijs, in Jānis Kronlins, *Gaišā ceļā* (New York: ALBA, 1964), 134.

23. Karl-Heinz Janssen, "Die baltische Okkupationspolitik des Deutschen

Reiches," in Jürgen von Hehn et al., eds., *Von den baltischen Provinzen zu den baltischen Staaten* (Marburg/Lahn: J. G. Herder-Institut, 1971), 224, 231.

24. Ibid., 229.

25. "Jelgava," in *LE*, I, 881.

26. Johannes V. Bredt, *Erinnerungen und Dokumente von Joh. Victor Bredt, 1914 bis 1933*, ed. Martin Schumacher (Düsseldorf: Droste Verlag, 1970), 128.

27. Ibid., 139.

28. David Footman, *Antonin Besse of Aden* (London: Macmillan, 1986).

29. Andrew Ezergailis, "The Causes of the Bolshevik Revolution in Latvia 1917," in Andrew Ezergailis and Gert von Pistohlkors, eds., *Die baltischen Provinzen Russlands zwischen den Revolutionen von 1905 und 1917* (Cologne and Vienna: Böhlau, 1982), 279; Uldis Ģērmanis, "The Rise and Fall of the Latvian Bolsheviks," *Baltic Forum* 5/1 (1988), 3–4; also Ezergailis, *The 1917 Revolution in Latvia* (Boulder, Colo.: East European Monographs, 1974), and *The Latvian Impact on the Bolshevik Revolution* (Boulder, Colo.: East European Monographs, 1983).

30. See the 1982 film on the Latvian Red Riflemen, *Strēlnieku zvaigznājs*, by Juris Podnieks, and the interview with him in *Baltic Forum* 5/1 (1988), 26–48. In her novel *Coup de grâce*, written in 1939, Marguerite Yourcenar singled out those Letts who had "served the Reds as hangmen." Trans. Grace Frick (London: Secker & Warburg, 1957), 11.

31. Edvard Radzinsky, *The Last Tsar*, trans. Marian Schwartz (New York: Doubleday, 1992), 343–44, 368. Vācietis was to be removed from his post when, according to Trotsky, it was noticed that he spent his evenings reading biographies of Napoleon. *LE*, III, 2543.

32. Aleksandr I. Solzhenitsyn, *The Gulag Archipelago, 1918–1956: An Experiment in Literary Investigation*, trans. Thomas P. Whitney (New York: Harper & Row, 1973), 189.

33. Leonard Schapiro, *The Communist Party of the Soviet Union* (London: Methuen, 1963), 474; Andrejs Plakans, *The Latvians: A Short History* (Stanford: Hoover Institution Press, 1995), 120–21.

34. Georg von Rauch, *The Baltic States. The Years of Independence: Estonia, Latvia, Lithuania, 1917–1940*, trans. Gerald Onn (London: C. Hurst, 1974), 36.

35. In conversation with Ved Mehta, *Fly and the Fly-Bottle* (Harmondsworth: Penguin, 1965), 113–15.

36. Pavel M. Awaloff, *Im Kampf gegen den Bolschewismus: Erinnerungen* (Glückstadt and Hamburg: Augustin, 1925), 176, 269; John Whiton, "'Das Haus am See': An Unpublished Memoir of a Baltic Baron," *Journal of Baltic Studies* 27/1 (1996), 82; J. Hampden Jackson, *Estonia* (London: Allen and Unwin, 1948), 143.

3. BALTIC BATTLES

1. Dmitri Volkogonov, *Lenin: Life and Legacy*, trans. and ed. Harold Shukman (London: HarperCollins, 1994), 482.

2. My emphasis. Harry Rudin, *Armistice* (New Haven: Yale University Press, 1944), 428–29. Also Robert G. L. Waite, *Vanguard of Nazism: The Free Corps*

Movement in Postwar Germany, 1918–1923 (Cambridge, Mass.: Harvard University Press, 1952), 100.

3. Erich Balla, *Landsknechte wurden wir* (Berlin: Kolk, 1927), 123–24; Ernst von Salomon, *The Outlaws*, trans. Ian F. D. Morrow (London: Cape, 1931); Waite, *Vanguard of Nazism*, 108–11. Also Hannsjoachim W. Koch, *Der deutsche Bürgerkrieg: Eine Geschichte der deutschen und österreichischen Freikorps, 1918–1923* (Berlin: Ullstein, 1978), esp. 140–43; Hagen Schulze, *Freikorps und Republik, 1918–1920* (Boppard am Rhein: Harald Boldt Verlag, 1969), 106; Werner von Harpe, "Baltisches Schicksal um 1919," *Baltische Hefte* 13 (1967), 111.

4. Lt.-Gen. du Parquet, *L'Aventure allemande en Lettonie* (Paris, 1926), 38, in Koch, *Bürgerkrieg*, 146.

5. In a letter, June 1919, in Nigel Nicolson, *Alex* (London: Weidenfeld and Nicolson, 1973), 54. Nicolson's chapter on the Baltic is full of frightful errors.

6. Diary, February 2, 1919, Harry Graf Kessler, *Tagebücher, 1918–1937*, ed. Wolfgang Pfeiffer-Belli (Frankfurt: Insel, 1961), 117.

7. Lloyd George told the Commons that he would rather see Russia Bolshevik than Britain bankrupt. House of Commons, *Parliamentary Debates*, 5th Session, April 16, 1919, vol. 114, 2942.

8. Stephen Tallents, *Man and Boy* (London: Faber and Faber, 1943), 267.

9. Archibald H. Young, ed., *The War Book of Upper Canada College, Toronto* (Toronto: Printers Guild, 1923), 50.

10. Herbert Bernsdorff, "Bilder aus Baltischer Landeswehr-Zeit, 1918–1920," *Baltische Hefte* 12 (1966), 125.

11. Joseph Chappey, "Au pays des Porte-Glaives," *Le Revue de Genève* 7 (1928), 194–95.

12. In Stanley W. Page, *The Formation of the Baltic States* (Cambridge, Mass.: Harvard University Press, 1959), 139.

13. Cabinet protocol, April 24, 1919, *Akten der Reichskanzlei Weimarer Republik: Das Kabinett Scheidemann, 13. Februar bis 20. Juni 1919*, ed. Hagen Schulze (Boppard am Rhein: Harald Boldt Verlag, 1971), 210. Erni Langewitz, "Die Bolschewikenherrschaft in Riga, 1919: Persönliche Erlebnisse," *Baltische Hefte* 20 (1974), 150. George Popoff lived through the occupation and gave his account in *The City of the Red Plague: Soviet Rule in a Baltic Town*, trans. Robin John (London: George Allen and Unwin, 1932).

14. Lenin to Molotov, March 19, 1922, in Richard Pipes, ed., *The Unknown Lenin: From the Secret Archive*, trans. Catherine A. Fitzpatrick (New Haven: Yale University Press, 1996), 154.

15. Popoff, *City of the Red Plague*, goes on at length about the Bolshevik "riflewomen," 161–62, 217, 328–29; also Tallents, *Man and Boy*, 312; and Klaus Theweleit, *Male Fantasies*, 2 vols., trans. Stephen Conway and Erica Carter (Minneapolis: University of Minnesota Press, 1987–89).

16. Paul Rohrbach, *Deutschtum in Not! Die Schicksale der Deutschen in Europa ausserhalb des Reiches* (Berlin: Wilhelm Andermann Verlag, 1926), 266–67.

17. "In women, the first theoretical realization of communist ideals always has to

do with the sexual drive." Delmar, *Französische Frauen*, 153, in Theweleit, *Male Fantasies*, I, 68.

18. See Ernst Heilborn's fine introduction to the work of Keyserling in Eduard von Keyserling, *Gesammelte Erzählungen in vier Bänden* (Berlin: S. Fischer, 1922), I, 1–31.

19. On Yourcenar, see Josyane Savigneau, *Marguerite Yourcenar: Inventing a Life* (Chicago: University of Chicago Press, 1993), 123–32.

20. Lytton Strachey, *Eminent Victorians* (Harmondsworth: Penguin, 1948), 223.

21. *The Globe and Mail*, September 29, 1960, 5. "Affecting the tweedy style of an English country gentleman, he brought to his undoubted Canadianism a very British tone," wrote Kenneth McNaught of Vincent Massey in his *The Pelican History of Canada* (Harmondsworth: Penguin, 1969), 277.

22. [Elizabeth Rigby], *Letters from the Shores of the Baltic*, 2nd ed. (London: John Murray, 1842), II, 20; on the delights of spring in the Baltic, Arthur Ruhl's *New Masters of the Baltic* (New York: E. P. Dutton, 1921), 123.

23. Siegfried Boström, "Aus meinem Kriegstagebuch," *Baltische Hefte* 14 (1968), 166.

24. Waite, *Vanguard of Nazism*, 118.

25. In a cabinet meeting on April 24, 1919, Foreign Minister Count Brockdorff-Rantzau had argued that an aggressive stand against Bolshevism would help Germany in the peace negotiations, but he was in a minority, and the cabinet had decided, on paper at any rate, to adopt a defensive posture in the Baltic. "On the question of Bolshevism, I don't consider it useful," said Colonial Minister Dr. Bell, "to pull the chestnuts out of the fire on behalf of the Allies." *Akten der Reichskanzlei: Kabinett Scheidemann*, 209–25.

26. Richard Walden Hale, ed., *The Letters of Warwick Greene, 1915–1928* (1931; Freeport, N.Y.: Books for Libraries Press, 1971), 82, 114; Koch, *Bürgerkrieg*, 157.

27. Waite, *Vanguard of Nazism*, 118–19.

28. In Tallents, *Man and Boy*, 310.

29. John Duncan Gregory, *On the Edge of Diplomacy: Rambles and Reflections, 1902–1928* (London: Hutchinson, n.d. [1929]), 187.

30. Nicolson, *Alex*, 54.

31. Randall White, *Ontario, 1610–1985: A Political and Economic History* (Toronto: Dundurn Press, 1985), 250.

32. In Koch, *Bürgerkrieg*, 162–63.

33. Ernst von Salomon, *The Outlaws*, trans. Ian F. D. Morrow (London: Cape, 1931), 101.

34. Tallents, *Man and Boy*, 362.

35. Pavel M. Awaloff, *Im Kampf gegen den Bolschewismus: Erinnerungen* (Glückstadt and Hamburg: Augustin, 1925), v, 151, 563.

36. Salomon, *The Outlaws*, 104.

37. Ibid., 84–85.

38. Awaloff, *Im Kampf*, 200.

39. Salomon, *The Outlaws*, 122.

40. Awaloff, *Im Kampf*, 209.

41. Salomon, *The Outlaws,* 119.
42. W. G. Smith, *Building the Nation: A Study of Some Problems Concerning the Churches' Relation to the Immigrants* (Toronto: Canadian Council of the Missionary Education Movement, 1922), 178; and Wellington Bridgman, *Breaking Prairie Sod: The Story of a Pioneer Preacher in the Eighties* (Toronto: Musson, 1920), 163–77, 244–46; also Donald Avery, *Dangerous Foreigners: European Immigrant Workers and Labour Radicalism in Canada, 1896–1932* (Toronto: McClelland and Stewart, 1979).
43. In Irving Abella and Harold Troper, *None Is too Many: Canada and the Jews of Europe, 1933–1948* (New York: Random House, 1983), 202, 235.
44. *The Globe and Mail,* June 28, 1947, in Jean Bruce, *After the War* (Don Mills, Ont.: Fitzhenry and Whiteside, 1982), 96.
45. In Milda Danys, *DP: Lithuanian Immigration to Canada after the Second World War* (Toronto: Multicultural History Society of Ontario, 1986), 252.
46. In ibid., 255.
47. The same was true in Britain: Joseph Behar, "'Essential Workers': The Foreign Labour Recruitment Policy of the British Government, 1945–1951," Ph.D. diss., University of Toronto, 1998, chapter 2.
48. Norman Hillson, *Alexander of Tunis* (London: W. H. Allen, 1952), 213.
49. David C. Corbett, *Canada's Immigration Policy* (Toronto: University of Toronto Press, 1957), 198; Mark Wyman, *DP: Europe's Displaced Persons, 1945–1951* (Philadephia: Balch Institute or Associated University Presses, Cranbury, N.J., 1989), 191; Donald H. Avery, *Reluctant Host: Canada's Response to Immigrant Workers, 1896–1994* (Toronto: McClelland and Stewart, 1995), 145.
50. Hauptmann a. D. Wagener, "Die Schlacht von Mitau," in Ernst von Salomon, ed., *Das Buch vom deutschen Freikorpskämpfer* (Berlin: Wilhelm Limpert, 1938), 208–213.
51. Salomon, *The Outlaws,* 131.
52. Diary, November 15, 1919, Kārlis Skalbe, *Raksti: Mazās piezīnes* (Stockholm: Daugava, 1953), 49.
53. Owen Rutter, *The New Baltic States and Their Future: An Account of Lithuania, Latvia, and Estonia* (London: Methuen, 1925), 129.
54. The photograph, deposited in the old Heeresarchiv and presumably destroyed during the Second World War, is reprinted in Salomon, ed., *Das Buch vom deutschen Freikorpskämpfer,* 213.
55. Edwin Erich Dwinger, *Die letzten Reiter* (Jena, 1935), 72.
56. In Peggie Benton, *Baltic Countdown* (London: Centaur, 1984), 55.
57. Rudolf Höss, *Kommandant in Auschwitz,* ed. Martin Broszat (Stuttgart: Deutsche Verlags-Anstalt, 1958), 34–35.
58. Mark Levene links the anti-Semitic outrages of 1919 in the Eastern European borderlands with the genocidal action of 1941: "Frontiers of Genocide: Jews in the Eastern War Zones, 1914–1920 and 1941," in Panikos Panayi, ed., *Minorities in Wartime* (Oxford and Providence, R.I.: Berg, 1993), 101–7.
59. Walter Duranty, *'I Write as I Please'* (London: Hamish Hamilton, 1935), 48.
60. In Nicolson, *Alex,* 64–65.

61. In W. G. F. Jackson, *Alexander of Tunis as Military Commander* (London: Batsford, 1971), 64.
62. The membership figure is from J. R. McDonald, *Baptist Missions in Western Canada, 1873–1948* (Edmonton: Baptist Union of Western Canada, 1948), 32.
63. Margaret E. Thompson, *The Baptist Story in Western Canada* (Calgary: Baptist Union of Western Canada, 1974), 190–91.
64. In Danys, *DP*, 172.
65. *Time*, January 7, 1946, 14, 16; in Norman Hillmer, *"The Outstanding Imperialist": Mackenzie King and the British* (London: Canada House, 1982), 5.
66. See Danys, *DP*, 96–97, 135, for other anecdotes.
67. In Bruce, *After the War*, 44.
68. Eric Wells, *Winnipeg: Where the New West Begins* (Burlington, Ont.: Windsor Publications, 1982), 8.
69. In David S. Foglesong, "The United States, Self-Determination, and the Struggle Against Bolshevism in the Eastern Baltic Region, 1918–1920," *Journal of Baltic Studies* 26/2 (1995), 114.
70. In Edgar Anderson, "The British Policy Toward the Baltic States, 1918–1920," *Journal of Central European Affairs* 19/3 (1959), 276–89.
71. Esmé Howard, *Theatre of Life*, 2 vols. (Boston: Little, Brown, 1935–36), II, 260.
72. In 1950 a Canadian Order-in-Council removed Germans from the "enemy alien" category and allowed them to emigrate to Canada. In Bruce, *After the War*, 110.
73. Fortnightly Report No. 6, Schleswig-Holstein, July 29–August 11, 1945, FO 1006/102, Public Record Office, London (hereafter PRO).
74. In Bruce, *After the War*, 48.
75. In Danys, *DP*, 94.
76. In ibid., 170.
77. Arthur Ruhl, *New Masters of the Baltic* (New York: E. P. Dutton, 1921), 191–92.

4. DISPLACED

1. Adolfs Blodnieks, a leader of the New Farmers and Smallholders Party, describes the land reform well in his *The Undefeated Nation* (New York: Robert Speller & Sons, 1960), chapter 17. By 1933 there were 109,000 holdings consisting of fewer than 10 hectares, 51,000 between 10 and 20 hectares, 24,000 between 20 and 30 hectares, 21,000 between 30 and 40 hectares, 18,000 between 50 and 100 hectares, and 2,000 with more than 100 hectares. See the Royal Institute of International Affairs publication *The Baltic States: A Survey of the Political and Economic Structure and the Foreign Relations of Estonia, Latvia, and Lithuania* (London: Oxford University Press, 1938), 107.
2. Ibid., 63.
3. Paul Rohrbach, *Deutschtum in Not! Die Schicksale der Deutschen in Europa ausserhalb des Reiches* (Berlin: Wilhelm Andermann Verlag, 1926), 261.

4. Edwin Erich Dwinger, *Auf halbem Wege* (Jena: Eugen Diederichs Verlag, 1939), 428.
5. Harold Troper, "Canada's Immigration Policy Since 1945," *International Journal* 48 (1993), 255–81.
6. In Robert Bothwell et al., *Canada Since 1945*, rev. ed. (Toronto: University of Toronto Press, 1989), 45–46.
7. Canada, House of Commons, *Debates*, May 1, 1947, vol. 256, 2646.
8. Stephen Tallents, *Man and Boy* (London: Faber and Faber, 1943), 275.
9. Memo of Lt. Col. F. C. Davis, August 3, 1949, to DP Div. ZEO, FO 1006/500, PRO.
10. In Jean Bruce, *After the War* (Don Mills, Ont.: Fitzhenry and Whiteside, 1982), 40.
11. John W. Holmes, *The Shaping of Peace: Canada and the Search for World Order, 1943–1957*, vol. I (Toronto: University of Toronto Press, 1979), 101.
12. Canada, House of Commons, *Debates*, May 1, 1947, vol. 256, 2645; Hugh L. Keenleyside, *Memoirs*, 2 vols. (Toronto: McClelland and Stewart, 1981–82), II, 297.
13. Massey, April 5, 1946, in Irving Abella and Harold Troper, *None Is too Many: Canada and the Jews of Europe, 1933–1948* (New York: Random House, 1983), 213; F. W. Smelts, December 16, 1946, in ibid., 235.
14. In Abella and Troper, *None Is too Many*, 217, 226. Similar views surfaced in official quarters in Britain. "In selecting the Displaced Persons we must give priority to Balts. We obviously want as few Poles as possible," said one official. Joseph Behar, "'Essential Workers': The Foreign Labour Recruitment Policy of the British Government, 1945–1951," Ph.D. diss., University of Toronto, 1998, 128–29.
15. *Perkonkrusts*, No. 14 (July 2, 1933), copied in R92/6, Bundesarchiv Koblenz (hereafter BAK).
16. *Perkonkrusts*, No. 26 (October 1, 1933), copied in R92/6, BAK.
17. FO 371/43050, PRO.
18. FO 371/47045, PRO.
19. During the last week and a half of March 1949, the Baltic states lost around 3 percent of their native populations. Romuald J. Misiunas and Rein Taagepera, *The Baltic States: Years of Dependence, 1940–1990*, rev. ed. (London: Hurst, 1993), 94–107; Toivo U. Raun, *Estonia and the Estonians*, 2nd ed. (Stanford: Hoover Institution Press, 1991), 176–81; Heinrichs Strods, "Die Zwangskollektivierung der Landwirtschaft in Lettland im Jahre 1949," *Acta Baltica* 32 (1994), 37–49.
20. Strods, "Die Zwangskollektivierung," 39; and Mart Laar, *War in the Woods: Estonia's Struggle for Survival, 1944–1956*, trans. Tiina Ets (Washington, D.C.: Compass Press, 1992).
21. John Duncan Gregory, *On the Edge of Diplomacy: Rambles and Reflections, 1902–1928* (London: Hutchinson, n.d. [1929]), 177.
22. In J. Hampden Jackson, *Estonia* (London: Allen and Unwin, 1948), 223.
23. D. M. Crowe, Jr., "Great Britain and the Baltic States, 1938–1939," in V. S. Vardys and R. J. Misiunas, eds., *The Baltic States in Peace and War, 1917–1945*

(University Park: Pennsylvania State University Press, 1978), 112–14. Also
Mieczyslaw Nurek, "Great Britain and the Baltic in the Last Months of Peace,
March–August 1939," in John W. Hiden and Thomas Lane, eds., *The Baltic and
the Outbreak of the Second World War* (Cambridge: Cambridge University
Press, 1992), 21–49.

24. Anthony Read and David Fisher, *The Deadly Embrace: Hitler, Stalin and the
Nazi-Soviet Pact, 1939–1941* (New York: Norton, 1988), 140.

25. See John Hiden, "Baltic Security Problems Between the Two World Wars," in
Hiden and Lane, eds., *The Baltic and the Outbreak of the Second World War,*
20.

26. Wolfgang Leonhard, *Child of the Revolution,* trans. C. M. Woodhouse (London: Collins, 1957), 73–4; Read and Fisher, *Deadly Embrace,* 293.

27. Albert Speer, *Inside the Third Reich,* trans. Richard and Clara Winston (New
York: Macmillan, 1970), 161–62.

28. Diary, August 25, 1939, Jürgen E. Kroeger, *Eine baltische Illusion: Tagebuch
eines Deutsch-Balten aus den Jahren 1939–1944* (Lüneburg: Nordland-Druck,
n.d.), 7.

29. Read and Fisher, *Deadly Embrace,* 248.

30. Many of the key documents are reprinted in Michael Rosenbusch et al., eds.,
*Schauplatz Baltikum: Szenarium einer Okkupation und Angliederung,
Dokumente 1939/40* (Berlin: Dietz Verlag, 1991).

31. Diary, August 28, 1939, Kroeger, *Eine baltische Illusion,* 8. On the heat and the
sun of the summer of 1939, see also Ingeborg Kentmann, *Eine Atempause
lang: Kindheit und Jugend im Baltikum zwischen zwei Weltkriegen* (Freiburg:
Herder, 1978), 219.

32. In his introduction to Armin Korn, *Lübeck zehn Jahre danach* (Lübeck:
Wullenwever-Druck, 1955), 3.

33. Fortnightly Report No. 6, for Schleswig-Holstein, for the period July 29–August 11, 1945, FO 1006/102, PRO.

34. Anthony Mann, *Comeback: Germany, 1945–1952* (London: Macmillan, 1980),
14.

35. Ince to Buxton, September 2, 1947, LAB 12/513, PRO; in Behar, "'Essential
Workers,'" 139.

36. *Army Talk,* November 30, 1946, 4–5, in Leonard Dinnerstein, *America and the
Survivors of the Holocaust* (New York: Columbia University Press, 1982), 52.

37. Ira A. Hirschmann, *The Embers Still Burn* (New York: Simon and Schuster,
1949), 72.

38. *Lübecker Nachrichten* (hereafter *LN*), March 16, 1948.

39. *LN,* June 26, 1948.

40. Michael R. Marrus, *The Unwanted: European Refugees in the Twentieth Century* (New York: Oxford University Press, 1985), 311–13.

41. In Bruce, *After the War,* 38.

42. Information on Dr. Callies was provided by Dr. Hans-Friedrich Schütt of the
Flensburg Stadtarchiv.

43. Dinnerstein, *America and the Survivors of the Holocaust,* 16–17; Marrus, *The
Unwanted,* 321–22.

44. In Read and Fisher, *Deadly Embrace,* 369. The texts of the agreements forced on the Baltic states are available in Rosenbusch et al., eds., *Schauplatz Baltikum.*
45. Lucy Addison, *Letters from Latvia,* ed. Rhona Chave (London: Macdonald, 1986), 17.
46. On the dilemmas posed by the Soviet ultimatums in June 1940, see Alfonsas Eidintas, "The Meeting of the Lithuanian Cabinet, 15 June 1940," in Hiden and Lane, eds., *The Baltic and the Outbreak of the Second World War,* 165–73.
47. Misiunas and Taagepera, *Baltic States,* 25–26; Georg von Rauch, *The Baltic States. The Years of Independence: Estonia, Latvia, Lithuania, 1917–1940,* trans. Gerald Onn (London: C. Hurst, 1974), 225.
48. In Frank Gordon, *Latvians and Jews Between Germany and Russia,* trans. Vaiva Puķite (Stockholm: Memento, 1990), 23.
49. George Kennan, *Memoirs, 1925–1950* (London: Hutchinson, 1968), 29.
50. Peggie Benton has a fine description of the street scenes and crowds in Riga in June 1940 in *Baltic Countdown* (London: Centaur, 1984), 110–12.
51. Menachem Begin, *White Nights: The Story of a Prisoner in Russia,* trans. Katie Kaplan (London: Macdonald, 1957), 90.
52. Published first in *Krasnyi Terror,* in November 1918, reprinted in *Pravda,* No. 281, December 25, 1918; extract in James Bunyan, *Intervention, Civil War, and Communism in Russia, April–December 1918: Documents and Materials* (Baltimore: Johns Hopkins University Press, 1936), 261.
53. Begin, *White Nights,* 154.
54. Memorandum, August 8, 1940, reprinted in Dietrich A. Loeber, ed., *Diktierte Option: Die Umsiedlung der Deutsch-Balten aus Estland und Lettland* (Neumünster: Karl Wachholtz Verlag, 1974), 252.
55. Rainer Schulze, "'Die Flüchtlinge liegen uns alle schwer im Magen.' Zum Verhältnis von Einheimischen und Flüchtlingen im ländlichen Raum," in *Geschichtswerkstatt,* Heft 13 (1987), 35–45.
56. See the long list of incidents in *LN,* May 21, 1945.
57. "Die Stimme der 134 Ermordeten," *LN,* July 8, 1948.
58. Ernst Hagemann, "Die Entwicklung der öffentlichen Grünanlagen und Friedhöfe in Lübeck seit dem Kriegsende im Jahre 1945," *Der Wagen* (1963), 75–82, esp. 77.
59. *LN,* August 16, 1947.
60. Letter from Dr. W. Greuel to the Ärztlichen Kreisverein, October 20, 1945, Folder A36 Militärregierung, Nordelbische Evangelisch-Lutherische Kirche, Archiv Lübeck.
61. James Stern, *The Hidden Damage* (New York: Harcourt, Brace and Company, 1947), 137.
62. *Lübecker Freie Presse* (hereafter *LFP*), August 16, 1947.
63. The extraordinarily perceptive report, dated March 22, 1941, of John Mazionis was included in a letter by the American ambassador in Moscow, U.S. National Archives 860m.00/471, and reprinted, with commentary, by Alfred Erich Senn, "Documents," *Journal of Baltic Studies* 26/2 (1995), 151–58.

64. "Bolsheviks Tortured, Slew Clergy, Commission Reports" (Reuters), *The Globe and Mail*, November 28, 1995. Dimitry Pospielovsky, *The Russian Church under the Soviet Regime, 1917–1982*, vol. I (Crestwood, N.Y.: St. Vladimir's Seminary Press, 1984), 174–75.

65. Edgars Andersons, *Latvijas vēsture, 1920–1940: Ārpolitika*, 2 vols. (Stockholm: Daugava, 1982–84), II, 522. Nicholas Tolstoy, *Stalin's Secret War* (London: Cape, 1981), 222–23, estimates that 61,000 Balts were deported. Raun, *Estonia*, 154, has counted 54,000 Estonians alone executed, deported, or forcibly mobilized by the Soviets between mid-1940 and mid-1941.

66. In Rainer Schulze, ed., *Unruhige Zeiten: Erlebnisberichte aus dem Landkreis Celle, 1945–1949* (Munich: R. Oldenbourg Verlag, 1990), 37. On the purported criminal activity of Poles and Ukrainians in the vicinity of Aachen, see Klaus-Jörg Ruhl, *Deutschland 1945: Alltag zwischen Krieg und Frieden in Berichten, Dokumenten und Bildern* (Darmstadt: Luchterhand, 1984), 203–6.

67. A. C. Dunn, regional supervisor, XV Corps, to J. H. Whiting, district director, November 6, 1945, UNRRA Archives, New York.

68. LN, December 20, 1947; LFP, December 20, 1947.

69. LN, January 8, 1948; LFP, January 4, 1948.

70. DPs' criminality was a major problem for the occupation authorities, less so because of the crimes themselves than because of their social and political reverberations. In fact, the statistics available suggest that the DPs were less involved in criminal activity than the Germans: OMGUS files 3/169–2/138, microfiche, BAK; Jerry M. Sage, "Germany's Displaced Persons," *New York Herald Tribune*, March 18, 1949; David F. Smith, "Juvenile Delinquency in the British Zone of Germany, 1945–51," *German History* 12/1 (1994), 39–63.

71. Read and Fisher, *Deadly Embrace*, 3.

72. Harrison E. Salisbury, *A Journey for Our Times* (New York: Harper & Row, 1983), 188.

5. BEAR SLAYER STREET

1. Proclamation of July 28, 1941, issued by Hinrich Lohse, Reich commissar for the Ostland, *Verkündungsblatt für das Ostland*, 1941, No. 1, 1; the Latvian version is available in R92/188, BAK; an English translation is in Raphael Lemkin, *Axis Rule in Occupied Europe: Laws of Occupation, Analysis of Government, Proposals for Redress* (Washington, D.C.: Carnegie Endowment for International Peace, 1944), 300–301.

2. Diary, August 23, 1941, Ruth Andreas-Friedrich, *Der Schattenmann: Tagebuchaufzeichnungen, 1938–1945* (Berlin: Union Verlag, 1977), 75.

3. Seppo Myllyniemi, *Die Neuordnung der baltischen Länder, 1941–1944* (Helsinki: Vammalan Kirjapaino Oy, 1973), 134.

4. Reports, on morale, of the Lübeck Police Group, December 21, 1948, and the Kiel Police Group, December 29, 1948, FO 1014/276, PRO.

5. "Der Kampf gegen die Kirche: Aus unveröffentlichten Tagebüchern Alfred Rosenbergs," ed. Robert M. W. Kempner, *Der Monat* 10 (1949), 36–7. Also

Gerald Reitlinger, *The House Built on Sand: The Conflicts of German Policy on Russia, 1939–1945* (London: Weidenfeld and Nicolson, 1960), 128–55.

6. Myllyniemi, *Neuordnung*, 200.

7. In Owen Rutter, *The New Baltic States and Their Future: An Account of Lithuania, Latvia, and Estonia* (London: Methuen, 1925), 152.

8. The renaming of streets was quickly seen by some German critics to have been an incredible administrative gaffe, a "political disaster," as the area commissar for Riga put it in a circular to other area commissars in the Ostland, November 10, 1941. See materials in file R91Mitau/16, and R92/61, BAK.

9. Unanimity in the RKO there was not. Regierungsrat Trampedach was appalled by much of the policy, the refusal to reprivatize and the attempt to eliminate Latvian national symbols. "In his need for recognition the Latvian is very sensitive, and in this sense should not be unnecessarily injured." See Trampedach's "Bericht über die politische Lage in Lettland," August 16, 1941, R90/115, BAK.

10. Myllyniemi, *Neuordnung*, 156.

11. Lagebericht, Gebietskommissar Riga, October 3, 1942, R91Riga-Stadt/2, BAK.

12. "The Homeless," *New York Herald Tribune*, May 17, 1947.

13. "Statement of the Executive Staff of UNRRA US Zone Headquarters," n.d. [1946], UNRRA Archives, New York.

14. *New York Times*, October 6, 1946, 35; in Mark Wyman, *DP: Europe's Displaced Persons, 1945–1951* (Philadelphia: Balch Institute or Associated University Presses, Cranbury, N.J., 1989), 186.

15. "First DPs to Sail for U.S.," *New York Herald Tribune*, October 9, 1948; Leonard Dinnerstein, *America and the Survivors of the Holocaust* (New York: Columbia University Press, 1982), chapter 7.

16. August 30, 1948; in ibid., 187.

17. Ibid., 251–52, for statistics, including religious breakdown.

18. In Nikolai Tolstoy, *Victims of Yalta*, rev. ed. (London: Corgi, 1979), 66.

19. The legionnaires' story is told by Per Olov Enquist, *The Legionnaires: A Documentary Novel*, trans. Alan Blair (London: Jonathan Cape, 1974). Also Tolstoy, *Victims of Yalta*, 487–88; Wyman, *DP*, 64. In 1996, on the fiftieth anniversary of their deportation, forty-one of these Latvians were still alive. Juris Reneslācis, "Piemiņas plāksne leģionāriem Zviedrijā," *Latvija Amerikā*, February 17, 1996, 4, 17.

20. Tolstoy, *Victims of Yalta*, 340.

21. William Sloane Coffin, Jr., *Once to Every Man: A Memoir* (New York: Atheneum, 1977), 77. On Vlasov, see Tolstoy, *Victims of Yalta*, chapter 12; Mark R. Elliott, *Pawns of Yalta: Soviet Refugees and America's Role in Their Repatriation* (Urbana: University of Illinois Press, 1982), 84–97; and Reitlinger, *House Built on Sand*, 317–96.

22. Nikolai Tolstoy has charged that this treatment, including the complicity of the Western Allies, "is fully comparable to Nazi treatment of the Jews." Tolstoy, *Victims of Yalta*, 29. He claims that many of those repatriated were shot literally within minutes of being handed over to the Soviets. See also the statistics in Elliott, *Pawns of Yalta*, 96.

23. In Ronald Steel, *Walter Lippmann and the American Century* (New York: Little, Brown, 1980), xvii.
24. Wyman, *DP*, 70.
25. Mendel Bobe et al., *The Jews in Latvia* (Tel Aviv: D. Ben-Nun Press, 1971).
26. The Pale consisted of 4 percent of the territory of Russia and held 94 percent of Russia's Jewish population. Bobe, *Jews in Latvia*, 34.
27. Bernhard Press, *Judenmord in Lettland, 1941–1945* (Berlin: Metropol, 1992), 17.
28. Hafrey arrived in the U.S. in 1940, became a journalist and then a foreign service officer. Ruth Seligman, "Libau: The Town that Never Died," *Midstream* 32/9 (1986), 38–39.
29. Press, *Judenmord*, 19.
30. Ibid., 24; Frank Gordon, *Latvians and Jews Between Germany and Russia*, trans. Vaiva Puķite (Stockholm: Memento, 1990), 23–25; Dov Levin, "The Jews and the Sovietization of Latvia, 1940–41," *Soviet Jewish Affairs* 5/1 (1975), 53.
31. In Alfred Erich Senn, "Documents," *Journal of Baltic Studies* 26/2 (1995), 153.
32. Copy, undated, in French translation, of a Soviet circular originating in the Soviet Ministry of the Interior and printed in issue 5 of "Moniteur Confidentiel"; AP PDR/1281/46, Archives de l'Occupation Française en Allemagne et en Autriche, Colmar, Ministère des Affaires Étrangères (hereafter AOF). The other documents in the file are from 1948–49.
33. "Government of Latvian Soviet Republic Appeals to Latvian DPs," *Repatriation News*, No. 14, June 14, 1947, 2–3, UNRRA Archives, New York.
34. Zonal Executive Instruction, on "Visits to Displaced Persons by Soviet Liaison Officers," January 6, 1947, FO 1006/291, PRO.
35. Andrew Ezergailis's *The Holocaust in Latvia, 1941–1944* (Riga: Historical Institute of Latvia, 1996) is the most detailed account on the subject, the result of great diligence in research, but it downplays the Latvian role in the events. By contrast, Mārģers Vestermanis highlights this role in "Der lettische Anteil an der 'Endlösung': Versuch einer Antwort," in Uwe Backes et al., eds., *Die Schatten der Vergangenheit: Impulse zur Historisierung des Nationalsozialismus* (Frankfurt: Propyläen, 1990), 426–49. A debate between the two authors can be found in *Latvijas Vēstures Institūta Žurnāls* 1 and 2 (1993), 108–30 and 122–38, respectively.
36. In Lothar Steinbach, *Ein Volk, ein Reich, ein Glaube? Ehemalige Nationalsozialisten und Zeitzeugen berichten über ihr Leben im Dritten Reich* (Berlin and Bonn: Verlag J. H. W. Dietz Nachf., 1983), 220–21. On other incidents in Rēzekne, see Ezergailis, *Holocaust*, 280–85.
37. *Der Prozess gegen die Hauptkriegsverbrecher vor dem Internationalen Militärgerichtshof* 29 (Nuremberg: Internationaler Militär-Gerichtshof, 1948), 1919-PS, 145. On Höss, see his *Kommandant in Auschwitz*, ed. Martin Broszat (Stuttgart: Deutsche Verlags-Anstalt, 1958).
38. Similar events took place in Lithuania: Alexander Slavinas, "Der inszenierte Aufstand," *Die Zeit*, July 2, 1993.
39. Ezergailis, *Holocaust*, 219; Press (*Judenmord*, 44) puts the figure much higher, at about 40,000 by early October.

40. Trampedach, "Bericht über die politische Lage in Lettland," August 16, 1941, R90/115, BAK.

41. Ezergailis, *Holocaust,* 173–202.

42. Hans-Heinrich Wilhelm, "Die Einsatzgruppe A der Sicherheitspolizei und des SD 1941/42," diss., Munich, 1975; Ezergailis, *Holocaust,* 226–29; Gordon, *Latvians and Jews,* 33.

43. Ezergailis, *Holocaust,* 239–70.

44. Press, *Judenmord,* 12.

45. On the "modern" aspects of Nazism, see Zygmunt Bauman, *Modernity and the Holocaust* (Cambridge: Polity Press, 1989); and Peter Fritzsche, "Nazi Modern," *Modernism/Modernity* 3/1 (1996), 1–21. On the links between planning and extermination, see Mechtild Rössler and Sabine Schleiermacher, eds., *Der "Generalplan Ost": Hauptlinien der nationalsozialistischen Planungs- und Vernichtungspolitik* (Berlin: Akademie Verlag, 1993).

46. House of Commons, *Parliamentary Debates,* December 15, 1944, vol. 406, 1484.

47. Irving Abella and Harold Troper, *None Is too Many: Canada and the Jews of Europe, 1933–1948* (New York: Random House, 1983).

48. *The Papers of Dwight David Eisenhower,* vol. VI: *Occupation, 1945,* ed. Alfred D. Chandler, Jr., and Louis Galambos (Baltimore: Johns Hopkins University Press, 1978), 358.

49. Memorandum of Dr. J. D. Castellanos to Laurence A. Dawson, June 5, 1946, UNRRA Archives, New York.

50. For statistics, see Gertrude Schneider's edited volumes, *Muted Voices: Jewish Survivors of Latvia Remember* (New York: Philosophical Library, 1987), 19–22; and *The Unfinished Road: Jewish Survivors of Latvia Look Back* (New York: Praeger, 1991), 190. On the food issue, see the account by Aizik Dimant-stein in *Muted Voices,* 121.

51. "Camp 553, Pasing," n.d., UNRRA Archives, New York.

52. In Milda Danys, *DP: Lithuanian Immigration to Canada after the Second World War* (Toronto: Multicultural History Society of Ontario, 1986), 76.

53. In Hans-Peter Schwarz, *Konrad Adenauer: A German Politician and States-man in a Period of War, Revolution and Reconstruction. Volume I: From the German Empire to the Federal Republic, 1876–1952,* trans. Louise Willmot (Providence, R.I.: Berghahn Books, 1995), 300.

54. The tensions between ethnic groups and criminality were cause for concern in the camp. See the correspondence on the camp in ZB892A, Archiv des Diakon-ischen Werkes der Evangelischen Kirche in Deutschland, Berlin (hereafter ADW).

55. Ira A. Hirschmann, *The Embers Still Burn* (New York: Simon and Schuster, 1949), 90.

56. "Statement of the Executive Staff of UNRRA US Zone Headquarters," n.d. [1946], UNRRA Archives, New York.

57. Myllyniemi, *Neuordnung,* 196. Clothing and shoes were in short supply; by October 1942, soles for shoes were selling for 70 reichsmarks. Lagebericht, Gebietskommissar Riga, October 3, 1942, R91Riga-Stadt/2, BAK.

58. See Dressler's defense of the song festivals in his letter to the area commissar in Mitau, June 17, 1943, R91Mitau/134, BAK; also the material in R92/33, BAK.

59. See, for example, the instructions sent out by the propaganda office of the Generalkommissariat Riga, March 4, 1944, in R91Mitau/27, BAK.

60. Myllyniemi, *Neuordnung*, 223–24.

61. His name and property, Lakstīgalas, are listed in the reprivatization file R91Mitau/173, BAK.

62. See the materials in R91Riga-Stadt/170, BAK; and *LE*, II, 1317.

63. The report is appended to a letter from the office of Reichskommissar Ostland to Generalkommissar Riga, July 13, 1943, R92/9, BAK.

64. Reitlinger, *House Built on Sand*, 147.

65. See the materials in R90/11, BAK.

66. "Vermerk," September 1, 1944, R6/266, BAK, 97–98.

67. Andrejs Johansons, "Latvian Literature in Exile," *Slavonic Review* 30/75 (June 1952), 472; Wyman, *DP*, 161.

68. Alexander Squadrilli, in Wyman, *DP*, 121.

69. Clifford Ansgar Nelson, "Supplementary Detailed Report of Survey Journey," n.d., Allg. Slg. C 121.3, ADW.

70. *Christian Science Monitor*, May 25, 1948, and materials in FO 1006/537 and 538.

71. Frederick Morgan, *Peace and War: A Soldier's Life* (London: Hodder and Stoughton, 1961), 239.

72. Kathryn C. Hulme, *The Wild Place* (Boston: Little, Brown, 1953), xi–xii, 67, 69.

73. On a scheme to smuggle DPs from the American zone to France, see the report of the 2ième Bureau, August 17, 1948, DG42/120/6, AOF.

74. Dorothy Macardle, *Children of Europe* (London: Gollancz, 1950), 11.

75. Churchill to Roosevelt, March 7, 1942, in Francis L. Loewenheim, Harold D. Langley, and Manfred Jonas, eds., *Roosevelt and Churchill: Their Secret Wartime Correspondence* (New York: Saturday Review Press, 1975), 186; and Winston Churchill, *The Hinge of Fate* (Boston: Houghton Mifflin, 1950), 327.

76. FO 371/43052, PRO.

77. Eden to Churchill, January 25, 1944, FO 371/43052, PRO.

78. Statement of the Latvian Social Democrats, sent on April 26, 1944, to Christopher F. A. Warner at the Foreign Office; the exchange between Warner and O. G. Sargent, deputy undersecretary of state, August 31, 1944; and Zarine to Warner, August 22, 1944, FO 371/43050, PRO.

79. Richard von Weizsäcker, "Forty Years after the War" (speech in the Bundestag, Bonn, May 8, 1985), in "Speeches for Our Time," *German Issues* 10 (Washington, D.C.: American Institute for Contemporary German Studies, 1992), 19. Also Christian Graf von Krockow, *Die Stunde der Frauen: Bericht aus Pommern, 1944 bis 1947* (Stuttgart: Deutsche Verlags-Anstalt, 1988).

80. Elizabeth Heineman, "The Hour of the Woman: Memories of Germany's 'Crisis Years' and West German National Identity," *American Historical Review* 101/2 (1996), 354–95.

81. Ibid., 381.

82. Curzio Malaparte, *The Skin*, trans. David Moore (London: Redman, 1952), 42.

83. Reports of the Black Market Information Committee, CCG, October 23 and December 6, 1945, FO 1014/64, PRO.

84. Wyman, *DP*, 116.

85. Heinrich Böll, *Missing Persons and Other Essays*, trans. Leila Vennewitz (New York: McGraw-Hill, 1977), 26.

86. See the Black Market Reports for Schleswig-Holstein in FO 1006/344, PRO.

87. R91Mitau/24, BAK.

6. ODYSSEY

1. Eleanor Hancock, *The National Socialist Leadership and Total War, 1941–5* (New York: St. Martin's Press, 1991), 107–8.

2. John Erickson, *The Road to Berlin* (Boulder, Colo.: Westview, 1983), 214; Alexander Werth, *Russia at War, 1941–1945* (London: Pan Books, 1965), 768–71.

3. In Gerald Reitlinger, *The House Built on Sand: The Conflicts of German Policy on Russia, 1939–1945* (London: Weidenfeld and Nicolson, 1960), 220.

4. The appointment order is reprinted in H. R. Trevor-Roper, ed., *Hitler's War Directives, 1939–1945* (London: Pan Books, 1966), 253–54. Schoerner (1892–1973) was captured by the Soviets at war's end and spent ten years in Russia as a prisoner of war.

5. F. W. von Mellenthin, *German Generals of World War II as I Saw Them* (Norman: University of Oklahoma Press, 1977), 186.

6. Reitlinger, *House Built on Sand*, 382.

7. Befehl, July 24, 1944, RH20–16, Bd. 430, Bundesarchiv-Militärarchiv, Freiburg im Breisgau (hereafter BAM). See also Schoerner's "Richtlinien für die nationalsozialistische Führung im Heere," March 28, 1944, RH20–16, Bd. 623.

8. Diary, March 2, Joseph Goebbels, *Final Entries 1945: The Diaries of Joseph Goebbels*, ed. Hugh Trevor-Roper, trans. Richard Barry (New York: G. P. Putnam's Sons, 1978), 26.

9. Erickson, *Road to Berlin*, 201.

10. See Artur Sahm, "Genealogische Beziehungen Rigaer und Lübecker führender Geschlechter. Ein Beitrag zur Kolonisation des Ostens," Kiel University diss., 1926.

11. Peter Guttkuhn, "28./29. März 1942: . . . und Lübeck sollte sterben . . . ," *Vaterstädtische Blätter* 33 (1982), 3–6.

12. Florentine Naylor, "Vom alten, vom zerstörten und vom auferstandenen Lübeck," *Der Wagen: Ein Lübeckisches Jahrbuch* (1982), 77–88.

13. The air war had killed 452 Lübeckers and injured 1,048.

14. Sigrun Becker, "Von Heimat zu Heimatstatt. Eingliederung in Lübeck," in *Dokumentation zur Ausstellung Eingliederung der Vertriebenen und Flüchtlinge in der Hansastadt Lübeck vom 9. bis 23. April 1989 im grossen Börsensaal des Lübecker Rathauses* (Lübeck: Senat der Hansastadt Lübeck, 1989), 74–76.

15. Wolfgang Grönke, "Vertriebene und Flüchtlinge in Lübeck — Notunterkünfte 1944–1967," in ibid., 63–68.

16. *LN*, July 31, 1946.

17. The reports are in RH20–16, Bd. 1004, BAM.

18. Diary, September 11, 1940, Virginia Woolf, *A Writer's Diary*, ed. Leonard Woolf (London: Hogarth, 1953), 347–48.

19. "Vermerk," September 1, 1944, R6/266, BAK, 102. See also the diary of Jürgen Kroeger, who was on Medem's staff: *Eine baltische Illusion: Tagebuch eines Deutsch-Balten aus den Jahren 1939–1944* (Lüneburg: Nordland-Druck, n.d.), 62–90.

20. The account that follows is based on several sources: the War Diary of the Sixteenth Army, RH24–16, Bd. 1, and the appendices in Bd. 4, BAM; the diary of my mother, Biruta Ekšteins, in private possession; and the oral reminiscences of another family member, who wishes to remain anonymous.

21. Josef Katz, *One Who Came Back: The Diary of a Jewish Survivor*, trans. Hilda Reach (New York: Herzl Press and Bergen-Belsen Memorial Press, 1973), 268–69.

22. Oberstleutnant Ruf, in his statement on August 7, 1944, to Oberstleutnant Panhoff, the officer investigating how the Russians got across the river in such large numbers, RH24–16, Bd. 4, BAM.

23. Kampf-Anweisungen, August 1, 1944, RH20–16, Bd. 430, BAM.

24. Korpsbefehl, Generalkommando Kleffel, August 2, 1944, RH24–16, Bd. 4, BAM.

25. Befehl, "Stellungsbau," August 6, 1944, RH20–16, Bd. 430, BAM.

26. Cable from Schoerner to AOK16, August 7, 1944, RH20–16, Bd. 433, BAM.

27. Tagesmeldungen, Oberer Quartiermeister, August 2, 12, and 14, 1944, RH20–16, Bd. 987, BAM.

28. General Kleffel, "Betr.: Evakuierung der frontalen Gemeinden im Korpsbereich," August 13, 1944, R24–16, Bd. 15, BAM.

29. FO 371/43052, PRO.

30. The war sermons of Rūdolfs Ekšteins are in my possession.

31. Tätigkeitsbericht des Gerichts, Abteilung III, AOK16, July–October 1944, RH20–16, Bd. 1032, BAM.

32. The difficulties in the railway network and in the transportation system as a whole in the summer of 1944 are described in the file of R91Reval/2, BAK.

33. For the impressions of a British journalist who reached Tallinn a few days after the Soviet occupation in 1944, see Paul Winterton, *Report on Russia* (London: Cresset, 1945), 84–90.

34. The Soviet legation in Stockholm claimed that all these people should be sent back to Russia because they were Soviet citizens. Swedish officials in turn were concerned that the refugees might form the nucleus for anti-Soviet agitation, thus harming Sweden's claim to neutrality. Sir V. Mallet, Stockholm, to the British foreign minister, Eden, October 5, 1944, FO 371/43533, PRO. On October 17 the newspaper *Ny Dag* reported that to date 30,000 Balts had arrived.

35. Of the Baltic refugees G. M. Wilson said: "I have a feeling that they will in fact

be pretty well looked after and that the more we keep out of it the better. We
shall have plenty of trouble on our hands here in course of time from the
Balts." Memorandum, October 23, 1944, FO 371/43533, PRO. See also Sir A.
Clark Kerr's dispatches from Moscow in late October, ibid.

36. The letter, dated October 24, 1944, was intercepted by the British, FO
    371/47045, PRO.
37. See the translation, by Charles Zarine, of the letter by J. Zalcmanis, president
    of the Latvian Union in Sweden, May 10, 1945, FO 371/47045, PRO. Also, V.
    Lasmane, ed., *Pāri jūrai 1944./45. g.* (Stockholm: Memento, 1993).
38. Renamed Kingisepp after the war, to honor Viktor Kingisepp, one of the
    founders of the Estonian Communist Party.
39. The Sõrve peninsula, jutting out to the south of Arensburg, the Germans
    managed to hold until late November.
40. Diary, August 24, 1943, Ruth Andreas-Friedrich, *Der Schattenmann: Tage-
    buchaufzeichnungen, 1938–1945* (Berlin: Union Verlag, 1977), 107; Magda
    Denes, *Castles Burning* (New York: Norton, 1997), 213.
41. Heinz Guderian, *Panzer Leader*, trans. Constantine Fitzgibbon (London: Mi-
    chael Joseph, 1952), 412.
42. In Dennis L. Bark and David R. Gress, *A History of West Germany*, 2 vols.
    (Oxford: Basil Blackwell, 1989), I, 19.
43. January 27, 1945, FO 371/47042, PRO.
44. John R. Deane, *The Strange Alliance* (New York: Viking, 1947), 43.
45. William C. Bullitt, "How We Won the War and Lost the Peace," *Life* 25/9,
    August 30, 1948, 97.
46. Marcel Reich-Ranicki, "Rede über das eigene Land," *Kulturchronik* 13/2
    (1995), 8.
47. Lagebericht des Generalstaatsanwalts bei dem Kammergericht Berlin, October
    1, 1944, reprinted in Hans Dieter Schäfer, *Berlin im Zweiten Weltkrieg: Der
    Untergang der Reichshauptstadt in Augenzeugenberichten* (Munich: Piper,
    1985), 199.
48. Christabel Bielenberg, *The Past Is Myself* (London: Corgi, 1984), 242–43.
49. Hans-Georg von Studnitz, *While Berlin Burns: The Diary of Hans-Georg von
    Studnitz, 1943–1945*, trans. R. H. Stevens (Englewood Cliffs, N.J.: Prentice-
    Hall, 1964), 214.
50. Diary, March 15, 1945, Goebbels, *Final Entries*, 146.
51. In Mordecai Richler, ed., *Writers on World War II: An Anthology* (Toronto:
    Viking, 1991), xxv.
52. Martin Middlebrook, *The Berlin Raids: R.A.F. Bomber Command Winter,
    1943–44* (New York: Viking, 1988), 46.
53. Wilhelm Wels, January 8, 1945, in R55/1295, BAK.
54. Diary, March 2, 1945, Goebbels, *Final Entries*, 24.
55. Diary letters, November 5, 1944, and February 18, 1945, Mathilde Wolff-
    Mönckeberg, *On the Other Side. To My Children: From Germany, 1940–1945*,
    trans. and ed. Ruth Evans (New York: Mayflower Books, 1979), 99, 110.
56. The mission is still in its old location. The Kronprinzenallee is, however, now
    the Clayallee, named after General Lucius D. Clay.

57. From the 1939 Grieben guide *Berlin und Umgebung,* in Hans Dieter Schäfer, *Berlin im Zweiten Weltkrieg,* 9.
58. In John Keegan, *The Second World War* (London: Penguin, 1990), 420.
59. In ibid., 421.
60. John Terraine, *The Right of the Line: The Royal Air Force in the European War, 1939–1945* (London: Hodder and Stoughton, 1985), 505–7.
61. In ibid., 476.
62. Martin Middlebrook, *The Battle of Hamburg* (London: Allen Lane, 1980), 276; Richard Rhodes, *The Making of the Atomic Bomb* (New York: Simon and Schuster, 1986), 474.
63. In Middlebrook, *Hamburg,* 279–80.
64. Ursula Gebel on the aftermath of a raid on Berlin in November 1943, in Middlebrook, *Berlin Raids,* 346.
65. Diary, February 4, 1944, Andreas-Friedrich, *Der Schattenmann,* 117.
66. In Middlebrook, *Berlin Raids,* 315. Middlebrook concludes that "the Luftwaffe hurt Bomber Command more than Bomber Command hurt Berlin" (325).
67. Diary, January 22, 1945, Andreas-Friedrich, *Der Schattenmann,* 175–76.
68. In Alfred M. de Zayas, "Die Flucht," in Frank Grube and Gerhard Richter, eds., *Flucht und Vertreibung: Deutschland zwischen 1944 und 1947* (Hamburg: Hoffmann und Campe, 1980), 139. "Dresden, like Prague or Venice, was one of the architectural wonders of the world. Its destruction was an act of perversity, like putting an ax to a Chippendale chair, or knifing a Michelangelo, or burning a priceless library." Ian Buruma, *The Wages of Guilt: Memories of War in Germany and Japan* (London: Jonathan Cape, 1994), 299.
69. Studnitz, *While Berlin Burns,* 250.
70. In Manfred Malzahn, *Germany, 1945–1949: A Sourcebook* (London: Routledge, 1991), 49.
71. Tätigkeitsbericht, July 1944, RH20–16, Bd. 1066D, BAM.
72. Recounted in diary letter, August 24, 1943, Wolff-Mönckeberg, *On the Other Side,* 77.
73. In Michael R. Marrus, *The Unwanted: European Refugees in the Twentieth Century* (New York: Oxford University Press, 1985), 325–26.
74. Norman M. Naimark, *The Russians in Germany: A History of the Soviet Zone of Occupation, 1945–1949* (Cambridge, Mass.: Harvard University Press, 1995), 133; and Agate Nesaule, *A Woman in Amber: Healing the Trauma of War and Exile* (New York: Soho Press, 1995), 59–70.
75. Report of Emma M., Bestand Ost-Dokumentation 2/130, 150–53, BAK, reprinted in Klaus-Jörg Ruhl, ed., *Deutschland 1945* (Darmstadt: Luchterhand, 1984), 49–51.
76. Aleksandr Solzhenitsyn, *Prussian Nights: A Poem,* trans. Robert Conquest (New York: Farrar, Straus and Giroux, 1977), 31, 37–9.
77. M. Koriakov, *I'll Never Go Back* (1948), 67, in Christopher Duffy, *Red Storm on the Reich: The Soviet March on Germany, 1945* (London: Routledge, 1991), 274.
78. In de Zayas, "Die Flucht," in Grube and Richter, eds., *Flucht und Vertreibung,* 134.

79. Milovan Djilas, *Conversations with Stalin*, trans. Michael B. Petrovich (New York: Harcourt, Brace and World, 1962), 95.

80. Marion Gräfin Dönhoff, *Namen die keiner mehr kennt. Ostpreussen: Menschen und Geschichte* (Düsseldorf: Eugen Diederichs Verlag, 1962), 37. A differently organized English version is available: *Before the Storm: Memories of My Youth in Old Prussia*, trans. Jean Steinberg, foreword George Kennan (New York: Alfred A. Knopf, 1990).

81. "The disaster that befell this area [East Prussia] with the entry of the Soviet forces has no parallel in modern European experience." George Kennan, *Memoirs, 1925–1950* (London: Hutchinson, 1968), 265.

82. Elisabeth Pfeil, *Der Flüchtling: Gestalt einer Zeitwende* (Hamburg: Hugo Verlag, 1948).

83. In Martin Gilbert, *The Day the War Ended* (London: HarperCollins, 1995), 374.

84. "Letter from Aschaffenburg," *The New Yorker*, October 30, 1948.

85. Leonard Dinnerstein, *America and the Survivors of the Holocaust* (New York: Columbia University Press, 1982), 16; Mark R. Elliott, *Pawns of Yalta: Soviet Refugees and America's Role in Their Repatriation* (Urbana: University of Illinois Press, 1982), 83.

86. Reitlinger, *House Built on Sand*, 395.

87. Dieter Wellershoff, *Die Arbeit des Lebens: Autobiographische Texte* (Cologne: Kiepenhauer and Witsch, 1985), 69.

88. "Dönitz as Head of State," *The Times* (London), May 2, 1945.

89. The numbers come from Wolfgang Kadasch, "Zum Flüchtlingsproblem in Flensburg in den ersten Jahren nach 1945," diss., Flensburg, 1976, 9–10; and Wolfgang Stribrny, "Vertriebene und Flüchtlinge in Flensburg," in *Flensburg, 700 Jahre Stadt: Eine Festschrift* (Flensburg: Gesellschaft für Flensburger Stadtgeschichte, 1984), 416–25.

90. "*Peace.* I would like to write this little word over and over again, a whole page full of nothing else until I myself were filled to overflowing with peace." Thus Wolff-Mönckeberg in her diary, August 14, 1945, *On the Other Side*, 147.

91. In Gilbert, *The Day the War Ended*, 174.

92. Clementine Spencer Churchill, *My Visit to Russia* (1945), 56–7, in Gilbert, *The Day the War Ended*, 174.

93. Diary letter, May 1, 1945, Wolff-Mönckeberg, *On the Other Side*, 117–18.

94. In Johannes Steinhof et al., *Voices from the Third Reich: An Oral History* (Washington, D.C.: Regnery Gateway, 1989), 527.

95. Günter Grass, *Two States — One Nation?*, trans. K. Winston and A. S. Wensinger (San Diego: Harcourt Brace Jovanovich, 1990), 96.

96. The figure normally given is twelve million. Alfred M. de Zayas, however, puts it at fifteen in *Nemesis at Potsdam: The Expulsion of the Germans from the East*, 3rd ed. (Lincoln: University of Nebraska Press, 1989), xix.

97. As reported in *LN*, May 21, 1947.

98. "Weekly Intelligence Sitrep," Hamburg Intelligence Office, January 20, 1949, FO 1014/276, PRO.

99. Diary letter, May 17, 1945, Wolff-Mönckeberg, *On the Other Side*, 123.

100. David G. McCullough, *Truman* (New York: Simon and Schuster, 1992), 407–8.

101. The bacteriological agent considered was code-named "N" and was probably anthrax. Anthony Cave Brown, *Bodyguard of Lies*, 2 vols. (New York: Harper & Row, 1975), II, 813–14.

102. Franklin M. Davis, Jr., *Come as a Conqueror: The United States Army's Occupation of Germany, 1945–1949* (New York: Macmillan, 1967), 105–6; and Rhodes, *Making of the Atomic Bomb*, 475–76.

103. This is Martin Walker's point in *The Cold War and the Making of the Modern World* (London: Fourth Estate, 1993), 25.

104. *LN*, February 8, 1947.

105. Solly Zuckerman, *From Apes to Warlords* (New York: Harper & Row, 1978), 322.

106. Ota Filip, "Meine drei Befreiungen," *Die Zeit*, May 12, 1995, 14.

107. In Hans-Peter Schwarz, *Konrad Adenauer: A German Politician and Statesman in a Period of War, Revolution and Reconstruction. Volume I: From the German Empire to the Federal Republic, 1876–1952*, trans. Louise Willmot (Providence, R.I.: Berghahn Books, 1995), 280.

108. James Stern, *The Hidden Damage* (New York: Harcourt, Brace and Company, 1947), 83, 119.

109. Ibid., 119.

110. Lucius D. Clay, *Decision in Germany* (Garden City, N.Y.: Doubleday, 1950), 21.

111. William S. Rogers, "The UNRRA Experience, 1945–1946," (1946) unpublished ms., 8.

112. Hans Rumpf, *The Bombing of Germany*, trans. Edward Fitzgerald (New York: Holt, Rinehart, and Winston, 1963), 126–28.

113. Heinrich Böll, *Missing Persons and Other Essays*, trans. Leila Vennewitz (New York: McGraw-Hill, 1977), 25.

114. T. S. Eliot, in his preface to *The Dark Side of the Moon* (London: Faber and Faber, 1946), 6–8. The preface is dated January 28, 1946.

115. Lord Tedder, *With Prejudice: The War Memoirs of Marshal of the Royal Air Force Lord Tedder G.C.B.* (London: Cassell, 1966); Zuckerman, *From Apes to Warlords*, 343–44; Albert Speer, *Inside the Third Reich*, trans. Richard and Clara Winston (New York: Macmillan, 1970), 224.

Index